THE BIBLE IN BUFFALO COUNTRY

OENPELLI MISSION 1925-1931

Aboriginal History Incorporated

Aboriginal History Inc. is a part of the Australian Centre for Indigenous History, Research School of Social Sciences, The Australian National University, and gratefully acknowledges the support of the School of History and the National Centre for Indigenous Studies, The Australian National University. Aboriginal History Inc. is administered by an Editorial Board which is responsible for all unsigned material. Views and opinions expressed by the author are not necessarily shared by Board members.

Contacting Aboriginal History

All correspondence should be addressed to the Editors, Aboriginal History Inc., ACIH, School of History, RSSS, 9 Fellows Road (Coombs Building), The Australian National University, Acton, ACT, 2601, or aboriginalhistoryinc@gmail.com.

THE BIBLE IN BUFFALO COUNTRY

OENPELLI MISSION 1925-1931

SALLY K. MAY, LAURA RADEMAKER,
DONNA NADJAMERREK AND
JULIE NARNDAL GUMURDUL

Australian
National
University

PRESS

Published by ANU Press and Aboriginal History Inc.
The Australian National University
Acton ACT 2601, Australia
Email: anupress@anu.edu.au

Available to download for free at press.anu.edu.au

ISBN (print): 9781760463984
ISBN (online): 9781760463991

WorldCat (print): 1198366907
WorldCat (online): 1198366865

DOI: 10.22459/BBC.2020

Cover design and layout by ANU Press

Cover artwork by Gabriel Maralngurra, 2020

Injalak Arts is an Indigenous not-for-profit community art centre based in Gunbalanya. It supported the development of this book through community consultation and cultural advice.

CONTENTS

ILLUSTRATIONS

FOREWORD

I am pleased to be able to write the foreword for our new book on Oenpelli's history. We call it 'Gunbalanya' today, but I will use Oenpelli because that was its name, way back when the missionaries first came here. As one of the Traditional Owners for Oenpelli, I am proud of this town and its history. My Mandjurlngunj people are in the minority here now. You might say we are multicultural here in Oenpelli with people from many different clan groups calling it home. They have their homelands too, but this is my homeland – Mandjurlngunj land.

My clan are Mengerrdji-speaking people and our country spans well outside of the current Gunbalanya (Oenpelli) township. It is home to beautiful billabongs, floodplains and many stone outcrops such as Injalak and Arrkuluk Hill. These places have always been our home.

Our recent history is complicated. Not all of it is nice to read about. But we survived the tough times and we are still strong as a community today. My father – Nipper Marakarra Gumurdul – was the Senior Traditional Owner for Oenpelli during the time the first missionaries came. He was also the boss when Paddy Cahill was here, before the missionaries. People still talk about him today. He was a serious but generous man.

People say that he looked after people from other clans who came to live in Oenpelli. He allowed them to stay here, even though it was not their country. He was a tough leader and made difficult choices sometimes. When he thought the *balanda* were going too far, he took steps to control it. I guess he was a diplomat, but he did use force sometimes!

I hope you enjoy reading about our history. The stories and the photographs are powerful and will bring back many memories for our people. We are glad to share them with you too.

Julie Narndal Gumurdul

ACKNOWLEDGEMENTS

We thank and acknowledge the Mandjurlngunj clan for their generosity in supporting this project and for sharing stories of their family. Oenpelli is situated on the unceded land of the Mandjurlngunj people and we pay our respect to their elders, past and present. We would also like to thank the Manilakarr clan whose land and people were also affected by the Oenpelli mission. We would especially like to thank Alfred, Leah and Connie Nayinggul for supporting this book, and for their advice and help with the photographs.

This book has been many years in the making and we are grateful to all our family and friends who have supported us on this journey. The community of Gunbalanya (formerly Oenpelli) have been a major part of this journey and have worked with us to bring this story together. In particular, we thank the dozens of community members who took the time to look at the old photographs and added names or other information. This is an ongoing journey and we look forward to continuing to work with community members to help document and share family and community histories.

We would like to thank Laureate Professors Paul S. C. Taçon (Griffith University) and Ann McGrath (The Australian National University) for their unwavering support of this research and encouragement to collaborate across Laureate programs. This research was funded by the Australian Research Council as part of research grants FL160100123 and FL170100121. We are grateful to the Griffith Centre for Social and Cultural Research (Griffith University) for providing funding towards the costs of copyediting and to the School of History (The Australian National University) for their ongoing support of our research.

We were lucky enough to spend time at the Northern Territory Archive Service while undertaking research for this book. We thank Francois Barr and Emily Prichard for sharing their knowledge of the Oenpelli collections and for assisting us over the years. Without your extensive knowledge of these collections, many photographs and records would have been missed. We are grateful to the Northern Territory Library, the National Museum of Australia, the National Archives of Australia, and the Pitt Rivers Museum, University of Oxford, for supplying high-resolution photographs and/or permission to use photographs from their collections.

Injalak Arts have been a partner in this research since we began. In particular, we appreciate the support of Alex Ressel, Kerri Meehan, Hayley Birchley, Gabriel Maralngurra, Benson Nagurrgurrba, A. Manakgu, Christine Nabobbob, Helen Nawirridj, Priscilla Badari, Sylvia Badari, Anne Gumurdul, Graham Badari, Josie Maralngurra, Felicity Wright and the Injalak Arts board members. Copies of the photographs were circulated in the community for over a year with names being added to the manuscript throughout this time. We will never know exactly how many people assisted with this process but we thank you all.

We thank A. Manakgu for checking over the spelling of Aboriginal names and words used in this book, especially within the Esther Manakgu story. We are grateful to the Bininj Kunwok Regional Language Centre for their support and advice, especially Murray Garde, Andy Peart and Jill Nganjmirra. We thank Rev. Lois Nadjamerrek from the Emmanuel Anglican Church in Gunbalanya for her insights into local history and her encouragement to bring the Church Missionary Society photographs back to the community and ensure this history is not forgotten.

Thanks also to Tracey Fairman at the Northern Land Council for facilitating permits during the course of this research.

Joakim Goldhahn and Robert Levitus read and commented on chapters of this book and we are grateful for their insights and suggestions. Robert Levitus also kindly shared his unpublished oral history recordings from 1981 with us and allowed us to quote from them. Thanks to Emily Miller who assisted with transcribing some of the archival material, Sandy Blair who provided early inspiration to delve into Oenpelli history, and Janet Davill who helped with archival research.

We are grateful to ANU Press and Aboriginal History Monographs for embracing this project, particularly Rani Kerin and Emily Tinker. We also thank Geoff Hunt for his careful and thorough copyediting.

Finally, the photographs and archival material are published here without restriction and with the support and permission of the Church Missionary Society of Australia. We thank Lyn Milton (CMS Archivist) for facilitating these permissions and Peter Rogers (CMS Director) for his support of this research.

A NOTE ON ORTHOGRAPHY

There is some ongoing confusion about the appropriate name for the township that Paddy Cahill first referred to as 'Oenpelli'. It is thought that 'Oenpelli' is a corruption of the original Erre name for the area, 'Uwunbarlany'. 'Kunbarlanja' is the current Kunwinjku name for the community while 'Gunbalanya' is the English version. As we are discussing the 1925–31 time period, in this book we use its contemporary name: Oenpelli.

Today in Oenpelli, many local dialects and languages are spoken – most predominantly Kunwinjku. English ranks low on the list of languages many people speak. Maintaining Aboriginal languages is culturally important. The missionaries discussed in this book had a complicated relationship with Aboriginal languages; they both discouraged people from speaking their own languages (Dyer never learned himself), but at the same time realised that using them helped to bring people to church. So, for example, some hymns were sung in a local language while, at the same time, Aboriginal people working on the mission were expected to learn and speak English. None of the missionaries during this early era could speak any local languages and there is no indication in our sources that they were trying to learn (although Nell Harris, who arrived when she married Dick in 1933, later made great progress eventually translating the Gospel of Mark into Kunwinjku together with Hannah Mangiru and Rachel Maralngurra). During the Dyer years, local Aboriginal people simply added English to their repertoire of languages rather than swapping it for their own languages.

For more information on local Aboriginal dialects and languages visit: bininjkunwok.org.au/.

1

ABORIGINAL HISTORIES IN THE MISSION RECORDS

In this book we share the rich documentary and photographic sources from the early years of the Oenpelli mission. Though it consists mainly of records produced by non-Indigenous missionaries, we consider this book a book of Aboriginal history. Why? The letters, reports and photographs that form its core were produced by missionaries who sought to convert and change Aboriginal people. We have done our best to contextualise these sources with Aboriginal perspectives and voices but, ultimately, the main voices represented here are those of the mission superintendent, Alfred Dyer, and his wife, Mary (known as 'Katie').

We hope that by sharing these documents and photographs readers will be able to see within them the ways that Aboriginal people were always present and working. They were working hard to make the most of a difficult situation for their community due to the newcomers on their land.

Times were hard. The invasion of Europeans meant that the community was facing health crises, separation from country, internal conflict and ceremonial turmoil – many of the things Aboriginal communities continue to battle. Through all of this, they were innovative, resourceful, flexible and smart. As Oenpelli (Gunbalanya) community members will remind you: back then, people were strong. They were strong in the mission days, that is how they survived. Of course, Aboriginal people living in and around the mission did not always agree with each other – some took one approach to dealing with missionaries, some took another – but they were always working to make the most of the mission times. In this chapter, we shed some light on the main themes emerging from the sources, beginning to re-read them, first and foremost, as telling a story of Aboriginal people.

Figure 1.1: Young men and boys at the top of Arguluk Hill looking down on the Oenpelli mission, 1930. Photograph by J.W. Bleakley.
Source: National Archives of Australia (A431, 8162283).

Figure 1.2: Alfred and Mary Dyer, date unknown.
Source: Northern Territory Archive Service (NTRS 694 Box 4a Item 201).

The missionary intent

The sources in this book also reveal what the missionaries thought they were doing. It was common for missionaries to embark on what they hoped would be a glorious adventure, reaping a spiritual harvest among the 'heathen', only to discover themselves overwhelmed with administrative tasks, abrasive personalities (who were often the other missionaries) and the monotony of the daily work that came with running a station. The Dyers had been missionaries in north Australia for decades when they arrived at Oenpelli, so they were not surprised that the daily experience of being a missionary was mostly just hard work. Still, they were not immune to disillusionment, nor to clashes with their colleagues. They also knew that it was unlikely Aboriginal people would flock to their mission or that they would see mass conversions rush through Arnhem Land (though they did record a number of baptisms). The work would be slow. They believed the mission would continue for decades before seeing its 'fruit'. As 'pioneer missionaries' they were simply 'sowing the seed'; later missionaries, they believed, would reap a Christian community in Arnhem Land.

This future for Aboriginal people, they imagined, would be as an independent Christian people. Like many missionaries, they believed that contact with white Australia was fatal for Aboriginal people. So, at this stage, missionaries were not self-consciously seeking to assimilate Aboriginal people into white Australia (though, they did attempt to reform Aboriginal family life and culture to white norms, which was, of course, a form of assimilation).

The sources here show that Dyer's ambitions were broader than simply converting Aboriginal people to Christianity or providing humanitarian aid to the 'remnant' of the race. Dyer wrote of his dream of an 'Arnheim Land State', commenting that 'a Native State is the only chance for these people'.[1] Through training Aboriginal people in pastoral work and agriculture, and by providing basic education, this state could be 'self-supporting'. Christianity, too, was essential to such an enterprise; it supposedly provided Aboriginal people with the moral fortitude and wisdom to resist temptations introduced by whites: alcohol, gambling and interracial sex. Aboriginal people's existing traditions, missionaries

---

1   'Report of the Policy for Oenpelli 1929 as discussed by Staff', Northern Territory Record Series (hereafter NTRS) 1099/P1 vol. 1.

presumed, were either useless in this respect, or so compromised by the pressures of colonisation that they could no longer provide moral guidance. Without this Native State, Aboriginal people were doomed to extinction; missionaries presumed they could not survive the onslaught of Europeans in their land. But fascinatingly, missionaries believed that Aboriginal people should have the right to a form of sovereignty – indeed, that sovereignty was the route to survival. The Oenpelli mission would lay the foundation for this state.

The need to negotiate

When the missionaries arrived, from the start, they needed to work with Aboriginal people. The missionaries began on the back foot. The Oenpelli community already had a bad impression of missionaries, having heard about other missions in Arnhem Land and Darwin. Local people would need to be convinced to cooperate with missionaries. As much as the missionaries dressed up their work in pious rhetoric, these sources show they had two main strategies for attracting people to the mission: tobacco and education of children.

The letters reveal Dyer's calculus of exactly how much tobacco would be needed to attract workers to the station. He wanted to give out as little as possible and had mixed feelings about addiction. 'I hate the stuff', he wrote.[2] Evangelicals did not smoke. The missionaries did use large Christmas banquets to attract people to the mission. But a general food ration did not work; the community could feast on ducks, wallabies, fish and fruit whenever they wanted, why would they want missionary food? Dyer did record an incident of a 'raid on the potato patch'.[3] But this was opportunism or even a protest, but not hunger. Addiction to tobacco, though morally questionable, Dyer found, had its uses: 'it is a very rare thing for any of them to desire the Gospel but they will travel miles for a bit of tobacco', he wrote.

The main reason the mission needed to produce food was to fuel its other strategy for attracting people to the mission: the education of children. As Dyer reported:

---

2   'Report for January 1926', NTRS 1099/P1 vol. 1.
3   'Oenpelli Report May 1926', NTRS 1099/P1 vol. 1.

We cannot follow them but we can attract them to us. They love to see their children taught & gladly leave them. Therefore I must make the home base a food producer, it is a big task but an Australian duty.[4]

It was very important to the Oenpelli community that their children learn to speak, read and write in English. As Frank Djendjulng later remembered, his father, Nipper Marakarra Gumurdul, sent him to the mission school to learn English:

Should have been staying in bush all the time ... but father brought me here ... Father brought everybody here to go to school and learn English. Learned little bit English in school.[5]

Others remembered the mission school as the missionaries' main gift to the community, even as it was important that they were still able to learn their own language and culture. As Frank Nalowerd remembered:

Dyer start school. Him best man. Big mob boys go to school. Went to school right through year. Learn both *bininj* [Aboriginal] and *balanda* [white] way. I been small boy Paddy Cahill time, but I been big man when Dyer come, but still go to school. We learned *bininj* way off mother and father.[6]

It was not that local people did not value their own languages or traditions around communication. They were already familiar with the benefits of being multilingual for negotiating with other groups (Arnhem Land being highly multilingual). So they quickly saw that adding English literacy to their existing linguistic repertoire would give their children an edge when negotiating with (or outsmarting) colonisers in the future. Only a few years earlier, a royal commission exposed how Thomas Cahill (the son of Paddy Cahill, the previous manager of Oenpelli) was exploiting Aboriginal workers. He was able to take their wages partly because they could not read; a bureaucrat signed over their money (forging their marks) on their behalf. Reading in English would give their children a better chance. It is also likely the community wanted their children to know something of the missionaries' spiritual knowledge. The missionaries seemed endowed with material wealth and power – knowing the source of their power might also be useful.

---

4   'Oenpelli Report for June', NTRS 1099/P1 vol. 1.
5   Frank Djendjulng, oral history interview with Robert Levitus, 20 July 1981.
6   Frank Nalowerd, oral history interview with Robert Levitus, 22 July 1981.

While it seems families were generally eager for children to receive education from missionaries, the Oenpelli community did not consent to being cut off from their children altogether. Some did not consent at all, as Priscilla Girrabul remembered:

> The missionaries would take kids into the dormitories from their parents. Parents were angry. Some mothers would take their kids out of the dorms and back into bush, kids of six or seven years of age. That's why many don't speak good English.[7]

Those whose children were held in the dormitory camped at the mission to keep an eye on their children's wellbeing. So when a flood hit the mission in 1930, families rushed into the mission to ensure their children were safe. The proximity of families suited the missionaries too; children were like a magnet, keeping the community within missionaries' sphere of influence. So many came that the mission sometimes struggled to provide work and food for them all:

> More are coming in than we can cope with. We take the children, but naturally some parents do not wish to leave the children if they cannot work themselves. More gardens are the solution & we have the soil to do it.[8]

Community frictions

The dormitory where the children stayed (originally Cahill's 'prison') was also useful to missionaries in their attempts to reform Aboriginal family life. It allowed them to focus their efforts on Christianising the children, as they believed missionaries would have little influence on the adults (rightly, as it turned out). Dyer wrote explicitly that the missionary influence would increase as the 'older ones die'.[9]

But here, again, these sources show that Aboriginal people had their own ideas about what was best for their community. Missionaries were especially concerned by the betrothal ('promising') and marriage of young girls to older men, particularly where men already had multiple wives. To them, this was a moral problem – it was a product of male lust and greed. To the extent that they recognised that Aboriginal

---

7   Priscilla Girrabul, oral history interview with Robert Levitus, 11 August 1981.
8   Dyer, 'Report of the Policy for Oenpelli 1929 as discussed by Staff', NTRS 1099/P1 vol. 1.
9   Dyer to R. H. Weddell, 1 February 1929, Mitchell Library (hereafter ML) MSS 6040/12.

marriage traditions were an expression of a kinship system that created intergenerational interdependence, they also considered this problematic because the interdependence of old and young prevented missionaries from influencing the younger generation. So missionaries used the dormitory to delay the girls' marriages until they were older, and to try to match them with younger men. Often the girls themselves preferred young husbands, but the changes created havoc in the broader community, which did not always agree. There are regular accounts of children being taken from the dormitories by parents or promised husbands. Missionaries did not always prevail in these disputes. Such was the power of community wishes that sometimes missionaries found they had to allow the girls to marry. Other times, it suited missionaries to exploit disagreements around marriage among locals. Marriage customs continued as a major source of friction, among Aboriginal people and between Aboriginal people and missionaries.

Another source of tension between the community and missionaries was spiritual. The community continued to practise their ceremonies right through the mission years, even though the missionaries considered them 'superstition'. The Dyers, it seems, were blind (perhaps wilfully so) to the ceremonial significance of sites around the mission. Dyer cut down 'sacred trees' late in 1929 to clear space for a new garden. Apparently, he did not learn that this was a sacred site until after the trees were already felled. Missionaries were ignorant of the spiritual significance of their surroundings, even of sites within the mission grounds. After community outrage, Dyer was compelled to burn the trees away from the mission. But the desecration of the site unleashed an epidemic of whooping cough – many babies died – and destructive floods quickly followed. Local people, naturally, turned to their own healers in the calamity and resented the missionaries. The missionaries blamed Aboriginal discontent on misinformed medical ideas. The cavalier missionary attitude to spiritual danger was more likely the cause.

Sometimes, when missionaries went too far, the community responded with overt resistance. Dyer recorded Aboriginal demands for higher wages and complaints that they were made to do things that were 'not their job'. He even conceded that they were only paid a 'small pocket money allowance', hoping simply that they would be grateful for the little they got. After the potato patch 'raid', Dyer cut off the tobacco supply. The community response was a general strike; these sources also reveal a history of labour relations that were inseparable from the colonising process. Though Dyer was against guns, he was willing to use corporal punishment. That time, the community gave in and the 'little boys' involved in the potato incident 'got the strap'. But even corporal punishment had limits in effectiveness: Dyer recorded instances of people simply 'running away' after punishment. The missionaries could only go so far if they wanted people to remain at the mission. Another time, the missionaries went on 'strike' after workers demanded higher wages. In this stand-off, Dyer refused to prepare breakfast until they gave up their demands. Through these stand-offs, with passive and overt resistance, on both sides, missionaries and Aboriginal people together negotiated the truces required to allow the little community to function.

When negotiations failed, the other option available to local people was simply to leave. Often they did. The mission model depended on the expectation that Aboriginal people would settle permanently at the mission, but not many did. The missionary records are full of references to Aboriginal mobility as people moved easily between the mission, the 'bush' and other stations. Missionaries found themselves constantly recruiting and retraining new workers as others 'went walkabout'. The constant movement of people, too, was a way of keeping missionaries on their toes and attentive to Aboriginal interests and needs. This is also partly why many other missions in the Northern Territory were established on islands. Missionaries hoped to keep Aboriginal people in and others out. Oenpelli was unusual in this regard and so required a higher degree of tact if it were to keep its contact with its Aboriginal flock.

As well as the complex relationships between missionaries and Aboriginal people, the sources also reveal that the missionaries themselves were not always united. This, too, presented an opportunity to Aboriginal people who developed close ties with some missionaries but not others, potentially playing them off against one another. There is evidence in Dyer's reports that other missionary staff sometimes cut him out of communication. Once he arranged a 'special meeting' to discuss policy, indicating that other staff were concerned about the direction of the mission. The Dyers, in their reports, seem more distant from Aboriginal people than their missionary colleagues. Unlike other missionaries who expressed their concern for and even friendship with individual Aboriginal people, the Dyers tended not to mention people by name in letters and reports. They were known to be socially awkward. Perhaps they were just very introverted. Maybe they had trouble relating to Aboriginal people. Mary described the people at Oenpelli as 'often very unlovable & unlovely' –

the relationship was not exactly warm – though perhaps it was actually she and her husband that went unloved.[10] Maybe Aboriginal people avoided them. This, too, was likely a strategy for upholding Aboriginal interests. The superintendent had little hope of knowing what was actually going on, let alone any hope of controlling Aboriginal people.

Photographic sources

Scattered through this book are 126 photographs primarily dating to the Dyer years in Oenpelli. Photography was used by missionaries across Australia to document their experiences and educate the church and the wider public on Aboriginal 'issues'.[11] Images were also great for fundraising. Missionaries all over the world had long used the latest technology to communicate their adventures to the masses, and photography was part of their modern missionary methods.

Of course, the effectiveness of photography also depended on the mission staff and their personal interests and skills with photography. But it seems that Alf Dyer had a good eye for photography. Given the quality of the photos, he clearly recognised the value of his photographic collection even as he was forming it. Around March 1929 he wrote to Rev. John Ferrier, 'put the films into my collection I hope you are guarding my trust as all these pictures are very valuable to me'.[12] At the same time, the mission reports and letters tell us that others may also be responsible for many of the photos in the collection, including Florence Sherrin and Dick Harris. Unfortunately, there is no record of who took each photograph.

The few mentions we have of photography give some insight into his motivations. Dyer complained of using old films and having little time to take photos. The shopping orders also include details of the type of cameras Dyer was using and his practice of developing the photos at the mission. Dyer used his own money to purchase (and presumably process) photographs taken at the Oenpelli mission.

---

10   Mary Dyer to Ferrier, 4 August 1929, ML MSS 6040/12.
11   Lydon, *Eye Contact*.
12   Alf Dyer to Ferrier, no date, ML MSS 6040/12.

The resulting photographs are a unique and invaluable collection for the Oenpelli community. They capture life on the mission and, to a lesser extent, life in the fringe camps around the community. They can also be technical images featuring boilers, boats and machinery. Yet, we use them here not simply to illustrate the mission records; they provide an important perspective on this early missionary period in Oenpelli. Of course, this is again a missionary perspective. They reflect what missionaries thought was worth documenting or that they believed might be useful in their publicity efforts. Whatever did not fit missionaries' narrative was left outside the frame. Nevertheless, they are useful to us because many reveal everyday life: children playing in irrigation trenches, women pounding antbed for flooring, and stockmen and their horses. Unlike the stiff and staged photographs of many anthropologists of the time, this collection is personal and full of life.

The photographs we selected for this book, therefore, tell their own story of Aboriginal lives and should be read as such. For local Aboriginal people, these images take on another level of significance. They bring forth a range of emotions ranging from sadness at the trauma being faced by many at that time, to joy at seeing the faces of relatives they may or may not have met. One of our key aims in writing this book was to bring these photographs out of their archival boxes and reconnect them with the Oenpelli community.

This book and its sources

The next chapters of this book provide the historical and cultural context for reading these sources. We outline the history of the Oenpelli region and its rich cultures that stretch back millennia. Then we turn to the arrival of Europeans on Aboriginal land and the establishment of the Oenpelli cattle station. The following chapter introduces the Church Missionary Society (CMS) as well as Alfred and Mary Dyer. Then we move on to the mission documents themselves, the backbone of this book. These are the reports and correspondence in the CMS collections held at the Northern Territory Archives Centre and Mitchell Library (State Library of New South Wales). We have arranged them chronologically (as far as we could discern the dating), blending the two archival collections together, such that you can see the mission story unfold at Oenpelli. Interspersed through these documents are the photographs dating to the Dyer years.

This remarkable, little-known archive is a visual testimony to the lives of the people of Oenpelli. Following the mission documents comes the testimony of Esther Manakgu in her oral history reflecting on the mission times. We hope her words might guide you in your interpretation of the documentary sources, and that her perspective might shed light on the ways Aboriginal people used and experienced the mission.

2

COUNTRY, CULTURE
AND KINSHIP

> I'll tell you a story about Yingarna, a woman who came here from
> the west. She carried many children in a large number of (string)
> bags. She came here to the flood plain after crossing over (the East
> Alligator River) and to this place where we live.[1]

Bininj (local Aboriginal people) have lived around the Oenpelli area
forever. The first people were placed there by the ancestral woman,
Yingarna (Figure 2.1). Yingarna emerged from the Arafura Sea before
she journeyed inland, deep into the Northern Territory, forming
landscapes, languages and their peoples as she went. Her story is long
and complex and relates to many other ancestral stories. In the words of
Thompson Yulidjirri:

> Yingarna, carrying all that dilly bag that woman. She had the
> woman and all them boys inside the dilly bags, and she dropped
> a few here, she went east, and then around south, just around
> the Top End here. And then Alice Springs somewhere and then
> I don't know, that's where she disappeared somewhere. She taught
> them language and clan and every dilly bag she would leave places
> like here.[2]

---

1   Thompson Yulidjirri, 2002, Sally K. May field notes.
2   Thompson Yulidjirri, 2002, Sally K. May field notes.

Figure 2.1: Rock painting of Yingarna, Injalak Hill.
Source: Sally K. May.

Figure 2.2: Northern Running Figure rock art from Injalak Hill.
Source: Sally K. May.

Yingarna laid *bininj* in their respective countries, gave them the language of the land and taught them to survive in that place. And they did survive, and thrive. Archaeologists have shown that *bininj* faced all kinds of challenges as their environment and its ecosystem changed over the millennia.[3] Recent archaeological research across the East Alligator River in Kakadu National Park confirmed the long antiquity of Aboriginal occupation of western Arnhem Land; *bininj* have been at the site of Madjedbebe in Mirarr country for over 65,000 years.[4]

More than mere survival in their country, *bininj* developed a beautiful artistic tradition. In fact, western Arnhem Land is also home to arguably the world's longest continuing artistic tradition.[5] For thousands of years people painted on rock surfaces, illustrating complex cultural belief systems, ancestral stories, intricate detailed information about animal species and more (Figure 2.2).[6] Art has always been an essential part of Aboriginal life in this region.

The entire western Arnhem Land landscape is imbued with cultural meaning. Every hill has a name and story, every river and waterhole is connected to the life cycle, and every animal and plant has a place within local beliefs. These stories often relate to the travels of the ancestral creatures, animals and people who formed (and often became) landforms such as hills or waterholes. The area surrounding Oenpelli is known for many *djang* (ancestral creation stories or 'Dreamings') sites, including places that relate to Adjumarllarl (an ancestral dog) and his sister Omwarl, Baladj (leech), Manimunak (magpie goose), Wurrkabal (freshwater long-tom), and Namardaka (catfish).

If these places are neglected, disturbed or damaged, the spirits will punish those responsible with dire consequences. Newcomers to this area did not often understand these rules and moved around the landscape without thought to cultural protocols. As we shall see, the missionaries themselves experienced death and destruction that might be expected from angered spirit beings when they cut down sacred trees.

---

3   See Clarkson et al., 'Human Occupation'; Jones, 'Recommendations for Archaeological'; Jones and Negerivich, 'A Review'.
4   Clarkson et al., 'Human Occupation'.
5   Chaloupka, *Journey in Time*.
6   For example, David et al., *The Archaeology of Rock Art in Arnhem Land*.

Figure 2.3: Painting by Tony Bangalang (2003) that represents the key cultural sites around the Oenpelli township through their associated ancestral beings.

Source: Sally K. May.

Anthropologists have written many books on the complexity of *bininj* cultures.[7] Local people take them for granted, but for outsiders *bininj* ceremonies, languages and social structures can be difficult to understand. The early missionaries could make little sense of them. Some of this knowledge is shared here to inform your interpretation of some of the events that are written about by the missionaries.

Bininj belong to various clans, with varying languages. You are born into your clan, inheriting your father's clan grouping. Yet your mother's and your grandparents' clans are also important throughout your life and give you rights and obligations to certain places and species of animal. Nipper Marakarra Gumurdul (skin name *Nawamud*) was a key player in the early history of Oenpelli, brokering the establishment of the cattle station under Paddy Cahill with local people. He was a Mengerrdji-speaking Senior Traditional Owner for Oenpelli and a member of the Mandjurlngunj

---

7   For example, Altman, *Hunter-Gatherers Today*; Taylor, *Seeing the Inside*; Berndt and Berndt, *Man, Land & Myth*; Spencer, *Native Tribes of the Northern Territory*; Mountford, *Records of the American-Australian*, Vol. 1.

clan, an identity he inherited from his father. His mother, however, was Kunwinjku-speaking. This meant Marakarra was not only a senior man for the Oenpelli area but that he also had rights and responsibilities for his mother's country. His particular kinship connections may also be a reason why the Kunwinjku people were first welcomed to Oenpelli and why they continue to be so prominent in Oenpelli today.

Kunwinjku Subsection System
("skin names")
showing patri-moieties and matri-moieties

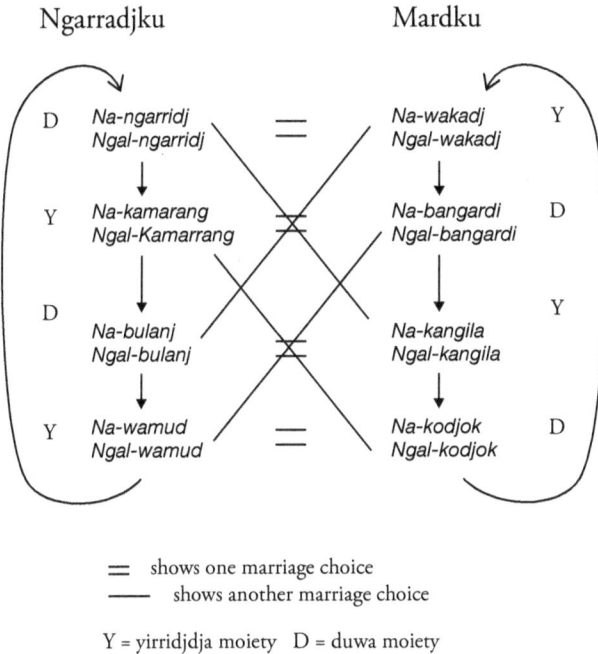

Figure 2.4: Kinship subsections of western Arnhem Land.
Source: Courtesy of Bininj Kunwok Language Project (bininjkunwok.org.au/information/kinship/).

All *bininj* relationships to others are determined not only by their clan but by their position within a comprehensive kinship system. For Bininj Kunwok speakers, this includes eight kinship subsections that help to classify and structure kin relations (Figure 2.4). This system determines your relationship to everyone else, including who you can marry. So, for example, if you are *Ngalkangila*, everybody with the skin name

Ngalbangardi is your mother (not just the woman who gave birth to you), your sons are all *Nakodjok*, your daughters are all *Ngalkodjok* and you must marry someone who is *Nabulanj* (or as a second choice – *Nangarridj*). This system is just as important as biological relationships and *bininj* must treat their kinship relations with appropriate respect.

The kinship system also determines your place within broader cultural systems. Everyone belongs to either the *Ngarradjku* or *Mardku* moieties, an identity inherited from their mothers. Likewise, everyone belongs to either the *Duwa* or *Yirridjdja* patrilineal moieties. You also inherit your 'skin' of either stone (*kunwardde*), sun (*kundung*), green ant (*kabo*) or fire (*kunak*) from your father.[8] These categories are important for ceremony including burial rituals. Throughout life, both men and women pass through different stages of ceremony. The documents in this book reveal just how important ceremonies were when missionaries first arrived (Figure 2.5). When they wrote letters about *bininj* going 'walkabout', it is likely that Aboriginal people were visiting their country to partake in trade and ceremony. The missionaries also noted that ceremonies were taking place in and around the Oenpelli station itself.

Figure 2.5: Men gathered for ceremony following a burial, c. 1926. Nipper Marakarra Gumurdul is pictured centre.
Source: Northern Territory Record Series (NTRS 694 P1 Box 4 Item 90).

---

8   Elkin, Berndt and Berndt, 'Social Organization'.

Since the first *balanda* arrived in western Arnhem Land, they affected and even interfered with this kinship system. As we shall see, Paddy Cahill tried to influence marriage arrangements, provoking retaliation from *bininj* elders. Later, the Dyers did not (or would not) understand this system and upset some *bininj*, especially when the missionaries encouraged 'wrong' marriages. Rites for deceased persons were also strongly contested, with missionaries insisting on burial, and *bininj* preferring, in some cases, for the body of the deceased to be placed in a tree or on a platform before their bones were removed to a cave.

Keep this cultural context in mind as you read the documents in this book. Local Aboriginal people were not 'childlike' or unsophisticated. They were, and still are, part of one of the most complex and dynamic cultural systems ever documented.[9] Dyer himself observed the way that Aboriginal social structures and norms created, on the whole, a peaceful and equitable way of life:

> The Aborigines have no police or prisons, no class/barriers, for all share their food (the old men keep the tasty bits for themselves). Their secret rites are to hold their power but their rulers receive no other compensation but the joy or worry of leadership. One king complained that he only had the worry of ruling and no wages or palace. They have no poor, no slums, no old age problem, no lunacy. They drink nothing but water, maybe the only race in the world. Their laws are kept. I never saw any wars for conquest, only over family vendettas or stolen wives and then they generally kill one on both sides and stop.[10]

Dyer's assessment here was coloured by both romantic and racist assumptions of Aboriginal childlike innocence. Nonetheless, his comments reveal some admiration for the ways Aboriginal people had so successfully organised their society, ways that Christians like himself could only aspire to emulate.

Until relatively recently, many *balanda* believed that Aboriginal people in Arnhem Land were doomed to extinction.[11] As late as 1951, writer Colin Simpson described the 'Australian Aboriginal' as 'a patient who years ago was marked down as "dying" and whose treatment since has consisted

---

9   See Berndt and Berndt, *Man, Land & Myth*; Taylor, *Seeing the Inside*.
10   Dyer Story, 22, NTRS 693, Item 8.
11   See Griffiths, *Hunters and Collectors*, 10.

mainly of pillow-smoothing and doses of pity'.[12] Dyer, too, doubted that Aboriginal people could survive contact, describing the Oenpelli mission as a 'real chance to make good'; that is, to provide some kind of compensation (albeit inadequate) for the evils of colonisation, 'even if it should be a failure to save a remnant of the race'.[13]

Despite such dire predictions, the Oenpelli community survives and continues to increase. Today in Oenpelli, the Mandjurlngunj clan continue their responsibility as Senior Traditional Owners. The descendants of many described in this book, such as Nipper Marakarra Gumurdul and his daughter Garabbunba ('Carabumba'), are esteemed community leaders. Dyer's strategy to entice Aboriginal people from across western Arnhem Land to the mission (and *bininjs'* calculated decisions to 'come in') has had lasting consequences. Today, people from over 40 different clan groups call Oenpelli home. It is a multicultural, multilingual community. While only a faithful few continue to engage with the Anglican Church there (now led by local Aboriginal woman and ordained minister Rev. Lois Nadjamerrek, and with the assistance of Church Missionary Society missionaries), nearly all uphold the kinship system. Ceremonial life is alive too, even as it has evolved to suit the needs of *bininj* today. The long *bininj* history of dynamic innovation and adaptation to new circumstances, even while upholding the fundamental changelessness of their traditions and identities, continues even now.

---

12   Simpson, *Adam in Ochre*, 186.
13   Dyer, 29 March, NTRS 1099/P1 vol. 1.

3

OENPELLI BEFORE
THE MISSION

The people of the Oenpelli region have been navigating cultural differences and negotiating with outsiders for centuries. Interactions between western Arnhem Land Aboriginal groups and foreigners began with South-East Asian mariners, at least 400 years ago (or possibly much earlier).[1] Aboriginal people painted images of South-East Asian sailing vessels or *prau* in rock art in north-western Arnhem Land. One example of rock art, found under beeswax, dates back to the mid-seventeenth century.[2] So far, there is no firm archaeological evidence for early interactions extending as far south as Oenpelli. But people living at Oenpelli certainly had heard about the sailors; the Aboriginal exchange systems, ceremonial gatherings and seasonal walking routes meant that information about these newcomers and Aboriginal people's interactions with them spread far and wide.

Then came fleeting visits from European explorers, such as Dutch explorer Maarten Van Delft who reached Melville Island in 1705.[3] Moving inland, later overland explorers made first European contact with Aboriginal groups across western Arnhem Land and what is now Kakadu. These included Ludwig Leichhardt in December 1845.

---

1   For example, Clark and May, *Macassan History*; Macknight, *The Voyage to Marege*; Taçon et al., 'A Minimum Age', 1–10; Theden-Ringl et al., 'Buried on Foreign Shores', 41–48; Wesley, O'Connor and Fenner, 'Re-evaluating the Timing', 169–95.
2   Taçon et al., 'A Minimum Age', 1–10.
3   Sheehan, 'Strangers and Servants of the Company', 6–34.

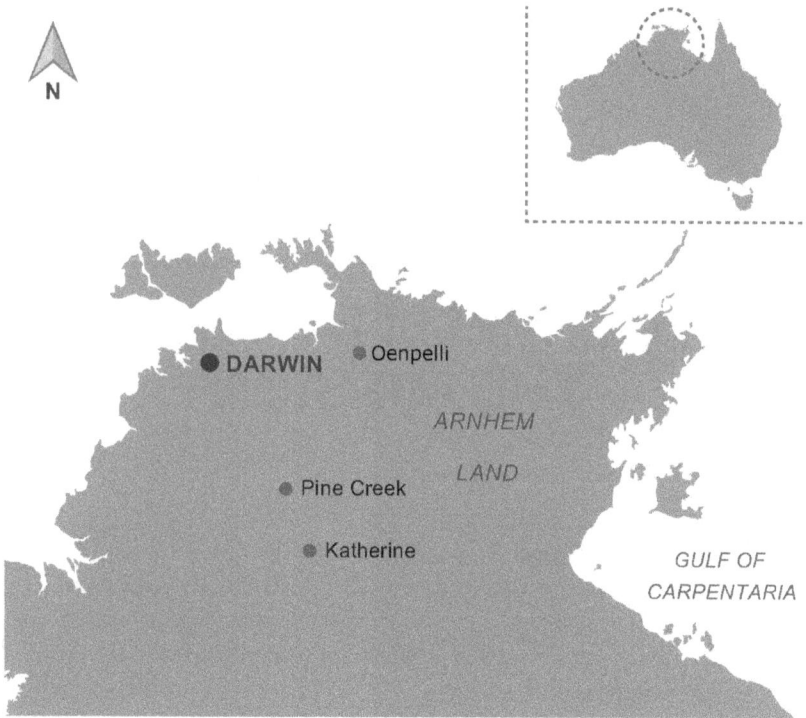

Figure 3.1: Map showing location of Oenpelli.
Source: Open source map edited by Laura Rademaker.

Nearing the end of his long journey, Leichhardt and his team were in the vicinity of the current Oenpelli township for a few days. Leichhardt complained that when he offered 'presents' (iron pieces, tin and leather belts) to a party of local people in return for fish, they became 'exceedingly noisy'. One of them, 'an old rogue', apparently began helping himself to Leichhardt's party's stores – a red blanket, spade, pot – so Leichhardt ordered the group be scared away. Trying to make amends later, Leichhardt's party offered them 'half a goose' that they refused, preferring their own food.[4] Undeterred, the group returned a few days later and became Leichhardt's guides. They showed him where it was safe to cross the East Alligator River. One man, Apirk, pointed them to food and water and gave them directions to continue safely on their way.[5] Apirk ushered Leichhardt north towards the British settlements of the Cobourg Peninsula and nearby islands. The 'explorers' were not so much 'discovering' routes across Arnhem Land as following instructions from those who already knew the way.

4   Leichhardt, *Journal of an Overland Expedition*, 512.
5   Leichhardt, *Journal of an Overland Expedition*, 513–15.

Figure 3.2: 'Native Camp, Port Essington', 1877. Photograph by Paul Foelsche.

Source: Northern Territory Record Series (PH1060/0057).

Buffalo era

The British had established garrison settlements on Melville Island in 1824 and the Cobourg Peninsula in 1829 (Figures 3.1 and 3.2).[6] When they failed, the British let their water buffalo loose. This suited the buffalo perfectly. Local monsoonal conditions meant they multiplied rapidly, spreading down the peninsula and across Arnhem Land.[7] By May 1839, Lieutenant Stewart sighted buffalo below the neck of the Cobourg Peninsula.[8] In 1845, Leichhardt noted Aboriginal people using the name 'Anaborro' (*nganaparru*) to refer to buffalo. Taking advantage of the buffalo's increasing numbers, shooter camps emerged along the river plains by the late 1800s.[9] Aboriginal men, women and children were the backbone of this industry, shooting, skinning and salting large numbers of buffalo (Figures 3.3 and 3.4).[10]

---

6   Levitus, 'Social History since Colonisation', 64–93.
7   Berndt and Berndt, *Man, Land & Myth*, 5; Mulvaney, *Paddy Cahill of Oenpelli*, 11.
8   Allen, 'Archaeology and the History of Port Essington', 352–53.
9   Leichhardt, *Journal of an Overland Expedition*, 524–25; Bowman and Robinson, 'The Getting of the Nganabbarru', 192; Levitus, *Everybody Bin All Day Work*, 13–21.
10   Albrecht et al., 'Convergence of Culture', 361–78; Berndt and Berndt, *Man, Land and Myth*, 5; Levitus, *Everybody Bin All Day Work*, 13–21; Mulvaney, *Paddy Cahill of Oenpelli*, 13; Robinson, 'Buffalo Hunting and the Feral Frontier', 893.

Figure 3.3: Reuben Cooper sitting on a wounded buffalo surrounded by the shooting and skinning team, c. 1914–17. Photograph by Edward Frederick Reichenbach (Ted Ryko).

Source: Northern Territory Library: Karilyn Brown Collection (PH0413/0044).

Figure 3.4: Buffalo shooters 'dining' on the carcass of the buffalo with photographer Edward Frederick Reichenbach (Ted Ryko) pictured front right, c. 1914–17.

Source: Northern Territory Library: Ted Ryko Collection (PH0055/0007).

Figure 3.5: Paddy Cahill and Quilp (on horses) with other buffalo shooters in the background near Oenpelli (Gunbalanya), c. 1901.
Source: Northern Territory Library: Peter Spillett Collection (PH0238/0707).

Among the European buffalo hunters was Patrick 'Paddy' Cahill (1863–1923). He was one of the first commercial buffalo shooters to work in western Arnhem Land. Cahill was, according to archaeologist John Mulvaney, a 'stocky, broad-shouldered extrovert'. Apparently he claimed, '43 buffalo with 52 cartridges was his best day's effort'.[11] Born in Queensland, in 1883 Cahill drove his cattle west with his brothers to the Northern Territory, working at Wave Hill, Delamere and Gordon Downs stations before being moving into the Oenpelli region in the late 1800s.[12]

There is some question as to how Cahill developed an interest in western Arnhem Land. Perhaps he was attracted by reports of up to 60,000 buffalo running wild on the plains of the Alligator River.[13] Mulvaney suggests that Cahill's interest was simply because the government made it available for lease. He knew the terrain and had seen its great agricultural potential. He knew many of the local people too; he had hired them to help with his buffalo-hunting enterprises.[14]

---

11   Mulvaney and Calaby, 'So Much That Is New', 302.
12   Clinch, 'Cahill, Patrick (Paddy) (1863–1923)'.
13   Clinch, 'Cahill, Patrick (Paddy) (1863–1923)'.
14   Mulvaney, Paddy Cahill of Oenpelli, 37.

CMS historian Keith Cole explains that the kinship connections of those he already knew, including Nipper Marakarra Gumurdul, attracted him to the region (Figure 3.6). Nipper's older brother Narpan had married a woman from Wave Hill and lived there while Cahill was based there. When Narpan was killed in a fight, Cahill moved to Narpan's country at Oenpelli.[15] According to Nipper's adopted son, Frank Djendjulng, Nipper considered himself as host to those on his country:

Figure 3.6: Senior Traditional Owner for the Oenpelli area, Nipper Marakarra Gumurdul, photographed in 1948.

Source: Mountford, *Records of the American-Australian Scientific Expedition to Arnhem Land*, Vol. 1, 14.

> Nipper was boss of these camps, because his country. This is where he was born. Happy to have mission on his country, happy to have people from other areas on his country.[16]

Cahill had connections with Aboriginal kin beyond Nipper and Narpan. He had an Aboriginal son born around 1900 to Kuludjba, a woman of the Wilirrgu clan who was living near the present-day Cahill's Crossing. This son was known as Paddy Cahill Junior Neyingkul, and he died in 1971. Neyingkul was raised by his Aboriginal relatives including the husband of Kuludjba, Bill Mayimarlba (Gerrmurrgu clan). His descendants still live in western Arnhem Land today. Cahill senior likely benefited from having an Aboriginal son. Perhaps his son eased the way for his long-term occupation of the area. Cahill's connection to the Oenpelli area was already well established by 1900, 10 years before the establishment of a permanent settlement.

15   Cole, *A History of Oenpelli*, 15.
16   Frank Djendjulng, oral history interview with Robert Levitus, 20 July 1981.

Figure 3.7: Left to right: Ruby Mudford (Roney), Paddy Cahill, unidentified man, Maria Cahill and Quilp (possibly) (date unknown).
Source: Northern Territory Library: J.A. Austin Collection (PH0412/0093).

Paddy Cahill (senior) had a non-Indigenous family too. Maria Cahill (née Pickford) was born in Stirling, Adelaide, in 1873 but lived in Darwin where her father was the publican at the Club Hotel. Cahill married Maria in 1899 and their only child, Thomas, was born not long after Neyingkul, in 1901.[17]

The Oenpelli settlement

After years of buffalo hunting in the region, Cahill and his business partner William Johnstone established a permanent settlement at Oenpelli in January 1910 (with the official lease granted in April 1910).[18] This included 640 acres of land, which was later reduced to 320 acres at Cahill's request. He also held a pastoral permit.[19] Ruby Mudford (later Roney), Cahill's niece, described this period in her oral histories (Figures 3.7 and 3.8). After the death of her parents, she had come to live

17   Mulvaney, *Paddy Cahill of Oenpelli*, 9.
18   Roney, NTRS 226, TS 735.
19   Mulvaney, *Paddy Cahill of Oenpelli*, 35.

with her uncle and aunt from 1904 until 1922. She described the family's arrival at Oenpelli and their dependence on local people throughout the early days of the settlement:

> In 1910, we packed up to go to Oenpelli and one January day, January in the height of the wet season, we went aboard this boat ... We left Darwin on the Sunday morning and we got to the East Alligator landing on Thursday where a lot of uncle's natives were waiting for us. How glad we all were to get off that boat. I remember some natives arrived and they had a tremendous big bit of barramundi on a pole which they carried on their shoulders for us. But the mosquitoes were very plentiful there too. We camped on the river bank that night and the next day we went up to the station. The boys brought some horses down. They already had my uncle's horses at Oenpelli. It was seven mile from the landing up to where we were going to live. We were glad to get up there and the natives and Johnson brought the stores later which we'd taken down, and the fowls. After a bit of a rest, this Johnson took the boat with a couple of native helpers back to Darwin and then brought everything else we wanted down and also our goats ...
>
> On Oenpelli we had fowls, goats, pigs and horses but there wasn't much of a living in it for uncle Paddy so when Doctor Gilruth visited us (I can't remember the year; it may have been '12 or '13), he decided to buy the place for the Government and appoint uncle Paddy a Protector of Aborigines which he did. Then he looked after the natives. He was pretty good with the natives, my uncle. He could speak the Kakadu language and they all knew him from when he was younger and single. When he was buffalo shooting in that part of the country, he knew many of the natives and spoke their language. So he looked after the natives there.[20]

It seems Nipper Marakarra Gumurdul saw some benefit in allowing Cahill to establish a settlement on his land – at least in the early years. Having an Aboriginal son and speaking the local language also allowed Cahill certain access that would have been otherwise unobtainable.

---

20   Roney, NTRS 226, TS 517, 16–19.

Figure 3.8: Paddy Cahill, his son Tom Cahill, Maria Cahill and Ruby Mudford (later Roney) with unidentified Aboriginal children, Oenpelli, c. 1912. Photograph by Elsie Masson.
Source: Pitt Rivers Museum, University of Oxford (1998.306.61).

During his 1912 visit to the station, anthropologist and Chief Protector Baldwin Spencer recorded its layout and day-to-day activities (Figure 3.9). He described a 'small house with a detached kitchen, built of stringy-bark, and sundry outhouses'. Around this, a 'large garden slopes down to the lagoon, nearly a mile long and a quarter of a mile broad'. Maria and Ruby, he commented, were 'just as keen on bush life as is Cahill himself, and both of them never so much at home as when they are on horseback, exploring the country for miles round the homestead'.[21] Carl Warburton, a traveller who visited in 1921, recorded Cahill as saying that Maria 'was the only white woman living who could speak the native language of the blacks'.[22] According to him, Cahill, too, associated closely with local people:

21 Spencer, *Wanderings in Wild Australia*, 742–43.
22 In Cole, *A History of Oenpelli*, 17.

Figure 3.9: The Cahill settlement at Oenpelli with Arrkuluk Hill in the background, c. 1912–14. Photographer is Mervyn Holmes or Elsie Masson.
Source: Pitt Rivers Museum, University of Oxford (1998.306.120).

> He never laughs at them; he speaks to them in their own language, and calls them by their native names. In return, they give him their confidence, and no ceremony is too sacred to be enacted before him.[23]

Both Paddy and Maria were resourceful. Their home impressed visitors (Figure 3.10). Warburton even noted that they owned an impressive library of several hundred books.[24] In 1915 Elsie Masson, a friend of Spencer and au pair for the children of the Administrator of the Northern Territory, briefly visited the station and described Cahill's work training the men to grow vegetables and build houses and the women learning domestic work in positive terms.[25]

23   Masson, *An Untamed Territory*, 103.
24   Warburton, cited in Mulvaney and Calaby, *'So Much That Is New'*, 302.
25   Masson, *An Untamed Territory*, 100–19.

Figure 3.10: Two unidentified Aboriginal men standing out the front of a house designed by Paddy Cahill and built by local Aboriginal people in Oenpelli (date unknown).
Source: Northern Territory Library: J.A. Austin Collection (PH0412/0192).

But it was not an easy life. Roney was bored and tired. She recalled that they played cards almost every night and that, when she finally left Oenpelli, she refused to play cards ever again. Maria treated her more as servant than kin. Roney recalled, 'I done all the cooking, bread and baking, all the mending, and making of my aunt's and my own underwear. I was always busy and darning all the socks and stockings'. Maria, meanwhile, apparently constantly found fault with her work: 'she didn't do anything at all, only complain'.[26]

> About two o'clock every afternoon, after I'd cleared away and washed up after the midday meal and set the afternoon tea tray ready for uncle and auntie, I went riding from two o'clock till five. I had a great time. I had plenty of nice horses to ride and I used to roam about ... It's lovely country down Oenpelli, beautiful country, lovely open plains and even sometimes I rode up to the ports and always enjoyed my get away from nagging and fault finding for a while.[27]

---

26 Roney, NTRS 226, TS 517, 23–24, 31, 38.
27 Roney, NTRS 226, TS 517, 21.

Trouble in paradise

Cahill's relationship with local people was not always rosy. In 1917 the Cahill family along with a non-Aboriginal assistant, O'Brien, two 'housemaids', Marealmark and Topsy, and the dog were poisoned with strychnine. It was in their butter. Only the dog died. But all were seriously unwell, and fortunately (for them) had medicine on hand. Cahill blamed Romula, a trusted Aboriginal friend, responsible for bringing mail to Oenpelli. Romula had accused Quilp, an Aboriginal stockman rumoured to be Cahill's son, of sleeping with his wife, Topsy. According to Cahill, Romula had wanted to poison them all because Cahill had prevented him from beating Topsy.[28] But some Aboriginal people thought that Cahill 'interfered too much' in their affairs and was too harsh in his discipline, and many were angry.[29]

There were violent reprisals. Thomas Cahill described how, after the butter incident, his father was about to chain Romula around the neck and flog him. Romula went to hit Paddy, when Paddy struck Romula's head with the chain.[30] Cahill wrote to Baldwin Spencer to justify his violence:

> I at once got a chain and padlock and arrested Romula. When arresting Romula he came towards me … I doubled up the chain and struck him on the head very hard; knocking him down. I at once fastened the chain on his neck and tied him up. You can imagine my feelings and the frame of mind that I was in. Mrs Cahill vomiting, O'Brien almost dead, the two lubras rolling on the ground vomiting and likely to die at any moment … When I got things fixed up, Romula said 'You look out boss nother one boy put poison in the water bag'.[31]

28   Cahill to Spencer, 30 June 1918 in Mulvaney, *Paddy Cahill of Oenpelli*, 125.
29   Cahill to H. E. Craey, 25 January 1917, National Archives of Australia (hereafter NAA) A3, NT1917/427.
30   Australia, Royal Commission on the Northern Territory, *Minutes of Evidence*, 28.
31   Cahill to Spencer, 10 October 1917 in Mulvaney, *Paddy Cahill of Oenpelli*, 119.

After the head injury, Cahill 'sent for the police' and 'committed Romula to Darwin' (that is, Fannie Bay Gaol).[32] Cahill also accused Nipper of being the ringleader, citing a rumour that Nipper ordered the other men to poison him after a group meeting in which they had expressed resentment at Cahill's discipline. Mulvaney inferred that 'as the owner of the land on which Cahill lived, Nipper may have suffered many slights and ceremonial discourtesies prompting his reactions in 1917'.[33] Soon after the poisoning, Nipper and Munnierlorko killed a cow. That was it: Cahill sent them to Fannie Bay Gaol too.

The poisoning of the butter, along with cattle killing, suggests that relationships between local people and Cahill were breaking down by 1917, most likely a product of Cahill's increasing assertion of control (Figures 3.11 and 3.12). Some of what was going on at Oenpelli was exposed in a 1920 royal commission. Cahill's violent treatment of Aboriginal workers was scandalous, even in its day.[34] Cahill acknowledged he used his role as 'Protector' to act as judge and jury over Aboriginal people, sentencing some to prison in Darwin, others to corporal punishment. When asked if his intent 'was to be Pooh Bah of Oenpelli', he admitted, 'yes; that was quite right. I wished to have power over the natives'.[35] A former Oenpelli employee, David Hogg, confessed that although he too had 'struck', 'hit' and 'punched' Aboriginal people for crimes such as 'not doing the milking', the Cahills were worse. One time, Thomas Cahill had put a gun to a teenage boy's face, cutting him. The boy was then chained to a beam for hours and, finally, given a 'good hiding'. The boy's offence: he had brought only 14 cows in for milking, not the 18 Cahill had requested.[36]

Following the disgrace of the royal commission, 2,000 square miles of land (including the Oenpelli area) were declared an Aboriginal reserve in 1920. Paddy, Maria, Thomas and Ruby remained until 1922 when the Cahills retired to the south of Australia. Paddy died the next year.[37]

---

32 Australia, Royal Commission on the Northern Territory, *Minutes of Evidence*, 135.
33 Mulvaney, *Paddy Cahill of Oenpelli*, 62.
34 Ben Silverstein, 'The "Proper Settler" and the "Native Mind"', 94.
35 Australia, Royal Commission on the Northern Territory, *Minutes of Evidence*, 144–45.
36 Australia, Royal Commission on the Northern Territory, *Minutes of Evidence*, 153–54.
37 Clinch, 'Cahill, Patrick (Paddy) (1863–1923)'.

Figure 3.11: Women and children gathered at the Oenpelli settlement, c. 1917. Photograph thought to be by Tom Cahill.

Source: Museum Victoria (Item XP 8454).

Figure 3.12: Four Aboriginal men competing in local 'games' possibly on Christmas Day, c. 1922. Paddy Cahill is seen standing at the back and his wife Maria is seated with an umbrella.

Source: State Library of South Australia (PRG 280/1/39/345).

Cahill was always afraid that if missionaries came to the region they would interfere with the traditions of local Aboriginal people.[38] According to Warburton, Cahill stated that, 'the only thing to do with them in the Territory … is to segregate them in areas and leave them alone'.[39] He did not seem to consider his own presence on Aboriginal land as interference, but it seems many local people thought otherwise. Years later, some in the community came to the conclusion that missionary discipline and interference was mild, at least compared to Cahill:

> Missionary people were good people, they were showing them good things. Paddy Cahill did hard things. Shot dogs. That's what I heard. Growl at them sometimes. Missionary people helped black people. Missionaries would send black away bush if they did wrong thing, like stealing.[40]

Loyalties and loss

On Cahill's departure from Oenpelli, the Mengerrdji-speaking people remained, while other Aboriginal families who had long associations with Cahill began to move away. Cole described an exodus of Cahill's workers and their replacement with others:

> Among other Aborigines who lived and worked at Oenpelli in Paddy Cahill's time had been Herbert Yupidj, Old Major (Burrirrlirl), Captain Madjarralaga, Garrinba, Mamuna, Marrawalawal, Arrawindji, Manujulug and Nawumirrili. When Paddy Cahill left, these and others left except Herbert, Old Major and Arrawindji (Lazarus) … As Paddy Cahill's workers left others filled their place as stockmen.[41]

Cahill would have hated that the station went to the CMS. Having observed the work of the CMS at the Roper River mission, he thought missionaries concentrated too much on piety, at the expense of practical work. His view was they achieved little other than 'singing and schooling – also prayers'. In terms of the 'industrial work', construction and 'cultivation', he thought missionaries were useless.[42]

---

38 Cole, *A History of Oenpelli*, 17; Warburton, *Buffaloes*, 141.
39 Warburton, *Buffaloes*, 141.
40 Hannah Mangiru, oral history with Robert Levitus, 27 July, 1981.
41 Cole, *A History of Oenpelli*, 23.
42 Cahill to Baldwin Spencer, 19 December 1912, in Mulvaney, *Paddy Cahill of Oenpelli*, 81.

Until the missionaries came in 1925, a government-appointed caretaker, Mr Donald 'Don' Campbell, managed the station with his wife.[43] Campbell had been a government stock inspector and had also served in the First World War.[44] A 1923 report in the *Northern Territory Times* described him as having a 'refreshing personality, whose vigour is indicated in his style and action'.[45] Mrs Campbell, on the other hand, is described as being in ill health but nevertheless had apparently 'done splendidly considering her lack of all previous experience of the loneliness and privations of outback life'.[46]

Dyer had mixed feelings about the Campbells. He found them personally supportive, writing in 1925 that Campbell has 'helped me much … he is an expert, I wish I were as capable'.[47] But he did not think much of his treatment of Aboriginal people. According to Dyer, Campbell was a threat to Aboriginal people:

> There are plenty [of natives] about. Mr. Campbell said he had about 300 last Christmas. His policy has been to hunt them, because of the cattle killing; as you read between the lines you will see plenty of problems for the Superintendent of Oenpelli – we will have an uphill fight.[48]

'Hunt' in Aboriginal English could mean simply to scare people away, though it implies the threat of violence. We cannot be sure in exactly what sense Dyer used the word, but it is clear Aboriginal people were unwelcome. When the missionaries arrived, the region was already under upheaval. Some families were fleeing, others were coming in, looking for work. Aboriginal people had good reason to mistrust the new missionary 'bosses', just as they had the Cahills and Campbells before them.

---

43   'The Maskee Returns', *Northern Territory Times and Gazette*, 2 December 1924, 4.

44   'Appointment', *Northern Territory Times and Gazette*, 23 December 1922, 3; 'A Long Tramp: Cooktown to Darwin', *Northern Standard*, 27 July 1923, 1.

45   'Bush Personals', *Northern Territory Times and Gazette*, 30 November 1923, 6.

46   C. J. Kirkland, 'A Trip to the Alligator Rivers', *Northern Territory Times and Gazette*, 5 May 1923, 4.

47   Dyer, 'First Report on Oenpelli', 21 September 1925, NTRS 1099/P1 vol. 1, Mission Reports.

48   Dyer, 'First Report on Oenpelli'.

4

WHO WERE THE MISSIONARIES?

Until the early twentieth century, Christian missions to Aboriginal people mostly failed within only a few years. Oenpelli was part of a new generation of missions, scattered across northern and central Australia, to Aboriginal people who lived on Country and who had few dealings with Europeans so far.

These twentieth-century missions started as humanitarian ventures. Of course, there was always the intention to convert Aboriginal people to Christianity, but the assumption was that Aboriginal people could have no place in white Australia. At the turn of the century, much of white Australia expected that Aboriginal people were doomed to extinction. Missionaries hoped that perhaps, by their intervention, they might save some. But contact with white 'civilisation', they believed, was toxic to Aboriginal people. Enticing and attractive, but like the forbidden fruit of Eden, it would be their downfall. As Dyer himself wrote, 'civilisation spells their extinction'.[1]

Christian churches and mission organisations, therefore, looked for isolated places where they believed they could attract Aboriginal people to missions, shield them from other white Australians, develop Aboriginal people's skills in agriculture, and conduce them to 'settle down' and, most of all, to convert to Christianity. Many established missions on islands, ideal for their isolation. The Tiwi Islands missions and Milingimbi missions in the Top End are examples.

---

1   Annual Report Oenpelli 1928, NAA A431/1.

THE BIBLE IN BUFFALO COUNTRY

Oenpelli, however, was not such an attractive location for mission organisations because it was too central and accessible. An island would be better. The Church Missionary Society, however, was convinced that the Arnhem Land escarpment was a sufficient natural 'fence' to keep Aboriginal people in and others out, and so seized the opportunity to establish a mission when Paddy Cahill's cattle station became available.

The humanitarian crisis for Aboriginal people in the Northern Territory was real. There were many massacres. In 1878, settlers shot and clubbed to death 17 Aboriginal people on the Daly River. Thirty were killed in another massacre on the Daly in 1884. About 100 Yolngu people were killed in a massacre between 1889 and 1896 near Milingimbi and, in 1903, 30 Alawa people were shot at Minyerri.[2] There were other massacres and murders that went unrecorded by Europeans but are not forgotten by communities today. In addition to violence, sexually transmitted diseases, malaria, influenza and leprosy were major health problems. Estimates were that 60 per cent of the population had leprosy in some form.[3]

So the CMS work in north Australian missions began with explicit humanitarian intentions. The Bishop of North Queensland, Rev. Frodsham, spurred evangelicals to work in Arnhem Land in 1906.[4] Frodsham called for missionaries of the so-called 'stronger race' to take action, constructing their mission in terms of humanitarian compassion, couched in racial hierarchies:

> Missionary work then may be only smoothing the pillow of
> a dying race, but I think that if the Lord Jesus came to Australia he
> would be moved with great compassion for these poor outcastes,
> lying by the wayside, robbed of their land, wounded by the lust
> and passion of a stronger race.[5]

Aboriginal people, he thought, might not survive the coming of the 'stronger race', but that race should, at least, show compassion to those they had supposedly conquered, went his argument.

---

2   Centre for 21st Century Humanities, 'Colonial Massacres Map'.
3   Cole, *From Mission to Church*, 124.
4   Dewar, *The 'Black War' in Arnhem Land*, 9; Cole, *A Short History of the C.M.S. Roper River Mission*, 5.
5   Frodsham, Bishop of North Queensland in Clarke, *Report of the Church Congress*.

The Church Missionary Society

The CMS was a product of the evangelical revivals in late eighteenth-century England. In 1799, a small band of evangelicals established their 'Society for Missions to Africa and the East', which later became the CMS.[6] The CMS went wherever the British Empire went, sometimes preceding it and preparing the way (as in New Zealand). Its original founders had Botany Bay in mind for a mission field. Despite this, it did very little in Australia in the early nineteenth century. It operated only briefly in the 1830s at the Wellington Valley mission. The mission provided food and medical aid and was a refuge from violent settlers encroaching on Wiradjuri land. Missionaries started learning Wiradjuri and, with Wiradjuri co-translators, translated some scripture. But then the missionaries kidnapped Wiradjuri children, so the Wiradjuri left. When the missionaries began fighting each other, the station imploded, and the mission closed.

In 1892, Church Missionary Associations (CMAs) were established in New South Wales and Victoria, both independent of the 'Parent Society'. These sent Australian missionaries all over the world but also operated missions to the 'heathen' Aboriginal people of Victoria (Yelta, Lake Tyers and Lake Condah).[7] In 1916 the associations came together to form the CMS of Australia and Tasmania (later simply 'CMS Australia'). Although CMS Australia remained autonomous, the Australians considered themselves 'a true heir to the Society of the 19th Century', sharing the heritage and evangelicalism of the 'Parent Society' in England.[8] It also distinguished itself from the other Anglican mission organisation in Australia, the Australian Board of Missions (ABM). The CMS was a democratic organisation governed by lay people, not the church establishment's bishops as in the ABM. It was also a Low Church evangelical society rather than High, so it emphasised personal conversion over sacramental styles of worship. This meant that the CMS could not always enjoy the support of bishops within whose diocese it operated (in the Northern Territory this was the Diocese of Carpentaria).

Following the CMS's failure at Wellington Valley (and the failure of many other similar missions), by the mid-nineteenth century much of white Australia suspected Aboriginal people could not be evangelised or 'civilised'.

6   Cole, *Sharing in Mission*, 7–8.
7   Johnstone, *A History of the Church Missionary Society*, 205–30.
8   Church Missionary Society of Australia, *Decade*, 6.

The churches taught that anyone, no matter their race, could potentially convert to Christianity, but the rise of social-Darwinist theories – that some races prevailed over others due to their superior intellect, bodies or culture – challenged this doctrine. Perhaps some races were simply too backward to understand Christianity. At the same time, Aboriginal people were dying at such a rate that others imagined there would soon be none left to evangelise. There was a second wave of missionary activity in the latter half of the nineteenth century. The most famous of these were run by German Lutherans in Central Australia. They also established their most successful mission, Hermannsburg (1877–1982) near Alice Springs, one of few to survive into the era of twentieth-century missions.[9]

For Aboriginal people, life on these missions was, sometimes, a last resort in a dire situation. Missions brought some opportunities. There was the opportunity to gain access to new knowledge (especially to learn to read and write in English). They could also be a refuge from violent settlers. But the missions also operated with strict discipline and work regimes. They were generally under-resourced and located on the poorest farmland, residents (called 'inmates') lived in poverty. Although missionaries respected Aboriginal people as equally human, they held patronising views of Aboriginal cultures as underdeveloped and unsophisticated. Most focused on children, believing adults were too steeped in their traditions to change. This could be devastating for Aboriginal families, especially when missionaries forcibly removed children or used dormitories, as they did at Oenpelli.

After the failure of the nineteenth-century missions, missionary organisations and churches took a new approach in the early twentieth century. It was a national and Christian duty, they believed, to atone for the evils of colonisation. They looked, with hope, to Aboriginal people in remote parts of Australia who had little contact with Europeans. Perhaps in these isolated places, where Aboriginal culture still survived (white Australia had little understanding of how Aboriginal cultures had adapted to change in the southern parts of Australia, believing Aboriginal society and culture were destroyed), missions might have a chance at preventing the destruction experienced in the southern states.[10]

---

9   See Hill, *Broken Song*; Austin-Broos, *Arrernte Present, Arrernte Past*; Kenny, *The Lamb Enters the Dreaming*.

10   For histories of these missions see Rademaker, *Found in Translation*; Loos, *White Christ Black Cross*; Ganter, *The Contest for Aboriginal Souls*; Choo, *Mission Girls*; Emilsen, *Fighting Spirit*; Pybus, *"'We Grew Up This Place"*; Morris, *The Tiwi*; Harris, *One Blood*.

Figure 4.1: 'Native Congregation, Oenpelli Mission', 1928. Photograph by John Bleakley.
Source: National Archives of Australia (NAA A1200/L26057 Minister and congregation, Oenpelli Church of England Mission, Northern Territory, 1928).

The Victorian CMA started their work in Arnhem Land in 1908 with the Roper River mission. Soon after, the Commonwealth Government carved up the Northern Territory for the churches, giving the Anglicans, Catholics and Methodists 'spheres of influence' in which to operate missions, provide welfare and keep Aboriginal people away from towns.[11] The Catholics had the west coast and Tiwi Islands, the Lutherans were in the centre, the Methodists took north and east Arnhem Land, the south-east went to the Anglicans. These spheres are still, implicitly, in operation today through the workings of faith-based social service agencies. With the assurance that its work would be protected as it expanded, the new united CMS of Australia and Tasmania began a mission on Groote Eylandt in 1921. When Oenpelli became available, it was natural it should go to the Methodist Church as it was close to their Goulburn Island mission and within their 'sphere'. But it was not an island. Thinking it would be too difficult to control who came and went, the Methodists rejected it, so did the Catholics. So it went to the Anglican CMS.[12]

---

11 Baker, 'Crossing Boundaries', 18.
12 Cole, *Oenpelli Pioneer*, 48.

The missionaries did not believe they came to destroy Aboriginal culture. The CMS articulated its approach in a 1931 policy document:

> We deplore any method which tends to detribalise the natives and suggest:
>
> a. A new method of approach to the Aborigines in their natural condition, that is by means of sporadic evangelism, in other words, a series of thrusts from strategically placed bases into the various tribal areas of Arnhem Land where the remnant of uncontaminated Aborigines of Australia is to be found. We feel that the stations at Oenpelli, Roper and Groote are so strategically situated, Mataranka being the convenient railhead.
>
> b. We are convinced that this will mean ultimately a very considerable saving in expenditure; a more efficient and worthwhile evangelising of the Aborigines; and a more effective and statesmanlike staffing, grouping and interchanging of Missionaries, especially with the aid of the aeroplane which is now in the field.[13]

The CMS, at this stage, did not intend to institutionalise Aboriginal people entirely but to set up strategic bases for evangelism, from which Aboriginal people would come and go, but eventually settle. Aboriginal people would not be 'detribalised'. By that, they meant that Aboriginal authority and social structure would be respected. Of course, this was with the proviso that Aboriginal practices did not conflict with missionaries' moral views, leaving missionaries considerable scope to assert their own authority (and missionaries were the ones with guns). Missionaries particularly targeted Aboriginal 'superstition' (ceremony) and patterns of family life as 'immoral', not accepting that these were in fact integral to Aboriginal people's social structure. Nevertheless, this method, the CMS hoped, would be more effective in converting Aboriginal people than previous mission attempts. It would also be cheaper.

---

13   Minutes of a meeting of the Federal Council, 3–5 June 1931, ML MSS 6040/1.

Tobacco was central to the whole enterprise. Missionaries had mixed feelings about it; they abstained themselves. But nothing worked better to attract Aboriginal people to the mission and induce them to work. The Aboriginal stockmen were essential workers, paid in small amounts of 'pocket money' and tobacco as well as sugar and tea (all addictive substances to varying degrees). Food was no incentive. The Aboriginal stockmen had no need for food; they knew how to live off the land. But the mission did provide meals for men, women and children as well as a general, smaller tobacco ration for those who worked at the mission in the garden or doing maintenance.[14]

Missionary women working as teachers and nurses and domestic staff formed the core of the mission staff.[15] Apart from tobacco, medical aid and education were missions' other assets for attracting Aboriginal people. On proposing the establishment of Oenpelli mission in 1925, Alf Dyer suggested the necessary staff would consist of himself, his wife (a nurse) and 'a lady teacher'.[16] The women's work was enormous. Female missionaries were constantly exhausted. Dyer, for example, reported that Florence Sherrin suffered a terrible string of maladies in her first 18 months: weight loss, whooping cough, malaria, pneumonia, a hearing impairment and stomach pains.[17]

The missionaries

Alf Dyer grew up in the suburbs of Melbourne. Born in Hawthorne in 1884, he left school at 13 and worked in the family-run hardware shop in Fitzroy. He said his family was not very religious.[18] They found his piety amusing and teased him that he would grow up to be a priest. 'Zealous and enthusiastic', but not too bright was the general consensus on his character.[19]

---

14   Harris, *My Story G.R. (Dick) Harris*, 18, NTRS 1105.
15   For a history of missionary women in Australia, see Cruickshank and Grimshaw, *White Women, Aboriginal Missions*.
16   A. J. Dyer to Hinsby, 20 March 1925, ML MSS 6040/3.
17   A. J. Dyer to Ferrier, ML MSS 6039.
18   Dyer, Manuscript, 1, NTRS 693 part 1, Item 18.
19   Henry Mercer, 17 May 1911, ML MSS 6039/39.

Figure 4.2: Mary and Alf Dyer (date unknown).
Source: Northern Territory Archives Service (NTRS 694 P1 Box 4e Item 681).

Dyer was convinced that God had called him to be a missionary to Africa, having been told in a vision in 1911.[20] He was so convinced of his call, he offered to work as a missionary for half pay, if funds were an obstacle. But money was not the problem. Dyer failed his theological studies.[21] He had no knowledge of any foreign language.[22] He eventually got the theological degree (he was 'not brilliant as a scholar' and only made it by 'perseverance in studying backed up by unceasing prayer' wrote his reference[23]), but, even after three abortive attempts, never passed ancient Greek. He was also single.[24]

The CMS was eager that more women should be posted on Aboriginal missions. The chair of the Roper River Committee even suggested to missionary Keith Langford Smith that the committee 'choose a suitable Christian girl and send her up to [him]' as a bride. Langford Smith refused, jesting that they should 'send a girl up on a thirty-day trial'.[25] Dyer's application was rejected by the CMS in 1913, partly because of his

20 Dyer, Manuscript, 2, NTRS 693 part 1, Item 18.
21 Questions for Candidates, ML MSS 6039/35.
22 Questions for Candidates, ML MSS 6039/35.
23 John Stanley Robinson, 18 May 1911, ML MSS 6039/35.
24 Dyer, Manuscript, 5, NTRS 693 part 1, Item 18.
25 Keith Langford Smith, 'Marriage', *Sky Pilot News*, Jan–Feb 1981, NTRS 337/P1.

lack of Greek, but mostly his lack of wife. That very year, the committee sent the woman he was later to marry – Mary Crome – in his place. For the CMS, missionary women had no need of husbands. The mission field needed single women, to teach and nurse. But missionary men needed wives to keep them in check from the 'temptations' of Aboriginal women. Single and without qualifications, Dyer had two strikes against him as a potential missionary.

Still, he was determined to make it. The CMS rejected Dyer from Africa but, eventually, the Victorian CMA invited him to go to the Roper River in March 1915. That the CMS chose to send a man with a notable lack of talent for language, and who they thought would not make it in Africa, indicates the regard they had for Aboriginal cultures and languages. Though the CMS accepted him, the Bishop of Carpentaria still had reservations. Dyer was not ordained as a deacon until 1927 as he had been directly blocked by the bishop when he hoped to be ordained in 1924.[26] Eventually he became a priest, in 1928, meaning that, finally, he could preside over Holy Communion at the mission. Photographs of his early mission years suggest he had a fondness for pith helmets. Perhaps he imagined he was in Africa.

Dyer had some skills that suited him to the mission. His hardware store experience meant he knew everything about tools, but nothing about cattle. He was stubborn, eccentric and obsessive, prone to overwork.[27] Other missionaries called him 'reckless'. A 'try anything once' attitude was the kinder way of putting it.[28] Such was his enthusiasm that when he visited Groote Eylandt in 1921, he was eager to translate the chorus 'Jesus loves me' into Anindilyakwa. Pointing to his chest, he thought he had learned the word for 'me'. Only later did he learn he was singing 'Jesus loves my chest hair'. The Anindilyakwa camp must have enjoyed themselves.[29] After his death, the preacher at his funeral commented on his 'strange personality', 'erratic, contradictory and elusive'. He was 'a very great man … so strangely shackled and frustrated by his chronic incoherence of expression'.[30] Alf was not a leader. But perhaps

---

26 Cole, *Oenpelli Pioneer*, 52.
27 Medical Form, ML MSS 6039.
28 Harris, *My Story G.R. (Dick) Harris*, 16, NTRS 1105.
29 Les Perriman Oral History, NTRS 226, TS 102.
30 Ralph Ogden quoted in Cole, *Oenpelli Pioneer*, 96.

his wife Mary was. One missionary remembered that 'everyone thought [Mary] was the boss of Oenpelli', and locals joked that she 'wore the trousers'.[31]

Alf met Mary Catherine Crome at Roper River. She was 'Katie' to him. They were soon deeply in love. Crome was a strange woman herself. The subsequent superintendent of Oenpelli, Dick Harris, described her as almost completely without personality:

> She reminded one of the one-time well known advertisement of Old Dutch Cleanser which pictured a starched, hooded Dutch woman cleansing dirt.[32]

Of course, those comments reveal as much about Harris's condescension to his female missionary colleagues as they do about Crome. But she was always working. A qualified nurse, on the mission she was also a seamstress, teacher, midwife and cook. Missionary Nell Harris described her as a strict, 'no nonsense' woman, but loving in her own way.[33] She was born in Northcote, Victoria, in 1874, so was a decade Dyer's senior. She began at Roper River mission when she was 39, full of enthusiasm for mission, although, until then, she had never met an Aboriginal person. Her diary reveals how she sank into depression during her first two years on the station. Missionary work was often lonely and monotonous for single women. It also reveals how she learned to find satisfaction in her work, growing less idealistic and more deeply committed to the mission.

Dyer and Crome courted secretly. Dating was improper. 'To walk out together or to kiss' was, in Dyer's melodramatic fashion, 'forbidden'.[34] With the permission of CMS, they married in 1917. Their love letters are still in the archives. She missed him intensely when he travelled:

> If you were only here now I would make you feel I love you it would be all I want humanly speaking just to feel that your arms were round me … you would get so many of these xxxxxxxxx.[35]

31 Nell Harris in Harris, *The Field Has Its Flowers*, 21.
32 Harris, *My Story G.R. (Dick) Harris*, 17, NTRS 1105.
33 Harris, *The Field Has Its Flowers*, 19.
34 Dyer, Manuscript, NTRS 693 part 1, Item 18.
35 Mary Dyer to Alf Dyer, 1 February 1917, NTRS 693 part 1, Item 4.

Figure 4.3: 'Mrs Dyer teaching in open air, Oenpelli' (date unknown).
Source: Item 431, Historical Oenpelli Slides, CMS, complied by K. Hart, A. Wilson and W. Kennedy, 1996.

Oenpelli station passed from the Campbells to the CMS on 18 June 1925. The Dyers, by then experienced missionaries, were appointed for the task. The happy missionary couple disembarked on the East Alligator River on 4 September and made their way to Oenpelli. First, they noticed its beauty. Surrounded by birds and flowers, nestled next to the billabong beneath red rocky hills, Gunbalanya is stunning. Assured by the Campbells that there were 'plenty of natives around the place', they began their work, optimistic about the future of this cattle station turned mission. By 1931, they were burnt out.

Alf Dyer's last hurrah was the Caledon Bay Peace Expedition in 1934. Together with a band of missionary men he went in 'peace' to persuade three Yolngu men accused of murder to face trial in Darwin. The supposedly 'peaceful' nature of the expedition was simply that it was not a massacre (which is what police had proposed). The missionaries were unarmed. But the episode ended in the death of one of the men – Dhakiyarr Wirrpanda – in Darwin. Dhakiyarr disappeared soon after his release, most likely killed by police.

The peace expedition was a publicity triumph for the CMS. But the Dyers' capacity was waning. In 1935, the Bishop of Carpentaria insisted that the Dyers must 'not return to the field'.[36] Alf had malaria and mouth ulcers. Mary was 'run down and tired'.[37] According to Cole, both had some form of cancer.[38] They retired from the CMS later that year, Dyer becoming parish minister in Guildford, Sydney. Ever committed to the mission and after decades of knowing no other work, this was not their choice but, in their words, 'owing to the Doctors' adverse report which forbids our return'.[39]

36 Minutes of the Oenpelli Committee of the NSW Branch of CMS, 15 April 1935, ML MSS 6040/4.

37 R. Long to Hewett, 22 March 1935, ML MSS 6040/35.

38 Cole, *Oenpelli Pioneer*, 92.

39 Alf Dyer to Hewett, 29 June 1935, ML MSS 6040/35.

5

THE MISSION DOCUMENTS

This chapter includes the reports and letters written from Oenpelli mission during the period 1925–31 that are in the CMS archives held by the Mitchell Library and Northern Territory Archives Centre. The spelling and grammar are unaltered except for some cases where we found it necessary to assist the reader by using square brackets to complete words or add punctuation. Most of the original reports and letters were typed, with occasional handwritten notes and some handwritten letters that are indicated in this chapter by italics. Where we could not make out what was written, due either to handwriting or wear and tear, we have indicated this using [...]. Most photographs from this era have little to no contextual information available. We have tried to place the photographs close to related discussions in the reports and letters. Where an original caption was available, we have included it in quotation marks. Captions added to the photographs by later researchers or archive staff have not been included. Appendix A includes a list of Aboriginal people mentioned in these records and Appendix B a list of known missionaries working at the Oenpelli mission during this time period.

***

Darwin
4/8/25

To the Government Secretary Darwin

DEar Sir

Oenpelli was formally taken over by the C.M.S. on June 18th 1925 from Home &Territories with all thereon as per inventory issued in 1,24 to us. Only the number of horses & goats were left to be decided by your department, with the clause inserted & sufficient number for the working of the working of the station to be given)

Yours sincerely
Alf Dyer[1]

*   *   *

Oenpelli
14/9/25

Dear Miss Harper

It is just a week since we arrived. Mr Dyer is away mustering with Mr Campbell, they may be back tomorrow. Mrs Campbell is here with me. I have been busy unpacking & trying to find places to put things. The landing is seven miles away & the horses cannot bring big loads in this heat. Two boys have done a trip and a day all last week & there is still two loads of flour to bring, the rest of the things are up & unpacked.

The grocery order is very good everything is in excellent order, I have never seen one better packed. There were one or two little things that my quantities were mistaken that was probably my fault. For instance I wanted 6 packets of blue I got 6 nobs. For 6 cakes of monkey soap I got 6 dox. If we had arrived here sooner I would have cancelled the order for Cream of Tartaric Acid, The rest of order is alright & if those things come it will not matter as they keep in jars & tins.

There was nearly a calamity with flour. It was in 50 lb bags but they were put 4 in a sack, which made them very awkward to handle. They have to be hand lifted from a launch or small boat on to […] through mud then up into shelter, from there to dray & finally from dray to store. The ends of sacks came undone & several bags burst.[2]

---

1   ML MSS 6040/31 Dyer, Alf.
2   ML MSS 6040/31.

Figure 5.1: Loading buffalo hides on ship (date unknown).
Source: Northern Territory Archives Service (NTRS 694 P1 Box 4 Item 74).

Figure 5.2: 'Buffalo shot for meat' (date unknown).
Source: Northern Territory Archives Service (NTRS 694 P1 Box 4a Item 191).

* * *

Oenpelli
20/9/25

Dear Friends

After our long wait we arrived here on the 4th. We had a very good trip, we left Darwin on 1st & anchored in the Alligator River the next afternoon. The launch was not working so Mr Dyer helped to fix it. Then we had to wait for the tide. We left the Kinchella about 3 30 p.m. on the 3rd. I wish you could have seen us. The big launch was packed as full as it would hold, also another boat carrying 5 tons .[T]here were 5 men Mr Dyer & myself. My husband acted as engineer to start. I was perched on the bow of the launch & did not feel too safe. However we had asked our Father, to help with the engine & He did so we just committed ourselves to Him asking Him to take care of us & to help us if need be to take the spoiling of our goods joyfully. Then we got on. So far there had not been much to see. The river is very muddy, mangroves along the banks & a very swiftly flowing tide. For some 10 miles we went along fairly well, though the tide had not turned. Then we got on a mud bank as the tide was near the turn we waited for a while & had some light refreshment, consisting of biscuit & water we had a cask on board, the river was so muddy I hardly liked to put my hands in it. We got off the bank just before the bore came up & we did spin along. Our next adventure was getting on another bank, it was nearly dark & very hard to see mud banks from the eddies made by the tide. We got off but the tow boat was on & had dropped her line so we had to go back for her; the tide was so strong that we had to go nearly a ¼ mile, before we could turn, we picked up the tow & on we went again. The moon came up & it was a little better but the shadows on the water were very deceptive. On we went ever on the watch for Canon Hill, so called from its resemblance to a big gun. Again we went on a bank very hard & the tow banged in to us, I thought all our goods would be in the water, but no all was good & she had given us a push that helped us & as the launch was well protected no harm was done[.] Another couple of miles brought us to the landing it was hard to find but one of the men jumped on shore & ran along & made a fire. So we were at the place we would be.

It took over an hour to unload the boats. I made a fire & boiled the billy for some tea; they would not wait but took it on board, as they wanted to go with the tide, so they went leaving us with all our gear on the bank and no one in sight. We just had a little prayer to thank our Father for all His goodness & guidance. Then a drink of tea & some bread & butter, made our beds, it was 1 a.m. & we were glad to lie down to rest. We were glad of our good net or the mosquitoes would have eaten us alive. I awoke very early & could not go to sleep again so we got up & Mr Dyer got got fires going to try & attract someone to the landing. He found the men on the boats were only a little way off they had found they could not keep going without great strain, they were very tired & & anchored for the night & were waiting for tide. So when my husband started on his seven miles walk I went over & gave them a wireless message to to let our friends know we had arrived. When I got back found the ants had fo[u]nd the bees & it kept me busy trying to keep them off. You would have smiled if you could have seen me black with Fire & dirt I had tried to wash pouring a little of my drinking water on a washer to wipe face & hands. We had opened a tin of fish with a shovel Mr Dyer had left his knife on the Kinchella[.] Spread bread with butter & fish using one solitary spoon, no plates no cups, the simple life if you like. About 2 30 p.m. Mr Dyer with Mr Campbell arrived & then I mounted a nice horse feeling a little nervous as it was sometime since I had ridden & in an hour I was home.

We like the look of the place very much. Of course it is too early to judge yet, but first impressions are very good. As I rode with Mr Campbell about 4 miles through beautiful grass flats, then through the bush with lots of shady trees &flowering shrubs I could not help contrasting it with Roper country. The gate of home paddock is about a mile from the house& you do not see it till nearly there. It is beautifully situated[;] there is a background of high hills, at the foot some grassy flats a lovely billabong in front & then the houses with some fine mango trees & bananas, also a few ornamental trees the Campbells have planted. The houses are very low roofed & rough, the best one in the engine house. However I can see ways of improving without much cost till we see how things are in the wet. One thing we have been assured there are plenty of natives round the place so we feel that we should go ahead. In the wet this part is an island, the river flats are all covered with water & the cattle get back between the hills. The bush people come down & camp the other side of the billabong, last year between 200 & 300 for 3 months[.] There are caves they can keep dry in & abundance of food. The bees we brought with us had a very bad time, but seem happy now & so far the birds have not been as bad as they were in Darwin. So we hope they will survive, they will be a great asset if they do.

I do not expect you will get this much before Christmas & we wish you all a very blessed & joyous one. Please pray much for us that we may be able to give these people some idea of what Christmas really means, they will hear it for the first time. Pray also about other workers that the Lord will choose out of those He wants & equip them Himself. We thank you for all your thought & interest in us for our work & pray that the God of allgrace will make you to abound in every good work & bless you abundantly. With our united Christian live & greetings to all co-workers.

Yours in His blessed service
M.C. Dyer[3]

Figure 5.3: Gurrwek (left) with baby Albert Balmana, and unidentified woman and baby (right) (date unknown).
Source: Northern Territory Archives Service (NTRS 694 P1 Box 4b Item 274).

* * *

---

3   ML MSS 6040/31.

First Report on Oenpelli, from Mr. A.J. Dyer. 21/9/25.

Oenpelli is a very beautiful place surrounded by hills. There are millions of birds feeding within the compass of a mile – thousands of ducks and pelicans are at our front door. Go for a walk and you see hundreds of wallabies; so the place abounds in native goods – I have seen no place in the North like it. The cattle around are feeding on lovely green grass – it does make pretty pictures wherever you look – a home for an artist!

Dr. Jones and Professor Watson had plans of building a large place here for tourists – game, fishing, scenery and health, with the added attraction of the blacks. Mr. Campbell was to look after the 3,000. odd cattle which are increasing rapidly – £900. worth are being sold this year, and there would have been over £1000. worth next year. Where the cattle are to be taken to, Mr. Campbell tells me he is afraid most of them will die, and he says it is too late to move mixed cattle now – the wet is upon us at any time now. He cannot understand Mr. Bishop's delay. The Campbells are anxious to get away now, but cannot till he arrives.

When I think of the number of people who wanted to buy the place I wonder the Government waited so long – the offer would not have held good for much longer, though. Even with 500. cattle, at the present rate of increase, Mr. Campbell tells me the place ought to pay for itself in five years' time. I want a man to look after them. With the boys he can shoot 100. buffaloes in a month, and the skins will pay his salary and the boys' expenses. They are worth at least £1. a hide, and he will have the opportunity of mission work with the blacks. Ivens might do this, if he has shown his willingness to serve in doing what he has been asked to do. He is keen for souls, and he needs to be for this work. If you decide anything, and he is willing, let him get cattle and horse experience and send him about April, as the cattle mustering starts about May, it is too wet before. I will help him all I can – Mr. Campbell has helped me much in this, as he is an expert, I wish I were as capable. I have been mustering with him and learning; we have been out past Cooper's Creek, and on to the King River – lovely feed everywhere, and Spencer's Range acts as a good fence, so we have no neighbours, nor can have for years to come.

<u>Natives:</u> Have seen very few yet, but there are plenty about. Mr. Campbell said he had about 300. last Christmas. His policy has been to hunt them, because of the cattle killing; as you read between the lines you will see plenty of problems for the Superintendent of Oenpelli – we will have an uphill fight. Over the ranges (our fence) are the buffalo hunters – men mostly of low morals; we will have to live down their tales. The natives themselves know something of Darwin and the other Missions – as far as I can gather, their impression is not favourable, insomuch that we cry, "Who is sufficient for these things?" Thank God we can look up! I want you to realise these things. The people are shy, the children more so, so our progress will probably be slow, but I trust sure – nay, we feel optimistic, for our God is with us, and this can be a great reserve for the people here and out beyond us.

<u>Buildings:</u> House is very poor, low-roofed, very hot, built by a man with no idea of system, comfort or order. The roof is tied on with logs and wire – hope it will hang out a bit longer. The other buildings have been put down anywhere – I shall put the whole place on a plan, and build and plant trees accordingly, as soon as possible, but this will be slow, as cattle and horses will take up a good deal of my time while I am singlehanded.

<u>Gardens:</u> There are some beautiful mango trees and bananas, which do very well. The white ant is not as bad as at the Roper, so we can grow trees. There are a few vegetables for house use – the rest of the gardens are wildernesses overgrown with weeds and grass – still lots to be thankful for. It is grubbed and fenced.

<u>Paddocks:</u> There are horse paddocks and cattle – several of them fenced – plenty of repairs to do. Mr. Campbell has done a lot of work building cattleyards and making gates – all these are great assets. There are three wells about the house, with good water. There are places that can be made good paddocks by fencing in between the hills. Mr. Campbell has recommended this, and I have the wire – this I will do as I have the opportunity.

<u>Labour:</u> There are several boys trained, and they have been paid a small wage – they do better work than many white men. The boys I must try and keep – others are anxious to get them. It will only cost a few knives and some clothes and other things which you can easily send. Some money has been banked for them, but this may not be necessary. There are a few women who are very good in the house and garden.

Equipment: We have a wonderful inheritance of tools, all of which were as per. inventory, generally more than on the list, and hundreds of valuable things not on the list at all – I do not think £500. would buy them. Of course lots of things are the worse for wear, while some are not much good. The machinery is in good order – I cannot speak of the boiler, it may not be much good, and a thorough inspection must be made before it is used.

Stores: There were a good number of them when we took over. I will wire to cut out the flour if not too late. I thought theirs would be finished, but there was half a ton in a tank, in good order, and free from weevils. Other things will keep. With clothing, etc., there would be £30. worth, so we will not need stores for some time. We have plenty of milk and eggs, game and meat – these keep down the cost of living. The Campbells have a few personal stores which I promised to buy, also a few cartridges, for shooting game for the table. There is about £20. worth of cartridges of various kinds. Mr. Campbell asked if he might keep a revolver, his only request, which I granted. Household goods were a very poor lot – Mrs. Dyer spent most of her outfit money in kitchen utensils, so we have a new start. A new stove was put in recently.

Staff: When I go away Mrs. Dyer will be alone in a place with many bad blacks about. Mr. Campbell was most anxious about Mrs. Campbell when alone – he says it is not right. He has cowed the blacks by threatening to shoot them, and giving demonstrations by shooting their dogs among them. Paddy Cahill always carried a gun, and one of the best boys here is going in with the Campbells to have his leg operated on for a wound inflicted by him. I do not believe in this – I have proved God in tight corners before at Groote Eylandt. but these people are apt to look on it as weakness on my part. We are not frightened, but we will be blamed if I leave Mrs. Dyer alone. There was an armed force sent to Goulburn Island because Miss Mathews was left alone.

The Bishop suggested a clergyman to be Chaplain and school teacher – if married, would solve the problem better. Yet for some time to come his work as teacher would be very limited, and we want a practical man, not afraid of hard work as part of his ministry. If a clergyman is not forthcoming, I would like a young man to help me with the stock – blacks can do the work, but they must have someone with them. Mr. Campbell has had long experience (14 years), and from what he has told me, and what I can see, it is imperative for successful work. If no one comes I will do my best and can see it through, but other things will suffer. We remember constantly the choosing of suitable workers – perhaps the Lord has already chosen. If you send anyone, they must come by the "Kinchella" before Christmas, otherwise not till next April, as we are cut off by water from the landing, which is seven miles away. We will be all right till then, as I cannot travel about in the wet.

Mr. Campbell has done good work about the place and worked hard. Everything is in good order – he has not been extravagant, which makes our task easier in many ways. He is very honest, and has not made many friends perhaps because of it. He has been exceedingly kind in giving me information and hints re. stock, etc., which will help me much.

We have a big inheritance of blessings, and many things to make us thankful and our work easier. But the city of Mansoul is strongly entrenched at every gate – we shall assault the city! Just at present we are looking at it till the Campbells go, when we shall in our King's Name begin the assault. Remember the front line![4]

---

4   NTRS 1099/P1 vol. 1, Mission Reports.

Figure 5.4: View of the old Cahill buildings when the Dyers first arrived (date unknown).
Source: Northern Territory Archives Service (NTRS 694 P1 Box 4a Item 258).

Figure 5.5: Narma Ramagul and Naganiki, 1925.
Source: Northern Territory Archives Service (NTRS 694 P1 Box 4a Item 100).

* * *

Oenpelli
Sept 29

Dear Mr Hinsby

Just in from branding yard & still at it branding C.M.S cattle luck nearly done now Mr Bishop not arrived yet but Kinchella is waiting to take Mrs Campbell to Darwin & mail. Everything is going along well but have not started our real work.

I want a grist mill to grind up corn; in this way I hope to be able to cut out a lot of the flour. The Enterprise Grist mill is a cheap line that does the work but if you can find a more suitable one it may be money well spent (for hand of for power).

1 cwt ea of those nails would never go amiss & they are a bit cheaper that way.

Never send goods to reach here later than the end of November or till June as the road is a bog & things have to be carried on the heads of natives & it is almost impossible to do it[–] this is important to remember.

You will get mail very rarely so dont get anxious[.] No new is good news.

There is a low down pump here in good order but the casting 1963 is broken[;] it is the casting to hold the piston of the pump in position[.] The piston works with a ratchet on handle. MYERS. BROS. U.S.A are the makers a big firm there are agents in Sydney.

1915 Pattern. Takes 2" Pipeing

Would you get 2 piston washers for the same please.

Just going Mr Campbell says he will not take the cattle this year. W[h]ether Mr Bishop will remains to be seen.

You can enquire. If so that means a muster again next year which is a bit of a bother but will make best of it. A Thought is going through my mind Mr Campbell says a lot of the cattle will die where they are going

If so you might come to some terms with the government which might suit Them better than mustering next year and offer to buy them on terms covering some years. we to submit report each year and as we pay expenses cut out the subsidy[.] This is only a suggestion[;] you must act as you feel led and I will follow on as you decide[.] Forgive scribble as they are yelling goodbye,

Cheerio
Loving greetings
Alf Dyer

PS: Will write again later at leisure if another boat comes

But dont act [...] later on say end of the year you will know then what has happened.[5]

* * *

C.M.S
Oenpelli
Sept 29th 1925

Dear Miss Harper

The boat has arrived & Mrs Campbell will be leaving this afternoon – there is nothing further much to tell, but I am putting in a few things not on order that perhaps some one may like to send later – thank you very much for that net. I am using it & it is just the thing till my mosquito net arrived – will you please thank Mrs Bragg for the handkerchiefs. That went to Roper it was kind of her to think of me & I had quite a Christmas parcel from Roper.

We will need continual remembrance there are many problems & also many advantages that we did not have at Roper – there is one thing we are not likely to get any mail once the Wet sets in till perhaps May & Mr Campbell says we certainly should not have stores brought out till the end of May as they have to be carried through water sometimes a couple of miles thick grass that boat cannot go through & the boys often fall & things are wet – there is no bath here – only a rusty shower bath that you haul up with a rope – I cannot manage it at all. Mr Dyer says he will make one sometime also chairs but I think it will be a long time before he will be able to spare time for that – with all the other things that need doing & teaching etc. Now I must stop...

Trusting this will find you well

Loving greeting – remembrances to all the Office & Depot staff from
Your fellow worker –
M.C. Dyer[6]

---

5   ML MSS 6040/31.
6   ML MSS 6040/31.

Figure 5.6: 'Three young hopefuls' (date unknown).
Source: Northern Territory Archives Service (NTRS 694 P1 Box 4a Item 164).

***

Oenpelli
17/10/25

To the Committee of C.M.S

Dear Fellow-workers

We are busy settling in. Since Mrs Campbell left we have refitted the kitchen with new shelves & benches. C.M.S. boxes came in very handy for this, & after whitewashing the walls & reflooring with antbed it looks quite decent it was very black & ugly before. We are doing up the whole place in the way of fittings to have a place for everything[;] it makes our work so much easier. Cattle work & other things have taken up a good deal of my time.

Mr Bishop has arrived he did not being a mail, so we will only get one in the next boat & then a six month's silence unless bad news forces us out, so no news will be good news.

We hope you have been able to send us a man to help with the stock. We hear numbers of natives will come as soon as Mr Campbell goes . At anyrate after the wet I will be able to give a definite report about them ,at present I cannot judge . We are glad of the respite to get things in order . There are so many things to repair . That will take me a year at least & like a farm it is never done .The mending of the harness alone is a big job .generally it is in good repair but most of it is very old . Attending to the horses for cancer & buffalo flys which are very bad here will take up a lot of my time here . Mr Campbell advises me to breed mules as the fly does not trouble them & they are stronger for packs & harness. I can get a donkey for £10 or £12[;] after the wet I will spend my Victorian money on that & 2 buffalo hides Mr Campbell has given me will pay the balance.

We have 400 odd goats I will breed up & Mr Campbell says there is a market for them in Darwin & the East . There are also pigs wild at present[,] plenty of bush food so the place rightly handled ought soon to pay its way . There are prospects of things here quite impossible at Roper or Groote & God helping me I want to make it a success & a real sanctuary for the natives. The ideal Aboriginal Reserve should pay its way & the prospects here are good with very little expense in outlay . I am not forgetting the stewardship of souls . These souls are very like the Cretes of old[–] they are attracted by their bellies . Grace follows after they come & to all we are guardians for they are like children. So Oenpelli can be a big thing. There have been so many tokens of God's leading in all the way that our hearts are full of praise & if we can only carry out the whole thing in that spirit surely He will bless us to the people , in the garden & with the stock, but it means hard work in the heat which is intense , so choose new workers wisely. For workers can make or mar a work . A practical man who loves souls & likes cattle is a real need. Mrs Dyer can manage school till the children grow in number .

Mr Bishop is taking away about 1300 head of cattle. I do not think he thought there were so many & he only has a small plant. Mr Campbell had branded 500 for C.M.S. before he came 18 bulls, 150males 324 females . Mr Bishop wanted all the males & good bulls , the cows & calves he was going to leave as they are difficult to travel with. We would have had more than 1000 in that way ; now he expects to come & get more next year &

leave what they call culls (oldcows) so even then we will get a very start & it is possible they will leave what are here now which make with ours 1500 . There has been much adverse criticism of the Government about it but the deed is done & we have a valuable property to use for the natives .

I want to get a lot of work done in the wet which is upon us . There is a lot of flour left by the Government which wants using up &plenty of meat ,it will give us a start to employ the natives & we will then be able to get in touch with the children & see how many are about . I will order a box of tobacco at Jolleys so you will understand why I have ordered it[–] we could not get it in time . I do not like tobacco but it is the recognized pay in this land[,] a stick every second day costing 4d . I will work to cut it down as much as possible with the young.

We expect a boat in November or early in December but it is always uncertain & we are taking this opportunity of sending mail & order .We will send a copy of it in boat in case of it going astray . The order is to reach us not before the end of May or June[;] the plains are a swamp & it might be lost before that.

Don't forget the circular saw & belt[;] we are very hard up for timber for shelving & fittings . There is plenty of timber & I have the spindle & can make a bench but it is hard to make it true. If you have the funds & could get a bench big enough to take a 2ft log (diameter) if you have the funds it would be a great help , Keep it in mind . I can drill the saw[;] there is a £50 drill here[,] a beautiful machine & lots of good things to work with but the saw was taken away some time ago .But please send the saw & belt.

Later Oct 19th Messenger arrived from Darwin this morning to bring mail[;] ours did not come overcarried. Mr Bishop's cattle leaving this morning under Mr Madrill . Mr Campbell was leaving tomorrow with the male cattle for Darwin market . Mr Bishop was going the next day to Pine Creek to arrange sale. Now Mr Campbell goes straight to Darwin. Mr Bishop has to take the cattle. They are not friends & there have been many rows but we have managed to be neutral & to kow tow to no one.

The branding of the 500 gave us male cattle that would have been taken[,] also some good bulls from South. This happened by office overlapping & personal feeling but we see the good hand of our God upon us . New officers in Darwin & Judge Roberts as Administrator may mean the remaining cattle will be left . The killers which have gone are worth about £5 per head but cows & calves are very costly to remove Mr Campbell says more than they are worth ,So we must just wait & see & pray .

We will report later developments when boat arrives. All things are working for good. Remember us continually as we do you.

With loving greetings & best wishes for a holy & happy Christmas Tide to you all.

Yours in happiest service
Alf Dyer[7]

Figure 5.7: 'Women pounding up antbed for flooring in place of cement' (date unknown).
Source: Northern Territory Archives Service (NTRS 694 P1 Box 4a Item 257).

***

7   ML MSS 6040/31.

Oenpelli
19/10/25

Dear Mr Hinsby

The report will give you the cream of the news. We are doing our best &will be glad to take over . There have been unpleasant scenes since Mr Bishop came .However it has not concerned us to turn to our good. We are getting well & the blacks are starting to come. We will be taking over altogether now . Mr Campbell has been managing most things & we have just been putting things in order & getting garden started . Most things are growing well . The bees are building up there hive .

I got ½ ton of salt from Roper in this way saved D Darwin fees . It cost £1 for freight . Mr Joynt will send on account . I have plenty now . He gave me seeds for Groote[;] I do not know if he will for here. Will you attend to this for me please & let me know what to do in future . (I missed him in Sydney .)

If you get the chance to get any dray & buggy harness also saddles do so . People taking on a car might help in this. Tarpaulin & fly covers are wanted . I am writing to Rev D Deasey of St Columb's Hawthorn re a Birkmeyer fly cover for my packs & camp when travelling in the wet . I will ask him to let you know if he can do this for you .He promised to help in ways like this .

There is a sulphuric acid tanning process(simple)[;] there is a tanning tank here & if I could get the process might be able to make my own leather. A book on tanning would be a help[.] There is also a book on general Useful Knowledge[,] Jack's I think[;] one often wants help & a book is our only means of gettingpoints. to help oneto be a Jack of all trades . I do want some good book to help me in Veterinary diseases especially tropical if procureable . I hope boat comes again this year . Try & arrange that the order is never later than November . Mr Campbell had to have his carried on the hand s of natives last December & lost some . Then end of May or June for following year . This is very important to remember . I will ask Mr Campbell to write to you if there is a saw bench procurable in Darwin .Also a pair of steel wheels & axles for carting in logs . Wooden ones go to pieces in no time here . A single furough iron plough too . These are all things which will be needed & you can get them as you are able .

Enclosing the order to be sent to Darwin for May or June

Mr Campbell has told me a way to firm up the wheels for the present. We will see Jolleys & they will write to you if there is a bench or plough in Darwin & the price.

Cheerio, hope you had a successful year. Greetings to all.

Yours sincerely
Alf Dyer[8]

***

CHURCH MISSIONARY SOCIETY OENPELLI REPORT FOR OCTOBER 1925

After Mr Campbell left we set ourselves the task of getting our house in order. Then the boat arrived with welcome boxes with all their good things for which we thank you & the Giver of all. The boat people naturally want to get off as soon as possible, especially so when one of the men had to walk 7 miles in the heat to let us know it had arrived. It was only the tide gave me a chance to hurriedly answer any mail by firelight.

We refitted the store, dining room, office then our own house, reantbedding the floors as they were as uneven as a choppy sea. So it has been mostly scrubbing brush, paint pot, hammer & saw work, with a growing family of children who have to be gently led on to discipline.

Outside garden work of all kinds going on also fencing. Reading between the lines you will see there are plenty of jobs. The feeding of 30 people. A fence is burnt, or harness breaks an axe or shovel is broken or something else so that some days one never touches the bigger jobs. In her spare time Mrs Dyer has been doing the store. The boy with the decaying leg takes time, teaching others to work & stirring up lazy ones also.

Workers had been getting ½ stick of tobacco till now. I have reduced this to 1.3 for camp workers so with the gift box we shall get a lot of work done. New faces have been arriving all through the month.

Alf Dyer[9]

---

8   ML MSS 6040/31.
9   NTRS 1099/P1 vol. 1.

Figure 5.8: House and other buildings, c. 1926.
Source: Northern Territory Archives Service (NTRS 693 P1 Item 21).

Figure 5.9: View of the early buildings with Arrkuluk Hill in background (date unknown).
Source: Northern Territory Archives Service (NTRS 694 P1 Box 4a Item 178).

* * *

CMS
Oenpelli
8/11/25

Dear Mr Secretary

Some boys from the Methodist Mission have come to get 50 goats & they will take this letter. We are very busy & have been working till late every night trying to get the place in order; it is a big task without the big family daily increasing & now between 50 & 60. Until we can get everything running smoothly it seems almost beyond us but we look up. So much of the gear has to be repaired that we get taken from the main task. However we are beginning to see daylight ahead of us & it is nice to see the people coming. The teaching of them is slow work. It was lovely to see the little blacks clapping their hands to time as I was trying to each them [']Jesus loves me'. We have had a very sad case brought to us. two black boys were wrestling in a buffalo hunter's camp about 20 miles away, with a rifle 303 which went off & shattered one boy's leg above the knee. The hunter did his best but the boy would not keep the splints on. The leg started to decay from the foot. When the boat came which brought our stores a Dr came to seek for lepers. He did not come here but went to see the boy on horseback[;] by that time the leg bones were showing almost to the knee. He should have taken the leg off but had no chloryform & the boy did not want to go to darwin, so he was brought to us. it is a terrible sight & a nasty case to treat[.] It makes one wish he were a Dr to help the lad. He is very cheerful & sings away without Grace putting to shame grumbling Christians. His mother is his nurse so faithful always on watch day & night to help; holding his bones like a faithful Rizpah when the leg has to be washed, these will come away in a few days & then we trust the healing with commence. He belongs to a family who have been very troublesome killing cattle etc. all the family are with us now & we hope love will triumph over evil. I was looking for a Bible picture book for him today but we have not any. One of young people had put a scrap book in our Christmas boxes, which arrived safely & in it were a few pictures of Chrsit which I have given him to look at. We do need pictures for this work[.] I did hope some lantern slides would have come[;] I have 15 Bible picture slides to carry on with till more arrive. If any of you can help us do so. Soldiers cannot work without ammunition, that is the task of the home base. This work is better than war. The Methodist boy's visit has been a help to us. one boy's testimony did some good[−] they turned up so early for work yesterday that I was not up myself. So we labour on in the day of small things.

Sent us reinforcements soon. Our thanks to all who sent parcels & boxes for Christmas we will write personally later this is only a chance mail.

Yours Faithfully
Alf Dyer[10]

Figure 5.10: Frank 'Naluwud' with decaying leg, 1925.
Source: Northern Territory Archives Service (NTRS 694 P1 Box 4a Item 184).

***

10   ML MSS 6040/31.

Oenpelli
Nov 8th 25

Dear Mr Secretary

There is no time for a report but this gives the news – We are well but tired. Weather is trying – I am enclosing negative of sick boy. With a little retouching you could use it, if not too ghastly – Have no time for photography yet – we are working late every night –

Mr Hinsby promised to fly up some Bible slides from negatives of Rev Kirkby of Bush Aid. – 6 their slides are useful too even if out of date as they have pictures – Children's Bible & other picture books are being useful.

There are plenty of natives about so future of work seems assured from every point of view –

I would like a windmill if you can get one not a high tower but the bigger the better as it means more water for irrigation. I have not had time to make an inspection of the boilers but am afraid they are not much good – I ordered a case of tobacco in Darwin to get a lot of stock done here this year – the garden is a wilderness & I want to knock it into shape. I am cutting a small stick into 3 pieces for myalls so that does 3 days work. Work is one of the best ways of helping them & we have got a lot done already.

The two saws sent from Darwin were without charge – but are no use – I hear Vesteys are closing down & selling off – Piping & things that would be useful here may be fairly cheap but next year – it a man is coming up ask him to inspect what is there. It might pay us to get some hardware etc there.

[Handwriting changes to Alf Dyers – until this point it is Mary Dyer's writing]

I have just been out chasing goats. We thank you all very much for the nice Xmas boxes. They will bring a lot of joy here this Xmas. […] & sweets were missing but one Victorian box sent 10 […] & 38 dress of which we are greatly in need of for the people.

Wishing you all a merry Xmas & a prosperous New Year.

Yours faithfully
Alf Dyer[11]

***

---

11   ML MSS 6040/31.

OENPELLI

REPORT FOR NOVEMBER 1925

A very hot month & trying, one rises praying for grace. A native arrived in the camp one day with a gun which I took from him. & gave him some work to do. Put up a washing shed. Have cleaned the steam boilers of the rust which was destroying them & painted engines so that I can inspect better later. Planted out bananas. A large part of the garden is ruined with a bad grass[:] nuts 2 ft deep in the ground very hard to fight, I am making new places so am pulling down old fences to get room for ploughing. Made a shade house for the people. Made the front verandah into a chapel also Communion Table & Reading Desk out of some Queensland oak I found here.

The Government suggested we let Goulburn Is Mission have some goats. 7 boys from there came & took 50 away, while here they helped in services. We have about 60 every night[–] an evangelistic service more of the Army style till we can train them for a church service. They love the lantern, dig up any of your old slides they all help.

The sick boy is much the same. The top of the leg is more normal but the decaying is slow I often feel tempted to cut it off. We have started to feed the children to feed the children twice a day to get them ready for school. We have been working from 5.30am & it is often 10 pm when we stop & fever occasionally makes the going harder but we see things growing around us & we could not carry on in a muddle.

Methodist boys arrived again[;] they were bad shepherds & had lost 30 goats so set them off again. Bees are increasing now. Most of the plants we brough are flourishing, so some things are fruitful. Of the seed of the Spirit we cannot speak they are singing, learning day by day so we go on sowing and praying.

Alf Dyer[12]

* * *

---

12   NTRS 1099/P1 vol. 1.

OENPELLI

REPORT FOR DECEMBER 1925

Mrs Dyer started school with 15 scholars I wonder how she manages it all, Grace she says. Started to plough with the Geelong plow, it is a great boon as there was none here. I had to make harrows. But the rain is late.

The boys returned from cattle trip with mail telling us first results of elections, so our little world closes around us. Then we mustered the cattle to hunt them off the plains before the floods.

Government report in the mail. Oenpelli gazetted a Reserve with myself as Protector. Most of the horses will be left on the Station. Mr Bishop recommended this but this is not final as the Administrator says the rest of the cattle will be mustered next year when everything will be finalized[;] whatever happens will have the 500 & their progeny & a number of culls., so we will have a good start. I am always thanking God for it, when I remember early Groote days & wallaby fare. Here we have lovely meat, milk & game. And so any tools[.] I am always finding new things even now thought I have a mental note of most things . £1000 would not buy the gear on this place.

We have over 100 people for Christmas which kept us very busy. The children enjoyed their bags & the people also. Services, lantern, games, a tableau of the Shepherd's & the Wise Men's visits, primitive but probably conveyed more than words.

Then again into garden, we are fencing in about 3 acres also a goat yard with drafting open. We want to get as much food stuff in as possible while we have the growing season. So ended our first year. A great deal has been done on the place. It begins to look a bit home-like.

Foundations for Spiritual work are being laid. The sick have been cared for. School begun. The Gospel preached. May He Who sees the need send us their blessings.[13]

***

---

13   NTRS 1099/P1 vol. 1.

OENPELLI

REPORT FOR JANUARY 1926

This month has been strenuous. Mrs Dyer lost her helpers as they went for their walkabout. With new workers & bread to make for 50 people besides other cooking, school & the sewing, & only a little colonial oven & a small stove to do it.

Every moment I could get has been put into the garden. Have put in ½ acre of bananas & about 5 acres of maize, cotton, kaffir corn, rice, Japanese wheat, potatoes, melons & pumpkins. That gift of tobacco has done that on the wages side. I hate the stuff & wish there was something else but it is the only thing they want. They get a 1/3 of a stick for a day's work. For the regular people I have introduced a system of payment that they buy what they like[–] I give the value of the tobacco & several of them are getting other things. I wish you people would help me in this. That old pair of scissors or razor, knives, bags, beads, ribbons, wool etc are all of value to them & help me to cut down expenses. Trousers & shirts that are shabby but will wear & pieces of cloth I want. The old station boys are used to clothes & except some old soldier's trousers I have none to give. The young people will be started with a regular dress boys with nagas, but stock boys must have clothes.

Have fixed up a boy's dormitory[–] the old room for butter making mosquito proof is their bed room & the other part for playing in. There are 15 of them.

For the girls I have fixed up the gaol putting in window & door also mosquito proof & they rushed to come in thinking it a mansion & are very happy except for scraps[–] for spears are not turned to reaphooks in a day. We have 23 children 12 station hands 5 old people & ten work people each day[;] these are changed daily to give all a turn & they rush the position.

About the station we have come in contact with over a hundred people. Before we came F. Birtles who set out to find the white women made a camp about 30 miles from here to take movies, he has a large number of natives there[–] one man told me over 30 children. He feeds them & gives them presents so a mission & work is not in it. At present we are not ready for large numbers. Beyond us there are plenty of blacks but they do not come here as it out of their country. That is why I want help to go to them for a present the Home Base needs all my labours.

Finished the goat yard & took heed to the state of flocks, have sent them to the hills & caves for the wet with a shepherd & wife. Found rain has been coming into boilers, had to attend to this & stop rust in its work, it has done a good deal of damage. Time would fail to tell of stopping stealing, taming cheeky ones, & all sorts of tries on with the new boss. The Apostle's injunction to rule with diligence is very necessary. Every time I went into the kitchen & saw them trying to cook with one little stove & a big open fire with colonial oven all falling in my heartnsmote me. Out in the bush I found an old Metter's stove No 3 all in pieces & oven gone so I gave blacks presents to find the bits, many were missing, no grates, top plates & only one bolt the size on the place[–] that is the time one wishes for a peep at George St. Two weeks of perspiration in the smithy between other jobs & she is cooking & along side her in the big open chimney because she looked lonely I am putting a baker's oven made of another old tank & antbed. The stove's oven is made of a tank[;] not one of those sheets of iron you can put your finger through so it may see us out.

Lovely rains, crops look well, cotton also. Next year D.V.[14] I hope to do something bigger did not have the chance this year. This sounds like smooth running, well, take the ploughing[:] I trained one boy to do it, there was some trouble about his little girl he ran away like Adam. I trained another he went off to look for a lost wife. The third is still going strong. Mrs Dyer has had much the same trouble with Eve. But they are beginning to find out it does not pay to run away as there are plenty of others to take their place.[15]

---

14 *Deo volente*, i.e. 'God willing'.
15 NTRS 1099/P1 vol. 1.

Figure 5.11: 'Gaol for cattle killers Service 4 languages bark verandah Oenpelli 1925'. Paddy Cahill's old gaol was used by Dyer as a girl's dormitory.

Source: Northern Territory Archives Service (NTRS 694 P1 Box 4a Item 174).

Figure 5.12: Young boys of the Oenpelli mission, most likely boys from the dormitory (date unknown).

Source: Northern Territory Archives Service (NTRS 693 P1 Item 21).

***

OENPELLI

REPORT FOR FEBRUARY 1926

Finished off the baker's oven[–] both it & stove are cooking well & overcomes the cooking problem. Mrs Dyer has only to make bread every other day now.

One family of blacks Mr Campbell had warned me about as cattle killers he had threatened to shoot them. We just asked our Father to overrule for us. Stumpy one of the family died here on the station this month. Another brother is the boy with the bad leg, the bones have fallen out now & he gets about on crutches. The other brother is working & he does not seem a bad sort so that problem is solved. We tried to make the poor chap understand, doing all we could for him. Then buried him all probably helping to confirm our message. Their burial customs are horrible[–] to[o] gruesome for publication.

I have parties out getting bark. Others at work in the garden. Everything is growing well as it has been a good season so far. Got in in more cows for milkers. Have had several horses with cancer to be cut out.

Having trained the people we started a shortened form of service every morning in the chapel[;] they march in & are very reverent. They hear twice daily so all this tells for the Word is quick still. We feel now that things are moving towards the goal. The children are getting on well in school. Now the station is moving more clocklike our work is becoming easier & we are getting over the rush. We have not been away from the sight of the house for a holiday since we started to dig in & there are lots of places we would like to see. But we praise God who has given us the strength to see it through. We feel now we would not mind a visitor coming in unawares.[16]

---

16 NTRS 1099/P1 vol. 1.

Figure 5.13: 'Cattle killers' (date unknown).
Source: Northern Territory Archives Service (NTRS 694 P1 Box 4a Item 226).

* * *

Oenpelli March Report 1926

Began the month by shooting a cancer horse, which we had cut several times. The bees made two swarms. We have had a number of watermelons, beans, maize bananas & custardapples. A long dry spell will spoil the results of the crops this year, we have not had half the usual rainfall. We have got 500 sheets of bark for building but cannot cart yet.

Rev H Reid sent his mail on to us, saying a boat is calling in April, at anyrate I sent back a copy of the order. Mrs Dyer has had school & general work daily. The boys have been breaking in horses & getting timber. The average attendance at service is about 60, no new children came in, but we have seen several smaller ones who will later.

I have started to attend to the engines, a report is enclosed which I have sent a copy of to the Government. The donkey engine is in pieces lying about everywhere, but I have found most of them now. The engine has some years of service yet, but the boiler is old, but seems fair. I am putting it up to put it through a test. If right I intend to erect by billabong to pump water as there is a good steam pump here on a well it would pump dry in ½ an hour. I will put the saw mill there also. It is a very big job made doubly hard because most of the bolts were cut off short & left to rust in, which meant drilling & retaping, but I am getting on.

The weeding of the garden has kept most of the bushmen (as the people call them) quiet. The place is overrun with a very bad grass & it will take some years to get it out. The gift box of tobacco has paid 8 workers per day since we started, they get a third of a stick, but it is finished now so I have had to put them off[,] much to their sorrow. They will not work for food, as they can get it easily in the bush. I have tried them but none offered. By a system of changing them daily we got in touch with a good number, & it helped to tide over the parents leaving their children. All workers go to service[17]

***

Report for April 1926

April closed the growing season. The results are very poor due to want of rain, we would have had a wonderful crop of peanuts, maize & cotton if what had formed had grown. It was hard to see them die. The rainfall for 1925 was

Janry	Feb	March	April	
1060	1103	1103	820	while for same time 1926
1466	828	615	42	Points

At anyrate we struck one of the worst years for a start.

I am erecting engine & pump on the billabong which I hope will overcome some of the problem, Put the boiler through a test which she stood without any apparent strain & have taken up the steam pump, will D V set up next month. It has been a very big job for me. I have taken every care but have had to make so many things & the 3", suction pipe I had to cut screws with a hack saw.

For the first time I have ridden round the Red Lily paddock. It has ranges which the cattle cannot cross on all sides but the river & half a mile of fencing. In some places it is 7 or 8 miles wide & in it a large billabong 7 or 8 miles long. This will carry 1000 cattle. So after the final Government muster all the cattle will go in there & a weekly inspection will save the mustering, at present they are roaming beyond the 2000sq miles but we have no neighbours & can't have because of the ranges. The Red Lily

---

17 NTRS 1099/P1 vol. 1.

paddock will also put an end to spearing of cattle. When the cattle increase there are other places where a short fence will give many sq miles of country.

Easter passed quietly, we decorated the Chapel the people joined in heartily. The lantern helped with pictures.

Have done a good deal of fencing, repairing harness, making ropes & whips, mending saddles & have also mended the dray, buckboard & buggy & painted them. A broken pump caused me a few days' work too.

We lost a good number of goats in the wet season. I had a bad shepherd & being on the hills could not give them the attention they needed, now they are back at the station am getting them in hand again. Mr Campbell advised me to send them over but I will not do so again. We got two buffaloes this month that saved the life of a killer. Have put off all bush workers as tobacco is getting low.

Mr Birtles writes he wants to visit Oenpelli for pictures. You have copy of my letter to him, I did not encourage him as you can see. Letter from Goulburn Is to say no boat coming, they had forgotten to bring our mail, we were a bit disappointed after waiting six months.

Mrs Dyer works harder than I do, cooking, sewing, cleaning & school. She reports good progress. The children sing very nicely now. The people from camp come well to the services & join in heartily. But we see no movement upon the face of the deep; darkness still reigns though there are tokens of coming dawn. After more than six month's hard work I got Mrs Dyer away for a day's outing to the waterfall. It also gave me a chance to inspect. There is 100ft drop from the top or more. Above this runs a creek between two hills for ¼ to ½ mile there is very little rise, rock bottom & 100 yds at the top to give a reservoir about 30 ft deep. Roll the stones down the hills & fill her up & you have millions of gallons of water for the dry to run down on the plain & power it. As Oenpelli grows this may help to make it well watered & a large cotton area.

Mosquitoes have been their worst this month. Fever has been prevalent.

Alf Dyer[18]

---

18   NTRS 1099/P1 vol. 1.

Figure 5.14: Goats on the edge of the billabong (date unknown).
Source: Northern Territory Archives Service (NTRS 693 P1 Item 21).

Figure 5.15: 'Bringing in a letter Oenpelli Native and White one. Bodies sprayed with paint blowed on by mouth' (date unknown).
Source: Northern Territory Archives Service (NTRS 694 P1 Box 4b Item 301).

* * *

Oenpelli Report May 1926

May has brought many problems of many kinds. Stealing in the kitchen Z (only milk) but it caused a great row & all the little girls ran away, but I had them fetched back, we found the culprit who was one of the old ones, who said she was shamed when found out & asked to go bush for a while. Later in the month all the little boys made a raid on the the potato patch, the big boys had set the example, I stopped their tobacco for a week & they went on strike leaving me 2 men to carry on with. But they soon got tired of it & came back still to face their punishment. The little boys all got the strap.

I had sent the head stock boy who has had many years of stock work to burn off around a stockyard & he burnt it down. It was a large yard with a dip but a cracked one & has not been used for some time. Also a fence which he has now the work of remaking. But I cannot attend to all these things myself & these people need constant supervision, with a very firm hand, the law; rather than grace but we have to combine the two.

Burning off everywhere & mustered about 1000 cattle & put them through the dip, then into the Red Lily paddock.

Made a cement & stone foundations for the steam pump & engine, there is several bags of old cement here not much good now. Have done a good deal of fencing about the house. Then I started in earnest on the engine I had to make firebars for the boiler a very hard job. I have laid down 300 feet of delivery pipe 2" to 1.1/4" at the top[.] With the few more lengths ordered I can irrigate anywhere in the garden. As I have a gradual fall both ways, I had to straighten old pieces of refrigerator pipe to do this & take pipe off other things & make screws without dies on some sizes & a few sockets, but I was fortunate enough to find most of the other fittings needed & taps out of our inheritance, could you buy it for £300?

On May 28th we gathered round & after a prayer for blessing on our irrigation & garden, Mrs Dyer turned on steam & a lovely stream of water came out of the 2" tap to make the dry place a garden of green & food for our little ones. It will also tide our cotton crop over a dry spell at any time which is the only real difficulty in cotton growing in the North. The pump is a double setting steam pump & fetches up a lot of water & works well on 20 lbs of steam. I have tested the boiler without & within & as far as I can judge she may work for some years on low pressure[;]

if Mr Warren comes he will have more experience. But if anyone would like to give a new one I will not say no as for the saw higher pressures are needed.

We garned in   21/4 Cwt of peanuts

2 " of maize

½ " of good cotton more of poor stuff

Over 300 watermelons & hundreds of custard apples & potatoes we are just starting to dig. No mail or boat arrived, but we sent mail to you via Goulburn Is Mission Lugger. Fever has been very prevalent & we have had our share of it, but your duties goad you on, when you feel like giving in, for conquest only comes through life given.

Yours sincerely.
Alf Dyer[19]

Figure 5.16: Boys with their garden harvest (date unknown).
Source: Northern Territory Archives Service (NTRS 693 P1 Item 21).

19 NTRS 1099/P1 vol. 1.

Figure 5.17: Babies in irrigation channel (date unknown).
Source: Northern Territory Archives Service (NTRS 694 P1 Box 4 Item 138).

* * *

Oenpelli Report for June.

July 7th still no boat & we have 5 bags of flour left, we use 3 a week, but we are rationing now & still stir up hope for if the worst comes we can live without flour; so we are not like London's poor. Up to our eyes in work & can't dodge it. Ah me I have never been in such a case, no socks darned for months no hope. I have had a bag of old socks a lady in Bendigo gave me & they have saved my feet[;] I wear them till I can't & dip into the bag again but it is nearly empty now. It is not Mrs Dyer's fault she simply has not time. Food shortage has brought cattle work to a standstill till boat comes. Have put about 1000 through the dip.

The old steam engine must have had 25 years service before she came here & has taken some repairing but I hope to get some sawing done with her. The pump is a new one & lifts 52 gallons per minute, so she shifts some water. One week she worked 40 hours. The garden will grow now but seeds have not arrived & it will be too late for them now. Cassava & sweet potatoes are growing nicely. We have lines of trenches where we are digging out the nut grass. Most of the trees & flowers are growing nicely. One tree is over 10 ft high from a seed planted since we came. We gathered 125 lbs of cotton to send away. We will do better as next year I can water if we do not have the rain.

Through June some days were 98% in shade. Generally the weather is pleasant. The children are beginning to read short sentences so are coming on. I have taken them through most of the narrative parts of Old & New Testaments.

We have come into contact with about 200 people round the place. They all assure me there are plenty out bush but they do not come here as it is not their country & our folk do not encourage them. This has to be lived down, then too they do not come unless there is something to be got & it is a very rare thing for any of them to desire the Gospel but they will travel miles for a bit of tobacco. But they need the Gospel of Christ, it is the only uplift. We cannot follow them but we can attract them to us. They love to see their children taught & gladly leave them. Therefore I must make the home base a food producer, it is a big task but an Australian duty. With Mr Iven's help we can do a lot. Home Base first then stretch out to the other sheep.

The site is as good as we can get in the North except the shipping still it is as good as most of the rivers & 7 miles is not a long distance, plenty of the stations have hundreds of miles to cart. Whether the number of people were here was the only fear after seeing the place but feel sure now that there are plenty more. Those about us are very cunning & make the task harder but they have lots of good points & all have souls to save & need help. We have done what we could but if more children are to come in it is quite impossible for Mrs Dyer to do all the women's side of the work. She is not very well now, it may be only fever & pass over but I am anxious knowing what she has done & that she is over tired. Then we are always on duty. I do not know what you have thought about it. We feel that as well as Mr Ivens there should be another married couple. If we are to cope with the work, buildings, garden, stock & itinerating 3 men are necessary & 2 women should be here. I expect the Bishop would like an ordained man. At anyrate you must solve the question yourselves in the way the Lord shall lead you.

Yours sincerely
Alf Dyer[20]

---

20   NTRS 1099/P1 vol. 1.

Figure 5.18: Young girls at Oenpelli mission, c. 1929.
Source: Item 698, Historical Oenpelli Slides, CMS, complied by K. Hart, A. Wilson and W. Kennedy, 1996.

* * *

Report for July 1926 Oenpelli

July has been just a month of holding the fort. The people have gone out for their dinner, except a few workers. Many have gone to the bush, but the children are all here. Four more boys have come in & we have seen several other children. Two men came to visit us from a distant tribe, one of our men described their numbers as millions, but he does not know what that number means; but it expresses a large number[.] I should have liked to have been able to have gone back with them but that is impossible till help arrives. Everything goes to confirm that there are plenty of people to touch. There is plenty of good soil here to grow food, so I have no fear of the future of the place now. We have dug 800 lbs of potatoes recently, that has saved a meal of flour a day for weeks. They were started from about 20 slips & I had to wait for them to increase. Next season I shall have a good start & hope to have tons D.V. [*Deo volente*] Have increased the 5 grains of kaffir corn to hundreds growing now with irrigation to get seed for the wet season, these will be our porridge for breakfast, if the gate is not left open & the goats do not get them. A man wants an eagle's elevation & his eye to do this job, also an eye in the back of his head as well, they are the most thoughtless people. The cool season is now gone, no boat, 4 months since our first trip was promised & I have lost all the crop of vegetables, as I have no seed, only two days from Darwin, that is when one wishes we had someone's pleasure launch to give it something useful to do. All my big jobs are held up as I have only wages for the few. Irrigated 2 days a week[,] often cutting the wood myself to spare the boys to muster for the Govt: some nights till 8 & 9 oclock to get done while I have steam up. The oldest & smartest girl in the dormitory was taken by a man who has 3 wives, she belonged to him[.] I asked him to let her have another year schooling as she is only young & he promised, but did not keep it[.] He is a leader here, & I know it was a try on, so I told him to clear out, or send her back[;] he went one of them told me he said he had been big fool, but he did not send her back, we were sorry for her, I have the future to think, so have to be firm

Made a jetty at the landing. I intended to make it of stone but found no foundation[;] the deeper we went the softer the mud, so made a wooden one, I hope flood proof[,] 3 days task. That is the place to see the air dark with mosquitoes at dusk. The slacker time has given me a chance to mend tools & get a place for everything so that I can check them. It is one man's task to keep things in repair alone. There are over 40 gates around the house & paddocks, I have remade three 3 the last few days & there must be 8 miles of fencing to look after[–] posts last about 3 years here. I have been watching everything & praying about putting the place on a plan, it had me beat for a while; as the buildings had been put up anywhere, but have it now; hope to send a copy when I get it all thought out.

A good deal of fever about this month, they give in easily we just have to fight it[.] Mrs Dyer has some hard tussles at times, I tell her that her jewel stone needs a lot of polishing, My November papers will be a bit stale when I get them. Mrs Dyer has attended to a lot of sick cases this month, the people says that she is all the same Dr[–] some of them have been in the hospital in Darwin. All this is very material, but the main motive behind it all is spiritual, we can only report sowing. "They that sow in tears shall reap with joy."

Still two bags of flour left[.] Cheerio, plenty of buffaloes & catfish.

Yours sincerely
Alf Dyer[21]

---

21 NTRS 1099/P1 vol. 1.

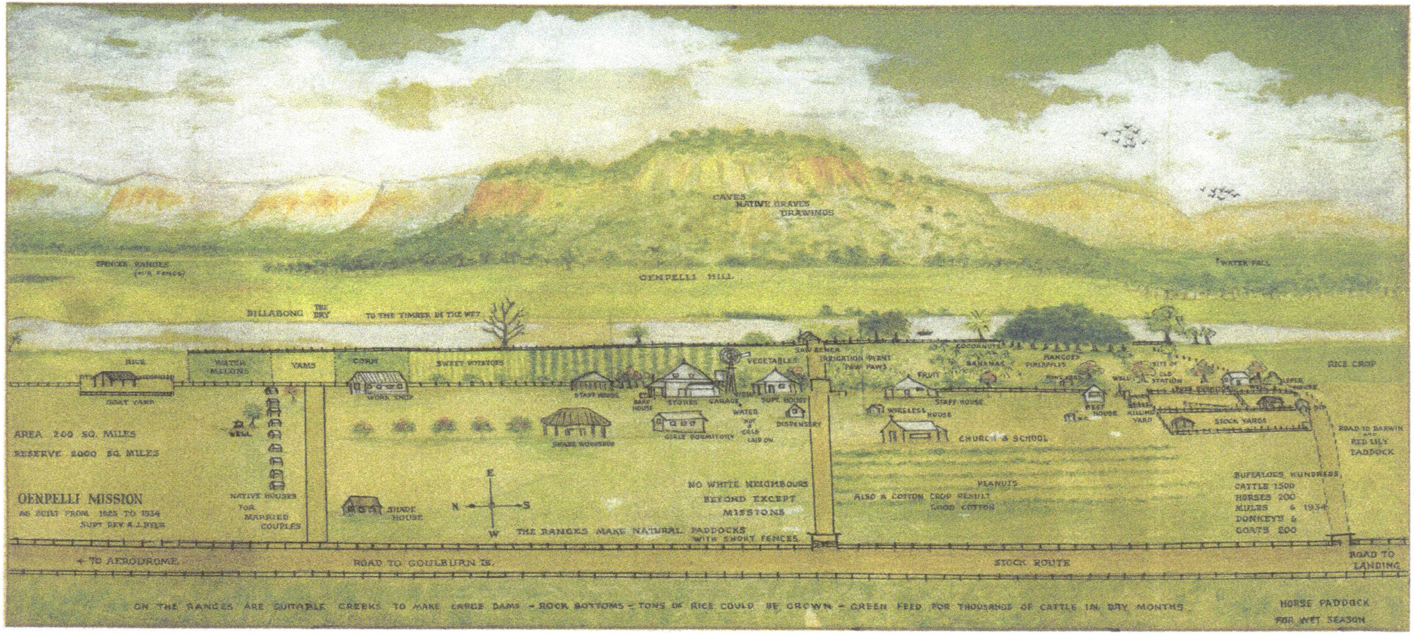

Figure 5.19: Alf Dyer's vision for Oenpelli, 1925.

Note: this plan does not represent what the Oenpelli mission looked like at this time.

Source: Northern Territory Archives Service.

***

Oenpelli Report for Month of August 1926

Began by just holding on doing necessary jobs. Mustering for 10 days about the King River, got a mob with 3 year old clean skins, dipped them & put them in the Red Lily. On the 5th a letter came from Mr Reid saying a strike was on in Darwin & they were on short rations but that he had 4 mats of rice for us. He asked for some meat & about cows as the boys were going with packs I thought it a good chance to fix up the matter, so sent 3 cows & a bull[;] one cow to kill as it was a dry one. They have been very kind to us sending & taking our mail & the rice, we will never miss the cows & have too many bulls. I did not feel we could charge seeing the Lord had been so good to us & it is worth while even to get our mail. The boys took them over & were back in a week, good going. Most of them are doing their work very well. Then the boat arrived[–] details you have. The week previous we had spent in the store, the old shelves in it were wide & useless besides being up & down like the waves of the sea. Had just finished remaking them & also put in a big window for light & ventilation when boat arrived we were so glad as it made the work of storing so much easier. It was nice to see some of the party to talk to after nearly 10 months. As the ladies were very tired, had been 3 days in the river on the mud, Mrs Dyer did not see them. Boat people had eaten some of our stores which they have promised to return. Unloaded on Monday & fed them up for which they were very grateful. They had a very bad trip back & did not reach the steamer till Friday. Our party brought stores to the Marion Sleigh on the Maskee because they were out of food. They arrived on the 21st leaving on the 18th. What a contrast to the other party who can doubt that prayer counts. How our tongues wagged in those days with fresh faces & all the new topics of conversation.[22]

***

---

22   NTRS 1099/P1 vol. 1.

Oenpelli
23/9/26

Dear Mr Hinsby

Am Sending herewith the report. Have tried to give a fair idea of the place. Will enclose a few negatives[;] not much time for photography yet. Please keep them for me. Some were old films hence are poor but they will show the buildings, which are mostly poor. I like Mr Campbell[,] he has told me alot about this place .Wheel within wheels[,] Holmes of Darwin offered him £500 to fix up that he should have the place. I have asked him to call & see you ,he is not a believer but I think he has done his best here .He certainly has helped me much[.] A little note of appreciation from you with an invitation to call in would not be amiss, I think he would value it. Donald Campbell Darwin would find him.

Will you keep in mind a circular saw bench for me to cut timber with when we start building. I have written to Col Story to see if there are any in Government Stores[;] it would save freight. The punt here is quite done[;] it is very useful to bring timber in especially in the Wet a dinghey would be useful. With the saw I could make one, it is most important to have one. A circular saw[,] small 36 ins diameter (I have found a small spindle) not drilled in centre as I can do that here right size. teeth for cutting boards. Some day perhaps a launch would be useful but I want to see what happens re Kinchella before I suggest anything. Mr Campbell favours a motor truck to the railway .A little work would fix the track. Water carriage is the cheapest[.] At any rate we must just think about these things &if anything suitable offers take it.

I mentioned Ivens because he struck me as a likely man for practical work. The cattle. The cattle will be a very asset but will need one' man's constant supervision as horses suffer from cancer (caused by wet) & must be watched day by day[,] also the cattle. Black are very good but fail in the details. Ivens seems to have a real call to Aboriginal work[.] Rev G Chambers is in touch with him.

If you think it is advisable send a copy of report to the Bishop. I will leave you to deal with him in the future. It is well to keep in with him,

Hope you have a successful Centenary. Greetings to all the staff.

Sept 24th Have been branding cattle all day & am out after more for several days so I must finish tonight. I am paying a cheque to Campbells for goods (invoice enclosed)[.] The Emasculator is for colts[;] we must have one and there is none on the place .He has put in a good many things several pounds in value to buy ,so I said we would take these.

Our expenses in Darwin were heavy & these later amounts £6.3.5 also &1.1.3 for mail bag & lettergram run into £49. There is the Melbourne credit of &9.7.5.for some special which makes £10 oddcredit. There will not be I hope any more expense for some time. After we get next boat it is not advisable for stores toarrive here before May as they have to be carried through the water and & liable to be spoilt.

I am adding several things we need as soon as possible

Yours sincerely,
Alf Dyer[23]

***

Oenpelli Report for September.

Mr Thorne was busy mustering cattle and putting them into Red Lily. On the 2nd Mrs Dyer & I camped in the Red Lily paddock for a holiday, we both needed it & enjoyed the few day's rest. The lillies were at their best & the colouring everywhere was beautiful, lovely plains of emerald green grass. I enjoyed doing a bit of sketching. I was able to see more of the area. On climbing a hill I saw another pocket which would easily carry 2000 cattle. The new party carried on with various jobs about the place. On our return an old woman died & we buried her, all passed off quietly this time as I had made sure of that first. A number of natives came up for a corroboree, had some lantern services for their benefit. Attended to goat herds, a good number of kids. Mr Ivin had been learning some of the woes of looking after the flock.

On the 14th after Mr Thorne had got the gear in order we went out for our first muster to the head of Cooper's Creek & the King River. Cattle mostly in twos & threes[;] this meant a lot of riding to get a few but we were able to make maps of the country which will help us in the future. We got 70 & know of about 30 more. Mr Thorne was away 11 days but

23   ML MSS 6040/31.

I had to come back earlier as Major Dudley had come out to see me on Abo questions. Mr Williams of Sydney Morning Herald was with him & Constable Pollard. They said they thought the progress made was good especially with all our setbacks of shortage etc. I was glad to meet the Major as he can help me in Darwin in many ways[;] he is going to try & get a saw bench for us. I expect Mr Williams will blow up his horn in Sydney but that does not count for much in these days of writing up. The Major wanted to get to Goulburn Is but could not get word over from the coast so had to return. They left here on the 25th for Darwin. On my way home I lost my teeth about 5 miles from the station. I sent the boys twice to track them but they failed. Then I went with them over 6 miles of track, so I had prayer with them for the return trip & I asked the Lord not to let me down & we found them 5 miles from home in grass & leaves, we had a prayer of thanksgiving, it all counts.

With Mrs Thorne's help Mrs Dyer has been able to do more in school & the progress is good. Mrs Thorne has taken over the dispensary work & has had a very busy time as many as 19 sometimes & some very nasty cases. Mr Thorne has ably relieved of all cattle worries & Mr Ivin of many others. We have 18 boys & 7 girls in the dormitories now. While out mustering I saw 6 more children[;] the parents wanted to know if I wanted them. New blacks keep coming we must have seen nearly 400 now. We had to ration again this month, the children get their dinner & come back for school. It makes problems & it is bad for teaching them to work & maintaining discipline. I am hanging on to the cattle work because I must, the boys are rationed & asking to go bus where there is plenty of food & not much work. For the rest of the work I have one whole man, most of his time is taken getting wood for house & engine, & another with one leg. The Major said he did not know when we will get anymore, cheerful. How can I do anything constructive? 6 months of this year I have been marking time.

On September 28 the hosts of darkness seemed to have their fling. The boys cut their way through the mosquito wire & the girls also[;] most of my morning went finding the offenders & laying on, some of the fathers helped in the punishment. Then the chief boy asked me to arbitrate, an impending fight over some trouble with the police boys & a lubra. However this trouble was overshadowed by a real fight[.] A new party arrived from beyond the head of the Alligator River toward Pine Creek, they rushed on to Dead Calf field in view of the house & the fight began before we knew. Some of our boys tried to stop them, but the fight went on, when we men folk go there one man on each side was laid out. One with a spear through his arm & into his body below the ribs. The other into his back & probably hit the floating rib. He was the man they were after[–] they blame him for a murder. The first man had one dressing on & has not troubled Mrs Thorne since, the other is a faintheart & will have to be pushed off his bed. It is very funny to see him held up by his youngest wife back to back, he will get his move on in a few days, he is the laziest black I have struck. A few nights later there was great commotion in the camp. men talked, women yelled, dogs howled. On enquiry next morning I was informed all over now, good friends, So things are done in the black world[.] The Palaver they had at Christmas has held good till now.

Finished up the month by getting ready for another muster as there are indications of an early wet.

It is now Octtober 19 th & for this year we have had 35 bags of flour & 4 mats of rice. I ordered 2 tons of flour for May as the least I could run the place on. I ought to be getting in timber but cannot employ the labour & am afraid it will be too late as they cannot bring it oover the plains when the rain comes. That will mean next August at the earliest, unless I had a punt but no saw no boards, However there are plenty of other jobs. Last week we had 163 points of rain & I should be ploughing & getting more ground ready. I am not complaining but it is hard to see everything hung up for the want of a few bags of flour.

Later Oct 23 a year since our proper supply of flour came in Oct 22 1925. Sleighs have sent one boat in a year & took some of the stores they brought, a cheerful state of affairs, I wish you people would do a stir up somewhere. H & T might do with a reminder

Alf Dyer[24]

---

24   NTRS 1099/P1 vol. 1.

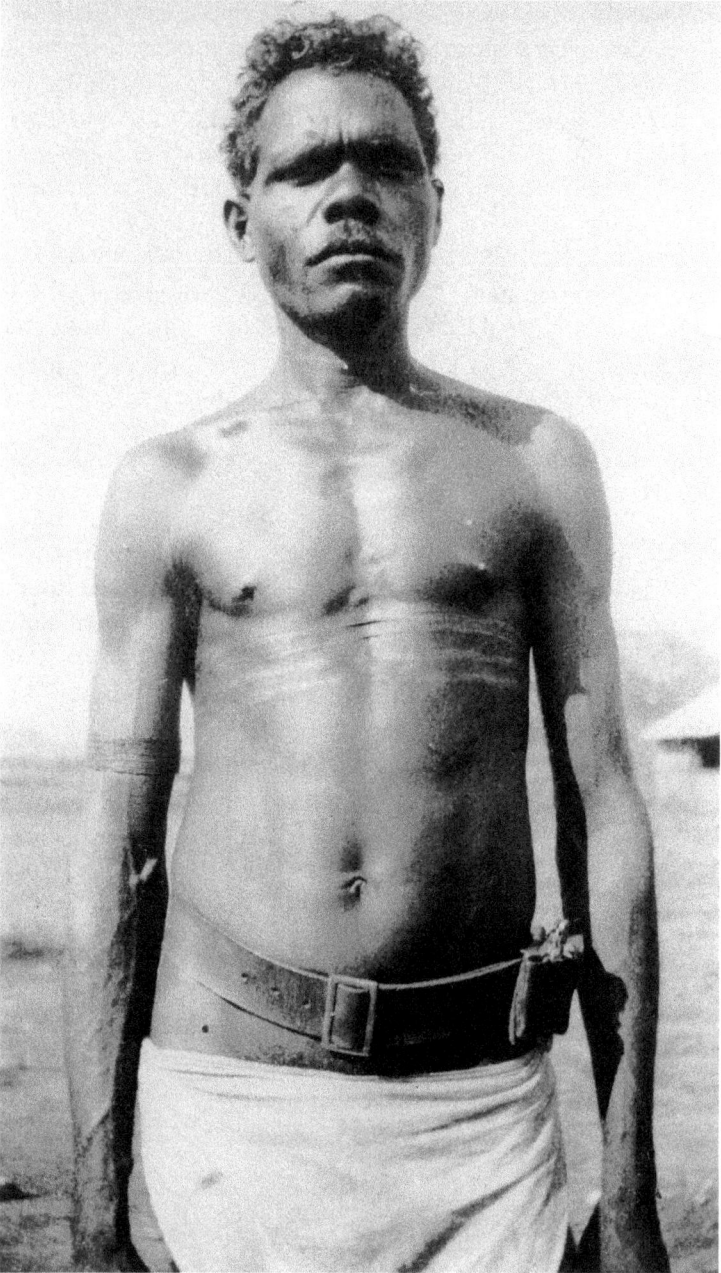

Figure 5.20: 'Harry' (date unknown).
Source: Northern Territory Archives Service (NTRS 694 P1 Box 4a Item 241).

* * *

Report for Oenpelli October 1926

For us men folk it has been largely a month of cattle work, mustering branding & dipping. Several times we have been mercifully spared from nasty accidents, handling big mickies. On some of the camps the water was hardly drinkable owing to the number of geese in the water. Of the cattle I need say nothing because you will have Mr Thorne's report in this mail. I endorse all he says, especially about the old cows. In previous reports I told you that there were a lot of old cows. Mr Campbell said they would leave behind as no drover would take them away, it is not a fair thing to include them in a purchase number.

Mrs Dyer has been able with Mrs Thorne's able help to do more in the school, & to get some of her back sewing more in hand. Dengue fever arrived from Darwin with the visitors & everyone on the station has had it, some very badly & we thought some of the old ones would die, but they pulled through, so Mrs Thorne has had a very busy time with the sick ones with a weary body herself. It also got its grip on me, I got a relapse & was imprisoned for a week. It is the last day as I do this & I feel better again. I have had bad ulcers in my mouth for months & could not eat my food properly, but this rest has healed them so I am very grateful.

We have 6 bags of flour left, Rice finished & sago. Have only necessary workers on. But if the boat does not come soon, I will have to send them all away. Have carted all the barbed wire in, it has been out in the bush for 10 years or more so the galvanising is off. I could not get it till the plains were dry. Also the bark, we mended the wheels, but a smash is impending soon so please remember the S.O.S as there is carting work to be done every day.

Alf Dyer[25]

***

---

25   ML MSS 6040/12 Oenpelli Reports.

Oenpelli Report November 1926

We carted timber in for building nearly every day. The month has been very hot & dry, water low everywhere, but rain has now fallen. This meant many cattle got bogged & had to be pulled out, one good horse was lost in this way. Mrs Thorne went with Mr Thorne on his last muster & enjoyed a few days away from the grind. Later in the month Mr Thorne put the cattle out of Red Lily. Between cattle work Mr Thorne pulled the old cart shed down[–] a terrible eyesore. In the big shed was a lot of waste space, by pulling down & rebuilding this he was able to put the 3 carts into this, which is a great improvement[.] Mr Ivin has been busy with many things. Getting timber, fencing irrigating & now rain has come he is busy ploughing. I have been busy with many repair jobs, to houses & tools & put an injector into the engine, which will save many loads of firewood. Mrs Dyer has kept school going & many other things. Mrs Thorne dispensary. There has been a lot of sickness & several lepers have come in lately. The Bishop say I am not to send them to Darwin, the Govt says I am, I am waiting. If I try to send them they will go bush so it seems as if I must make a separate place for them, some are so pitiful. Services have been held daily[,] sometimes we have over 70. We see many improvements in the people & one feels it is good to have been sent to labour here for God, regeneration is His own work & will come in His season. Most of workers are away owing to food shortage, we can only give a little piece of bread each, but make up with meat. Mr thorne is fencing with a boy[.] Mr Ivin is ploughing & one of the boys should be doing that, the other two are carting & I have no one to help me. I am building the Thorne's new house according to the new plan of the station to be. All the staff think the site is ideal. Leper section, girls dormitory & Church are urjent needs but hope to get these on the way soon. We hear the boat has gone to the Roper & will call in here on her way back, so we live in hope with the fear that if she does not come soon, we shall not be able to get them; or ruined with the rains, but there is a little season of grace yet & we pray that it will not be too late. Generally our health is fairly good. With every good wish for 1927 as this will be the last report you will get for some time. We trust all your needs have been supplied[;] we feel grateful for all His many blessings our last Gleaner was August so we are a bit behind.

Yours sincerely
Alf Dyer[26]

---

26   NTRS 1099/P1 vol. 1.

Figure 5.21: Man with family being treated at the dispensary (date unknown).
Source: Northern Territory Archives Service (NTRS 694 P1 Box 4 Item 139).

* * *

Church Missionary Society
Oenpelli November 1926
East Alligator River N.T.

I beg to submit report for 1926, During the year about 400 blacks have visited the station, coming and going. There are 18 boys & 8 girls in the dormitories & a dozen children who will come in later & more further out again. Generally speaking I think their impression of the station is favourable.

Two different tribes have come up to settle old scores with this tribe, the first one after conference peaceably, the other with a fight in which two men were speared & afterwards patched up. After this they informed me it was finished now. All these things help break down tribal differences, many have been killed here in the past from what I can gather from the blacks, there is no reason why this Reserve rightly handled should not make a good one for numbers of blacks.

During the Wet we were principally growing food stuffs. I had in about 5 acres of Cotton, Maize, Corn, Peanuts, Potatoes, but the crops were very poor owing to the rain ceasing early in March. This involved fencing & clearing. I hope to do better this year as we shall have a better start & shall have my own seed.

I have erected an old donkey engine left here in pieces from milking days. Most of the bolts were broken off on the boiler and bed & I had to drill them all out with a little hand drill & retap which made it a very big job for me, But I succeeded & it now works a double acting steam pump on the billabong which lifts 52 gallons a minute. We can now irrigate to tide over a dry spell.[27]

* * *

Oenpelli Report December 1926

Began the month telling the children & most of the people they must get their own breakfast. They were quite cheerful over it as there was plenty of fish just at our doors. Some of the older people said when we opened the last 50 lb of flour, you keep it for yourselves. We gave them a good meat tea, & the children came back for afternoon school. They are very fond of school & we have had no runaway trouble Which is remarkable for these people. They seem keen to learn.

Mr Thorne finished off the horse paddock fence which was very sick, this keeps the horses in a small area in the Wet, also away from the leeches, they are a supposed cause of cancer. Good rains have come & Mr Ivin has been ploughing. this is a job blacks can do[;] shortage means always we have to do tasks they can do, & other things are left undone. When I was able I was working on Mr Thorne's house, & when he finished the fence he joined me. We had just got the framework up when the boat came on Dec 13, details of this you have already had in letters sent. This put a stop to building, as carting & putting away had to be done. Then Mr Thorne & the boys mustered in the horses, a report of these has been sent.

---

27   ML MSS 6040/12.

As no cultivator came I had to make one & succeeded in making of all iron & steel& it will serve us for many years I trust. Then came Xmas preparations, while doing this we got a pleasant surprise, after our disappointment when the boat came with no groceries, hardware or mail, on Dec 18 our letters came via Goulburn Is Mission. All this I have answered & sent to the Secretary. Many general jobs have been done also. The ladies work has been done faithfully, but does not lend itself so easily to report, but I expect we would not get very far without our meals & our sewing, Mrs Dyer has kept school going till Xmas preparations stopped it. Mrs Thorne has treated a number of sick cases day by day & many are very unpleasant ones & the household work.

One thing that pleased all, was that the working boys told us they wanted to give all their money (pocket) to buy a bullock for the blacks for Xmas. I had intended doing this, so I thanked them for the thought & told them we could not give them much for their labour, but I would give them a beast for the way they had done their work. So they killed it & we gave out no meat for two days as everyone shared. Of Xmas itself Mrs Thorne has kindly written a report of which I will send a report typed, so there is no need to say anything further of that. We did not have a great number as I could not send out early invitations this year owing to shortage, but we had over 120.

We have a good start with the garden this year, have in about 3 acres, & prospects of a good year, but could have been much further ahead, if we had not had the shortage & an early start means a great deal when the rains come with it. Have planted out trees along the two main drives of the new station to be, & am starting a botanical garden also, the place D.V. should be something to please the eye in a few years time. So closed the year 1926, some have gone beyond lately whom we have pointed to the Lord[;] they seemed to grasp a little of the way of light. The year has brought many setbacks, but very many more blessings, to the Giver of All be the praise.

Alf Dyer[28]

---

28   NTRS 1099/P1 vol. 1.

Figure 5.22: Man with fish caught in nearby billabong (date unknown).
Source: Northern Territory Archives Service (NTRS 694 P1 Box 4 Item 141).

Figure 5.23: Fishing in the Oenpelli billabong. Elizabeth Garabbunba ('Carabumba') stands in the foreground possibly with her husband 'Gamarad' (date unknown).

Source: Northern Territory Archives Service (NTRS 694 P1 Box 4 Item 67).

***

March Report . . Oenpelli 1927

Mr Ivin & a party of blacks were barking for nearly two weeks & got about 700 sheets for building purposes. All through this month Mr Thorne has continued his improvements to the cattle yard & reconstructions[,] also the milking shed with odddays of harness repairs. He is still suffering the effects of the strain of landing stores[.] The ladies have fulfilled their general tasks & dispensary & school. Methodist Mission sent mail to say 2 of their party on Crocodile Is had been attacked by blacks & that Mr Robinson had been speared in the arm , the blacks were caught & were being sent to Darwin in their lugger which would also take in our mail waiting there since January & on their return they would bring out our mail. This also gave us the chance to send our mail over to catch their next boat so we kept the boys for a few days till out mail was ready, we sent away over an 100 letters between us. Mr Reid in his letter said he had heard of cattle killing so Mr Thorne & self decide to have a look around & warm the & punish some whose names we had if we found them. We spent a week but did not see any signs of killing except the cases reported. We visited two pockets with a little fencing across which will make good paddocks to keepthem in during the Wet, this will save mustering & will make spearing very difficult to put over. On our return we found mail awaiting us & a chance of getting our mail away. My time has been taken up largely with repairs & general tasks, the I made another start on the lazarate to have it ready before I go away. Mr Iviv also made a start to fence in Waterfall pocket which willmake a large paddock near the station for cattle we want to keep apart for breeding a better class of cattle. Got in the first batch of kaffir corn. On the 30th Mr De Lancourt arrived walking, they were bogged in Red Lily & only have one donkey left, Mr Francis remains with the gear, the[y] had to swim therivers & had a very rough time.

Alf Dyer[29]

Figure 5.24: Man making bush string while another holds a spear, bush camp near Oenpelli (date unknown).
Source: Northern Territory Archives Service (NTRS 694 P1 Box 4 Item 89).

***

29   NTRS 1099/P1 vol. 1.

April Report Oenpelli 1927

De Lancourt & Mr Francis arrived on the 1 st of April with only one donkey, the rest having bogged & died on the road between us & the railway, this will give some idea of the difficulty in travelling in the Wet season, & it took him 9 weeks to do what can be done in on week. They departed on April 27th. We decided to give them two old horses to help them on their journey. He made several reports of Oenpelli for the papers South[–] all very wordy. H was n not very anxious to start on the rest of his long journey, Mr Thorne has to move him on as I had already left for Darwin as he was to move off a few days after we left. Mr Thornes work has been on yard construction, breaking in horses, & the usual many tasks cropping up on a station. Mr Ivin has found the garden required most of his attention as irrigation had to be started again, a start was also made on the Waterfall pocket paddock which will take about 4 miles of fencing[,] the ranges making another paddock. Self on general tasks & engine repairs, was able to fix up the knocks on the steam engine & overhauled the pump & put in ne[w] washers. Both visitors report favourably on the condition of the boiler ~~was~~ one was a mining engineer. Finish off the lazarette & put in three boys. Then had to get ready to leave for Darwin on the 20 th of the month via Goulburn Is. Mrs Thorne has ably carried on her many duties in the household & dispensary. Mrs Dyer general & school work till she went with me to Goulburn Is for a short change by horses[–] this meant a 50 mile ride[;] she managed to see it through. G Is people have been very kind to us, we were disappointed to find the Is so barren making the problem of the future very great without agriculture for food. It made us count our blessings. I left Mr Thorne in charge while we were away.[30]

* * *

May Report Oenpelli 1927

Mr & Mrs Thorne & Mr Ivin carried on the of the station while I was away in Darwin. General supervision takes a lot of time[.] Mr Thorne did a lot of repairs to harness & saddles etc for the coming cattle season, also continued with yard construction & breaking in mules & horses. Mr Ivin's work was principally garden & a new fence around the reserve. Peanuts & Kaffir corn & cotton had to be gathered in. One bale of cotton

---

30   NTRS 1099/P1 vol. 1.

was sent in to be ginned, both seasons have proved that good cotton can be grown here, but for the present food stuffs must be my principal object. peanuts we keep for our own use here an extra for Sunday we bagged cwt lbs. Kaffir corn report later we had a very good crop, this will be a rice saver. Mrs Thorne carried out all the women's side of the work until Mrs Dyer returned, dispensary is always a busy time here & Paddy's sickness made the task heavier. Mr Ivin went to bring Mrs Dyer from Goulburn Is & spent 2 nights there & returned on the 11th. Mrs Dyer painted the inside of our house & started school on the 16th again. Mr Thorne cleaned out the dip & refilled it. There were several lots of stealing in the garden which Mr Thorne promptly punished. Mr Ferrier & self arrived on May 29 th overland 7 days trip. The boat did not come in time so we came on ,but it arrived after we left and brought our stores .However it gave several more days here & we saw the overland track & the difficulties of the many crossings & boggy places for motor service[;] we will stick to the ship ladsto save our lives. Everything was in good order on the station & I thanked the staff for the able way they had carried on. Mr Ferrier will make his own report no doubt for better or for worse. I was ordained deacon May 15 th at Christ Church Darwin. With the £ 35 given to me personally for the work I was able to get a 3 Furrow Mouldboard plough Stump jump for £10[;] it had never done any work it was only a little rusty. The present price South is £36 & this saves freight £15 for a good saw bench at Vesty's with the balance belts rails wheels a shaft & pulleys iron etc & 2 Cir saws. both of these wer urgent needs. The plough will break up many more acres for growing food next season ,we hope for rice also. The saw for buildings etc A chartered lugger made no difference in freight so the Lord did prosper me. Finished the month by planting out the new seeds & overhauling the pump which was in trouble. Quite a lot of new people coming about & many more children so we are evidently winning the parents approval, so we must press on till they find the Truth.[31]

***

Oenpelli report June 1927

Mr Ferrier was with us the first few days & he suggested a six monthly meeting to discuss policy of the mission. The first meeting was held while he was with us. Report of this to follow. The boat arrived on the 2 nd our coming overland gave Mr Ferrier a few extra days, & also he was able to

---

31 NTRS 1099/P1 vol. 1.

see the station more normal in working. We had to use a new track as the other was still bogey , being full of holes the waggonette sick wheels suffered & one ceased to be a wheel. The lorry also suffered the front forecarriage breaking & a general twist up[–] a report on the condition of the lorry on arrival enclosed. Unpacking & putting away always means a few days. The flags presented by Sydney Grammar Schools were handed over by Mr Ferrier to the children & hoisted. Earth - quake shock on the 4th long & violent the children were very scared. On Sunday 5th aftermCommunion Service Mr Ferrier left[;] it was good to have him with us & to have our first communions on the Station. On the 7th our best loved boy & best stock boy died, as he had confessed a simple trust in the Lord Jesus I asked him if he would like to be baptized[,] he said yes, so he was baptized before all on his deathbed[–] my first official act as deacon on the station. With the new pipe up from the landing we were able to complete the present scheme of irrigation. Mrs Thorne has had a very busy month in the dispensary besides her household duties[,] some days over 60 for treatment. Mr Thorne took her away for a change but not much of a rest, on a burning off around the cattle yards, with repairs being away for 8 days, he reports all the yards safe & in order. Mr Irvin has been away with a fencing party to fence in the Water fall Pocket ,the whole length of the fence in about 7 miles, this will use up most of the Govt barbed wire, we had hoped to have enough to do another pocket at Fish Creek but there will not be enough to do this. This makes a paddock of about 5000 to 7000 acres as the fence is only on one side[,] the ranges do the rest[.] Mr Thorne will use this to keep cattle in in the Wet season to save mustering. He will finish this in early July. This will save lots of work in days to come & help in improving the bre[e]d by selection. While the party were away I mended the lorry, taking the best part of a week with supervision of the family ,was able to make a fair job of it & then took a party down & repaired the road filling up all the bad holes & burning off around the Red Lily fence & brought home the waggonette. Mr Thorn[e] & self then set to work on the buckboard & the waggonette for a complete overhaul to change over the wheels & put on the new set[;] this will make two useful vehicles he really did most of it as the garden took most of my time with irrigation, we have a nice lot of vegetables coming on .I also had to reset the pump on her foundations, owing to being unduly raced. The horses are in very poor condition so Mr Thorne turned them out till next month, there is too much water about yet for mustering. We are badly off for horses as Mr Ferrier has been informed. Mrs Dyer has done her many general tasks & school of which Mr F. will no doubt report on. Have had trouble with the goat herd we fear s some are stolen ,but cannot locate the trouble ,but are watching. Finish up the month by pulling out my first Abo's tooth, a big one, he came, most things do if you pull hard enough, so pull the Heavenilies are behind us.

Yours Sincerely[32]

Figure 5.25: Men and boys at Oenpelli, standing around large wagon (date unknown).
Source: Northern Territory Archives Service (NTRS 694 P1 Box 4 Item 13).

Figure 5.26: Raising the flag, Oenpelli mission (date unknown).
Source: Northern Territory Archives Service (NTRS 694 P1 Box 4 Item 689).

---

32 NTRS 1099/P1 vol. 1.

Figure 5.27: Pulling teeth (date unknown).
Source: Northern Territory Archives Service (NTRS 693 P1 Item 21).

Figure 5.28: Stockman breaking in horse, Arrkuluk Hill in background (date unknown).
Source: Northern Territory Archives Service (NTRS 693 P1 Item 21).

* * *

Oenpelli Report for July 1927

Mr Ivin fencing till the 21st this finished off the Waterfall pocket paddock. Being the vegetable season I have been irrigating twice a week. Getting the seed this year we have had a nice lot of Southern Vegetables[;] the soil suits them very well. For me the month has all been repairs[,] nothing constructive. The house pump went wrong[,] being a lathe job my efforts only produced a small flow of water. Mail came on the 3th from Mr Ferrier & South. Goulburn Is people report De Lancourt playing up with the blacks[–] we were suspicious of him. Mr Thorne finished off the yard gates, & gets ready for the mustering season on the 14 th[;] he went mustering with a circus start off 2 falls & Mr Thorne was knocked down by a horse[,] all lucky escapes, he returned on the 20 th branded & bangtailed & later again reports on the numbers will follow later. Mr Ivin pulls down the old garden fence & is setting up a new one to take in 3 more acres[;] it will also make a better ploughing paddock for the 3 F plough. We have harvested over a 1000lbs of cassava with about another 1000to get 1600 lbs of potatoes this is about half & 1500 lbs of kaffir corn & 2½ cwt of peanuts. Quantaties of watermelons pawpaws toma toes cabbages lettice beans etc. This is reducing flour consumption considerably ,so I feel we have done well with one little plow. I think it is helping them to see the advantage of work. We have good rice land also, so when we get our new plough going & more garden we shall do better. The steam pump caused me some trouble to get in order, but succeeded after trying various causes. The boiler then sprung a leak in the firebox on the bottom seam ,this meant taking it all down to see if I could mend it. I could not bend iron plate to the 4 angles, but Mrs Dyer's nurses plate did the trick with iron over the top of it then then run 2" of lead inside all along the seam[,] put on 3 patches & drill 30 holes with my baby drill still going strong. Old age now being acute on the house pump we fill the tank with buckets[–] very slow but there was an old low down pump here broken in the main casting in 3 places so we put a plate on join them together & solder the cracks & she goes, but this is costly in my time & I ought to be building. Mrs Thorne has had her usually busy time in the dispensary[;] there are always plenty of sick folk about & household duties. Mrs Dyer general & school. She also had made over a 1000lbs of soap. the usual services have been held the camps visited ,also the sick. The children now know 34 hymns by heart & Scripture. In school they are picking up short sentences.

Yours faithfully
Alf Dyer[33]

Figure 5.29: Two men examining a paw paw tree (date unknown).
Source: Northern Territory Archives Service (NTRS 693 P1 Item 21).

* * *

Oenpelli Report August 1927

Mr Thorne has been busy mustering, branding, & dipping cattle with the usual repairs to gear & saddles. He also made a set of bars for a four horse team for the plough & a new fence around the yard & started a new fowl yard & house. Mr Ivin took the little boys for their first holiday in the bush to their great excitement. He has been fencing in the new garden area & winnowed the Kaffir corn which harvested 1500lbs[.] Numerous other tasks have been done, getting in bark firewood timber garden & irrigating[–] we have had a lovely lot of vegetables this month. Between many tasks I have started a new well[–] put in cement walls down to the hard clay. (Govt cement) left here but has nearly lost its life still does some jobs alright. Also acement foundation for the saw bench with shafting & extra pulleys to work other machinery as necessary in the time to come. The making of couplings & large pulleys to smaller shafts made the task much longer & harder. We are also making a semi-shade house for nursery & vegetables in the hot weather. Carambumba was sold for a mosquito net & blanket to a black for a wife by her father[;] he did not consult me as he promised, but we were able to fit it up that a young man named Nagal whom she wanted to marry should marry her soon, this is a begining to overcome one of our greatest difficulties: young girls promised to old men. Mrs Thorne has had her usual many tasks always (plenty) of sick folk[.] Buranali who was speared last year died, a real lizard but even lizards have their place in creation, he had a stroke at the last & could not talk, but always had a smile as I talked & sang to him. Mrs Thorne scalded her foot badly which laid her up for a few days, then she took the girls to the Waterfall for a camp to their great delight ,but was unfortunately marred by bad eyes. Mrs Dyer has had her usual many tasks & school[.] On the 31st Mr Thorne & self left on a mustering trip for humans & cattle along the Goomardar [Goomadeer] River on out eastern border which we have not seen yet.

Alf Dyer[34]

***

---

34   NTRS 1099/P1 vol. 1.

Oenpelli Report September 1927

Mr Thorne (& self) go for a mustering trip to the Goomardar River which is on our eastern boundary., we had not been so far out before. We find a few cattle had gone out this far, but that they mostly remain about the Cooper & the King. By inviting blacks to our camp with the promise of a buffalo which we were able to fulfil, getting our own cuts; & the[y] had the rest. I was able thus to see a number of blacks[,] some not seen before & children who were very scared at first, some had not seen whites before, peanuts & pictures made an opening & one night the little boy danced a corrorbee in our honour. These will come in later as we are able. We mustered up the country all the way back, collecting over an hundred with a fair number of cleanskins among them, but the yard broke the last night so we lost most of the wild ones, returning on the 16th with 60 odd. Goomardah [Goomadeer] is well watered with some good country. Mr Thorne was able to make many additions to his map.

Mr Ivin & the ladies carried on the work of the station, they have had their usual many duties not written up. Mr Ivin fencing grubbing & general with garden[;] lots of vegetables that Gen Sec was doubtful of. I had the misfortune to scald my foot in camp which laid me up for a few days but mail & plans kept me from idleness. After banding & dipping Mr Thorne & the boys went mustering again to the N.W. till the 28 th brands & makes repairs to gear. Self kept out of mischief by a few repairs to the lorry[–] a broken wheel on the waggonette. Fix the saw bench for running also the grist mill for power also put my tools in order to get on with building. We strike water in the new well which will supply the water for the new buildings. Plenty of problems, but things are moving on slowly towards the ideals in view so we look up & take courage; God is over all.

Yours sincerely
Alf Dyer[35]

---

35 NTRS 1099/P1 vol. 1.

Figure 5.30: Mrs Dyer, dormitory girls and Aboriginal women from mission. Elwyndiwyndi can be seen at back left (date unknown).
Source: Northern Territory Archives Service (NTRS 694 P1 Box 4 Item 33).

***

Oenpelli Report for October 1927

Mr Thorne & the boys mustered around the Cooper again, but was not able to complete it owing to the horses being too tired. We have not enough working horses, his report will cover details. Between times repair jobs to the yard ,fencing & completed fowl yard & house. Mr Ivin garden & irrigation ,but rains have stoppd this ,he also went with boys & got timber which with bark we have been carting in almost daily. We started the saw bench going & he cut up some firewood[;] the saw worked well. Self made windless fixed up the saw bench pulleys & fittings. Erect the first house for the people to their great delight on a 406feet square to have 20 houses on two frontages & 10 on the other two with road - way between. Cleaned up & marked out cementry. Marked out squares for the new station. Started to pull down the old school building to reerect in the new plan. This iron will do 3 native houses. the hall of the future & school which will also have to serve as a Church for the present as we have outgrown our present Chapel. The Church end will be scre[e]ned off to keep sacred. Have allowed a block 150' x 60' for the Church. The boat arrived when the school was almost down so I must leave it to Messrs Ion & Phil Taylor who have come to help with buildings & generally. Also Miss Sherrin who will take over school & sewing. No tides hinder us going so we are able to help unpack the boxes with all their loving gifts from those who labour with us in the Lord to Him & them we offer our thanks. The ladies have done faithfully their many tasks in dispensary school & household. We have been able this month to start a reading class in the S.school [Sunday School] [.] Several new children & babies have come in & newpeople keep on coming. we must now have seen on the reserve about 500 people who come & go. This is an indication of their approval of what we are trying to do for them.

Produce grown in the garden with one small plough is as follows

1590 lbs Kaffir corn
2848 " Cassava about 1000lbs to dig yet
3455 lbs Sweet Potatoes
92 Dozen Bananas
475 Pawpaws
2896 Lbs Pumpkins
108 lbs Tomatoes
1 Cwt Cotton
1 do maise
2½ Cwt Peanuts
Numerous melons cabbages lettice carrots turnips beans mangoes

This is encouraging &with our 3furrow ploughwe should do better[;] about 4 more acres have been cleared ,horses are our problem, a tractor would soon save for the flour it would save. Looking back over the past we see many changes both in the people & in the station generally & we all feel it has all been well worth while. This spiritual is not yet but who can tell but God what is germinating underneath so to Him from whom all life comes we give thanks for all His many gifts & leave the future in His hands.

yours sincerely
Alf Dyer[36]

---

36 NTRS 1099/P1 vol. 1.

Figure 5.31: Building Aboriginal houses (date unknown).
Source: Northern Territory Archives Service (NTRS 693 P1 Item 21).

Figure 5.32: Aboriginal stockmen preparing horses for cattle mustering (date unknown).
Source: Northern Territory Archives Service (NTRS 694 P1 Box 4a Item 264).

* * *

OENPELLI C.M.S. ABORIGINAL MISSION STATION, NORTHERN TERRITORY –

REPORT FROM OCTOBER 1925 TO OCTOBER 1927

When we took over Oenpelli there were nine people employed in the place – no children, and two or three old people in the camp. One was getting regular food, as she was blind. We sent out invitations telling the people we would employ any who wanted work, that we would start school for the children, and any sick ones could get medicine, and if necessary, food. Since that time about five hundred natives have come and gone.

School was started in November, with eleven pupils. Since May 1927 there has been an average of thirty pupils, and during October, thirty-five. The have two hours each afternoon in school and our aim it's the three Rs. – that they may read, write and count, to understand the value of money. As they are able for it, and we have the time, we hope to increase the school hours. In October 1927 several of those who came in the first six months were reading short sentences, which considering they knew no English at all is not slow progress. The change in the children's habits, i.e., cleanliness, industry etc., makes the work among them most encouraging. With babies and children who are too young for school, there are resident on the place nearly fifty children.

Garden: The old garden was full of nut-grass, which is very hard to get rid of, so we removed to a new area which has been cleared and fenced, about ten acres being ready, for the present wet season, to be ploughed. I was fortunately able to get a three furrow plough in Darwin cheaply. Horses are a problem, though as they cannot stand much in our climate, we have hopes of getting a tractor. Lat wet, on about seven acres we produced some six tons of food-stuffs, including Cassava 3,841 lbs. – Sweet Potatoes 4,000. lbs. – Pumpkins 2,896. lbs. – Corn 1,500. lbs. – Maise 1 cwt. – Peanuts 2½ cwts. – Tomatoes 108 lbs. – Pawpaws 475 – Bananas 92 doz., besides other vegetables and fruits and a sample of cotton, 1 cwt. Of which we sent to London. This reduced greatly our flour bill, and is a very real factor in teaching the people the advantages of industry. Meat is raised on the reserve.

Cattle: The Government gave us 500. when we took over, and we purchased 800; during the first year at least 200. died of old age. This year we have mustered with calves branded 1,800. and hope next This year to have we will have our first sale of cattle. New yards have been made to handle the work more easily. seven miles of fencing was done with wire left on the place, around a large pocket where the ranges make one side of the fence. We have two large paddocks now for improving the stock, but new blood is needed to improve the herd. Mr.F.Thorne, who is Overseer of this department, is a very practical man.

Horses: We have some 60. but 30. of those are breeding mares, and some are old, so there were only about 20. available for work. And mustering over 2,000. square miles, the cattle being wild, need horses. They were too tired to complete the muster, but we were able to estimate the totals.

Constructional: The old buildings are hopeless and will be pulled down shortly[.] The new station is already planned on lines which allow for expansion. Squares of 406 ft. with 40 ft. roadways and tress on either side are laid out. Two new houses are up and a third was started when we left. Two young men, Messrs.I.& P.Taylor, who went up to help in this work, will continue during our absence, and this part should go ahead; we were hindered by many other tasks. An old donkey engine left behind by the Government has also been erected near the billabong, and with a steam pump serves for irrigation during the dry season, and has enabled us to grow things there. Besides many new fences, repairs, goat yards and a horse paddock. We also secured a small saw bench in Darwin and erected that.

Medical Work: This takes a good deal of Mrs. Thorne's time. She is a trained nurse, and each morning a sick parade is held and all who need treatment are attended freely. During the year well over 5,000. dressings etc., have been given. Many old and infirm have been helped, while the do not grasp much, they are grateful, and their darkness has been lightened. Several lepers are attended to also, and all those too old to work are fed.

Services are held daily. The children are losing the look of fear present in the faces of those who fear evil spirits. The expression of their faces shows that good seed is growing up within, and it shows outwardly in the way they apply themselves to their work. We do not mean that they are saints; good and evil is present in the best of humanity.

Confidence and appreciation of people: we feel the willingness of the parents to leave their children with us and the fact that none of the latter have run away shows we have gained their confidence, and that they appreciate our efforts to give them a better life. Only a few days before we left, Mr. Thorne, our Stock Overseer, who is not a missionary, remarked – "It is wonderful the way these people have come in from the bush to settle down to routine and labour." And in that we believe lies the hope of a future for these people of the stone age.

In presenting this short report of what has been attempted and done, not in our own strength, for acknowledgement is due to Him Who has been our help throughout, we would thank you for sympathy and help given in several requests we have laid down before the Government from time to time.[37]

Figure 5.33: Planting rice, 1927.
Source: Northern Territory Archives Service (NTRS 694 P1 Box 4 Item 12).

Figure 5.34: Tractor with dray (date unknown).
Source: Northern Territory Archives Service (NTRS 694 P1 Box 4a Item 145).

* * *

37   NTRS 1099/P1 vol. 1.

OENPELLI NOVEMBER 1927 REPORT

The lugger "Mary" arrived with stores on the 28th October after spending 5 days negotiating the passages up the river, even then she did not get to the Landing and we had to unload her about three miles down stream where she struck hard and fast. Mr & Mrs Dyer left on the 9-11-27, the lugger having to wait until then for the tides to float her off, and the intervening days were spent on carting up all the stores. I sent two boys down river with them and they returned on the 16-11-27 reporting the lugger as clearing the river on the morning of Monday the 14th inst.

The balance of the month the horses and mules have been worked to their fullest capacity carting timber which Mr Ivins party had cut last month, we got in approximately 500 sticks but fully 50% of them are very thin and not of much use. The plains being flooded to a depth of 15 inches or so[,] we cannot cart any more.

Mr Ivin was sick with, we think Rheumatics, contracted last wet season and he had to spend a week or so in bed.

All garden work has been confined to planting Cassava and weeding. We planted out 720 Cassava shoots and these with what we hav[e] give us a total of over 1200 plants, and these ,renewed as they are used should give us a plentiful supply.

We have had the following produce from the garden during the month CASSAVA 377 lbs PAWPAW 81 BANANAS 46 doz[;] also all hands have had mangoes 14 times which totals approximately 1250 mangoes

Messrs Taylor have been engaged in erecting the new building which is to act as school and hall and I expect to be able to advise completion of this on th[e] next report. Mr I.Taylor also assisted in the garden during the period of Mr Ivins incapacity.

Owing to the increased number of children Miss Sherrins time is fully occupied with school, school preparation, preparation for and taking services, sewing and assisting Mrs Thorne on washing days. She has found it necessary to have a kindergarten class in the morning[.] Miss Sherrin and Mrs Thorne are endeavouring to teach some of the women sewing.

Mrs Thorne has had a very busy time with Dispensary ,Baking[,] Housekeeping, washing, sewing and general supervision. Some of the trained kitchen staff have been ill and some have asked for and gone walkabout.

My own time has been occupied with cattle drafting, branding etc, assisting in school, in garden and general supervision.

The "Maskee" arrived here on the 19th inst looking forthe "Mary" and left again on the 21st having presumably crossed each other on the way over.

Also during the month I have extended the present girls dormitory giving it an extra 55 square feet of floor space and putting in two wire windows for air, also the boys dormitory by 9 feet giving an extra 90 feet of floor space. This I have always considered an absolute necessity in view of the face it will be fully two years before the new dormitories will be ready for occupation.

F.A. Thorne[38]

Figure 5.35: School class, 1927.
Source: Northern Territory Archives Service (NTRS 694 P1 Box 4a Item 202).

---

38   NTRS 1099/P1 vol. 1.

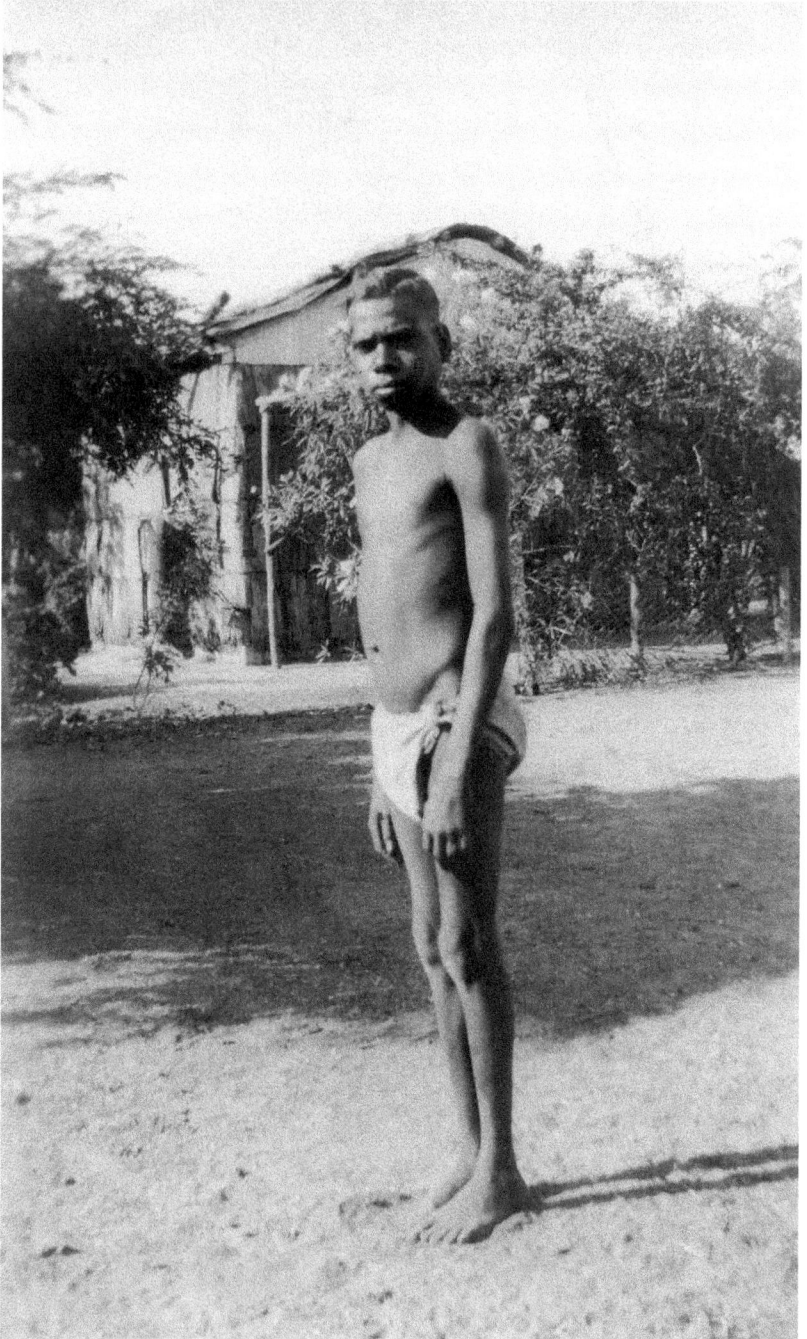

Figure 5.36: 'David' Namilmil (date unknown).
Source: Northern Territory Archives Service (NTRS 694 P1 Box 4 Item 76).

Figure 5.37: Mission garden (date unknown).
Source: Northern Territory Archives Service (NTRS 693 P1 Item 21).

Figure 5.38: Mission gardens/crops (date unknown).
Source: Northern Territory Archives Service (NTRS 693 P1 Item 21).

Figure 5.39: Working in the mission gardens (date unknown).
Source: Northern Territory Archives Service (NTRS 693 P1 Item 21).

* * *

OENPELLI REPORT DECEMBER 1927

The rainfall for the month was 12.71 points and we only lost four or five half days, most the rain falling at nighttime.

On the 2nd boys out behind Argolook, getting firewood broke the pole of the lorry and this gave us a good repair job to start the month.

The old antbed oven by the meathouse (which Mr Ferrier will probably remember) was pulled down and as a material was good I used it in part on the floor of the new School and Church building., the Taylor bros completed this on the 17th of the month though the ant-bedding took several more days to dry, We decided to use the building for the Xmas tree on the 24th and officially open it with service on Christmas day, this was done and are now using it for morning service each day.

The garden work has been a constant fight against weeds and Mr Ivin has had his hands full keeping the workers going, during the month he planted about 240 watermelons of which very few have come up, also about 200 pumpkins[–] most of them so far are doing well, and a number of paw-paw, but they mostly died and we are now awaiting further rains to put out a new batch of seedlings.

On the 30th and 31st we planted out about ¾ acre of peanuts and we are looking for a good fall of rain to shoot them.

On the 14th we started ploughing and found that the undergrowth absolutely choked the plough so we had to put on all hands clearing the rubbish, this entailed a vast amount of really gruelling work, but we completed the patch on the far side of the road by the end of the year and harrowed it also, the patch where the peanuts are sewn was worked over five times in all before they were put in.

Five days were spent in repairing the Horse paddock fence, but the wires are badly corroded and will not stand any strain.

We completed the new fence along the South side of the roadway and hope during the coming month to make and hang the gates for same.

Before any harrowing could be done the old harrows had to be repaired, and it took me nearly three days to make a new leaf and bars so that we could use the two together, this gives us quicker and better work. I also improvised a fixture to hold the handles on the new cultivator which is doing good work.

On the 18th we marked out four more people houses and the Taylor Bros have been on these until the end of the month.

The Horehound spread extremely rapidly and took a lot of pulling out (roots and all– this is the only way) in the garden and round the area for the new houses also outside the wing entrance to the stockyard. We have not been able to do any more and I think next year provision will have to be made for a special gang of about twenty men to work on it exclusively and pull it out by the roots, it is very hardy and like all pests spreads with startling rapidity.

Mr P. Taylor is writing up an account of the Xmas festivities, we think the people had an enjoyable time, there were 146 and 27 picaninnies and about that number or a few more at the Xmas tree and attending for a few days afterwards.

On the 26th a small boy–Narlbrett– who had come into the Dormitory a few days previously, got in the way of a horse ridden by one of the stock boys and got his arm fractured. Mrs Thorne set it for him and he is now going along splendidly.

The average for meals for the month has been 91 or 273 meals per day, some days we had up to 99; with the flour available also the cooking facilities and kitchen staff this is far too many and we must reduce numbers, this

I would have done earlier, only it is Mr Dyers wish to encourage them to come in at Christmas time so I gave all who wanted it work until after the holidays.

The daily average medicines was 25per a.m. and 10 at p.m. and of these quite a number are very big dressings that have to be done twice and some three per day.

Since Mrs Dyers departure Mrs Thorne has found the old arrangrmnt of sick parade after service not practicable, the kitchen work at that time of the morning requiring constant supervision and so she entered into an arrangement with Miss Sherrin to get the Staff breakfast (myself supervising the preparing and giving out of the peoples breakfast) and Mrs Thorne now does the major part of the dressings before 7 a.m. and finishes giving out medicines immediately after service thus leaving her free to take over the kitchen about 8-15 a.m. and we find this arrangement working satisfactorily.

Mrs Thorne has had a very busy month with Xmas preparations[,] making cakes and puddings in accordance with usual customs. There has been a great deal of sickness necessitating many visits to the camp and this combined with several of the trained women being sick and going "walkabout" necessitated taking in new women to train.

The new workers were naturally very disappointed at the non arrival of the mail, so as the Wet was before us I very reluctantly (from a horseflesh point of view) sent horses over to Goulburn Island for the mail and they arrived back on the night of New Years day.

Miss Sherrin continues to be extremely busy with her school, preparations,- and sewing.

The flour question is again going to be a matter of serious consideration but I am going into it thoroughly and will advise you further in the next report.

The new plough purchased by Mr Dyer in Darwin is doing good work and with increased motive power will be able to do quite a lot of work.

F.A. Thorne[39]

---

39   NTRS 1099/P1 vol. 1.

Figure 5.40: A later photograph of Nangalbered ('Narlbrett'), 1950.
Source: National Archives of Australia (A1200, L13067, 11656518).

Figure 5.41: 'Butter Factory, boys on Xmas day 1925'. The old Paddy Cahill–era butter factory is in the background. In the foreground, the children are playing with their Christmas presents.
Source: Northern Territory Archives Service (NTRS 694 P1 Box 4a Item 151).

* * *

OENPELLI REPORT JANUARY 1928.

January has been a month of struggle and dissapointment,– instead of being a month of good heavy rainfall it was very dry and hot, up to the 18th we had only a couple of small sharp showers, less than an inch which scorched everything and did more harm than good. The days were very hot, up to 110% in the shade, with a terrific amount of humidity in the atmosphere. The total rainfall for the month was only just over five inches instead of about twelve

We had to stop ploughing on the 10th owing to the ground getting too hard to continue.

I append a list of seeds, cuttings etc sewn for the month:-

1st & 7th	Lettuce
4th & 6th	Pawpaw
5th & 6th	Maize
9th	Pumpkins

12th	Tomatoes
16-17th & 18th	Kaffir Corn
17th	Mangoe trees
17th	Trees along roadway – replacements.
25-27th &28th	Sweet potatoes– approx 4550 cuttings.
27th &28th	Peanuts

Of the sewings the lettuce and watermelons are a complete failure.

The pumpkins and peanuts are replacements of previous failures fully 80% in each case.[40]

Most of the maize pulled through, being sewn on the new low lying ground and the Kaffir corn and trees luckily struck rain the day after they were planted[,] also the sweet potatoes, but we require a lot more steady rain to pull us through.

The Taylor Bros completed the four new houses for the people on the 19th inst and since then have been engaged on odd jobs connected with buildings.

Owing to the dry time and the bigger area cultivated[,] the Bandicoots and rats seem to have taken refuge in the Cassava and they have eaten quite a lot of it. This is a very heavy loss and is causing us great anxiety.

We have been harrowing and cultivating all the ground ploughed right up to the time of sewing to try and kill the growth of weeds which has been prolific.

There is about 3 to 4 acres of Kaffir corn in and it is showing up nicely.

We have had the following out of the garden during the month,:- 394 lb CASSAVA – 18 Pawpaws– 56doz Bananas– 44 Pineapples beans etc.

During the month I made and hung two pair of gates on the new garden fence, one at the square where the road goes down to the engine, and one at the back of the fowl house, also replaced post and rehung big yard gate– it fell down– the old post being eaten thro with white ants. Have also cut 20 cancers and regret to say that there still more to be done.

---

40   NTRS 1099/P1 vol. 1.

Trenching for the sweet potatoes is and has been a big job especially with our reduced numbers owing to the flour shortage (see special report).

The Horse padock fence has also taken a lot of watching and we have had to remuster the bullocks three times and repair the fence seven times.

The 24th being Mr P. Taylor's 21st birthday the brothers went out for a ride and Mr I. Taylor has been off ever since being completely incapacitated with headache, at the time of writing he seems to be slightly improved. We surmise it must have been a touch of sun.

We only had one death this month, on the 14th, that of an old man Billy (Narlumbeal)[.] Mr Dyer will remember him.

Miss Sherrin reports substantial progress with her school work

Narlbrett– broken arm reported in December – am pleased to report that the setting of the broken arm was a complete success.

Early in the month I was approached by the Staff regarding a midday prayer meeting which Mr Ivin stated Mr Dyer had asked him to carry on – My Wife andI had no knowledge of any such meeting other than what we have read in reports of the Mission, they had been carrying it on so therefore I placed on record a midday prayer meeting to be held at 1-50p.m. each day for those who wish to attend. WE do not.

Dispensary:- When we moved up .to the new Hall for services I converted one end of the veranda and fitted it up as a dispensary and Mrs Thorne finds it a very satisfactory change from the former quarters which Mr Ferrier will remember were totally inadequate.

F.A. Thorne[41]

***

---

41   NTRS 1099/P1 vol. 1.

OENPELLI REPORT FEBRURARY 1928

The rainfall for the month was only 773 points, which with January's low fall puts us a long way behind, however the growth of everything was fairly good, including as usual a prolific crop of weeds.

Mr Taylor was off until the 7th (from 24th Jan) Since when he and his brother have been making the Dining room flyproof, as both they and Miss Sherrin feel the insects and mosiquito's very much, this occupied them until the end of the month.

During the month we have sewn the following: -

approx 8500 sweet potato cuttings

> 350 Pawpaw
>
> 20 Pineapples
>
> 100 Cassava cuttings
>
> 150 Tomato plants

approx 250 Pumpkin seeds and also further wheat, maize and kaffir corn.

The majority of the pumpkins and pawpaw failed and the wheat did not show up at all.

The cuttings of the sweet potatoes planted to date is approximately 13000 cuttings.

The Kaffir corn, Maize and Peanuts areall doing well and with good future rain we are hoping for a big crop.

All available hands have been busy weeding, but owing to our compulsilarily reduced numbers we are not making much impression on them.

We have had the following out of the garden during the month:-

Cassava	276 lbs.
Pawpaws	22
Bananas	33 doz,

I have cut several more cancers this month making a total of 27 cancers cut out this wet.

We have also repaired several collars and winkers and restuffed two saddle and sundry other small repair jobs

On the 29th inst I started rebuilding and repairs to yards and am still on them.

On the 16th the only death of the month occurred, when Nagals baby died.

On the 23rd I was informed that the outside blacks were spearing the bullocks in the Waterfall paddock and after enquiries found that there were three boys implicated, two of whom were caught and brought in and I have warned them off the reserve as neither of them was the ringleader, he cleared out bush but will be punished if and when he shows up again.

We lost at least three good bullocks and the remainder were badly frightened and have lost a lot of condition.

The medical work has been pretty heavy this month, with one outstanding case of Leprosy, the woman–Gurijula– lost he big toe soon after coming in and her dressings took fully an hour daily.

We had the engine going this month twice to test it and to saw up some small timber

F.A. Thorne[42]

---

42   NTRS 1099/P1 vol. 1.

Figure 5.42: Child on edge of billabong (date unknown).
Source: Northern Territory Archives Service (NTRS 693 P1 Item 21).

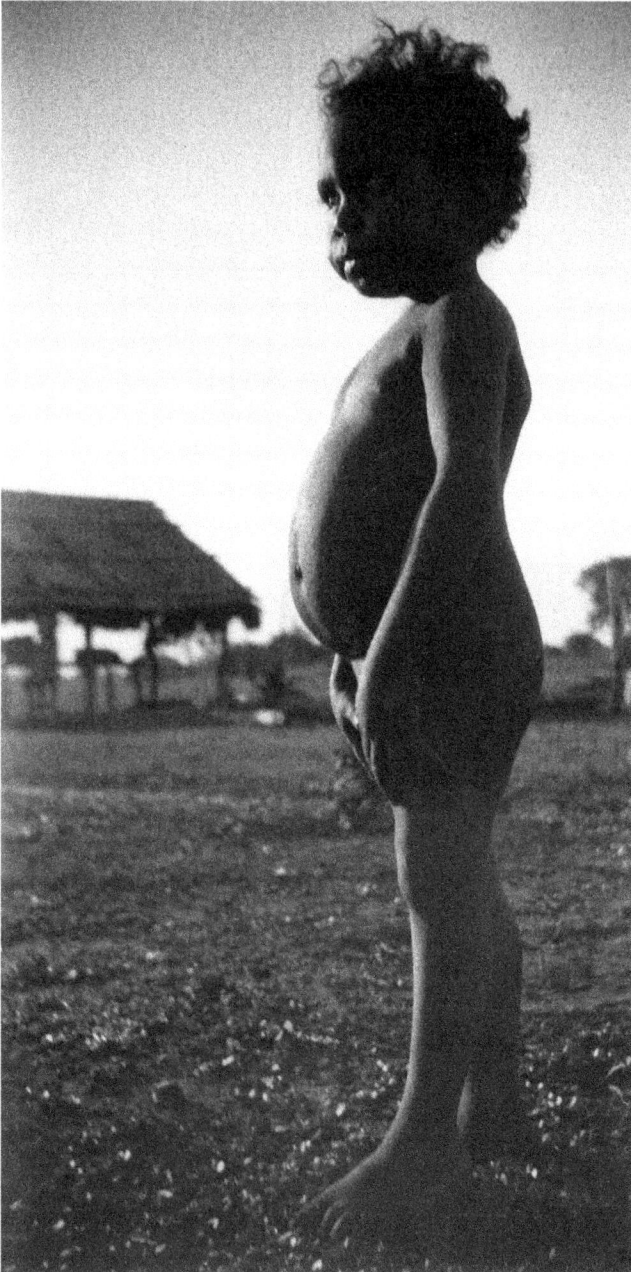

Figure 5.43: Young child at mission (date unknown).
Source: Northern Territory Archives Service (NTRS 693 P1 Item 21).

***

OENPELLI REPORT MARCH 1928

The rainfall for the month was 1383 points, which forded along all garden growth and of course the never ending crop of weeds.

On the 15th we had a severe storm of 560 points and in the flood, the water being right up through the Mangoes and around the foundation of the pump also right out across the plains and in the Paper barks on the other side, it stayed at about this level for eight days when it gradually started to reduce.

After serious discussions we decided to risk a bag of flour to go out and get some bark cut and on the 29th of Feb Mr Ivin and Mr P.T. Taylor took out a party of boys and cut approximately 675 sheets returning on the 10th inst. Mr Ivin went out as Mr I. Taylor volunteered to do his work in the garden to free him to go and he was working in the garden until the 14th inst

During the month we have planted the following:-

Peas failed.

700	Cotton
40	Pawpaw failed
130	pines a lot of replacements
40	Bananas
100	Cassava replacements
700	Sweet potatoes all replacements of failures

We banked up the peanuts and they look like being a good crop

The flood waters played havoc with the cassava and pumpkins on the low lying ground[;] in fact everything that was covered with water was a total loss, approximately 200 strong pumpkin plants and fully 205 cassava were killed

I have again had to cut several cancers some of them for the second and third time, this emphasises the need for a paddock for the horses for the wet season where they cannot get into the still swamp water where the leeches are.

The stock boys have been engaged most of the month on yards repairs and on the 26th I sent them out for a few days to look round the cattle and see if there were any signs of spearing outside, they report all in good order, though all my work of last year drafting out the bullocks is lost as they are out again in the bush.

We have had the following out of the garden during the month:-

> Cassava 283 lbs
> Pawpaw 32
> Bananas 42 doz.

The medical work has averaged about 25 patients per day. The Leper woman reported last month is responding slowly to treatment but will of course never really recover.

Mrs Thorne has had a very busy month with Housekeeping, Dispensary and general supervision. At the end of this month she had a severe attack of Dysentry and she had to have two days in bed.

Miss Sherrin reports School work progressing favourably.

F.A. Thorne[43]

---

43   NTRS 1099/P1 vol. 1.

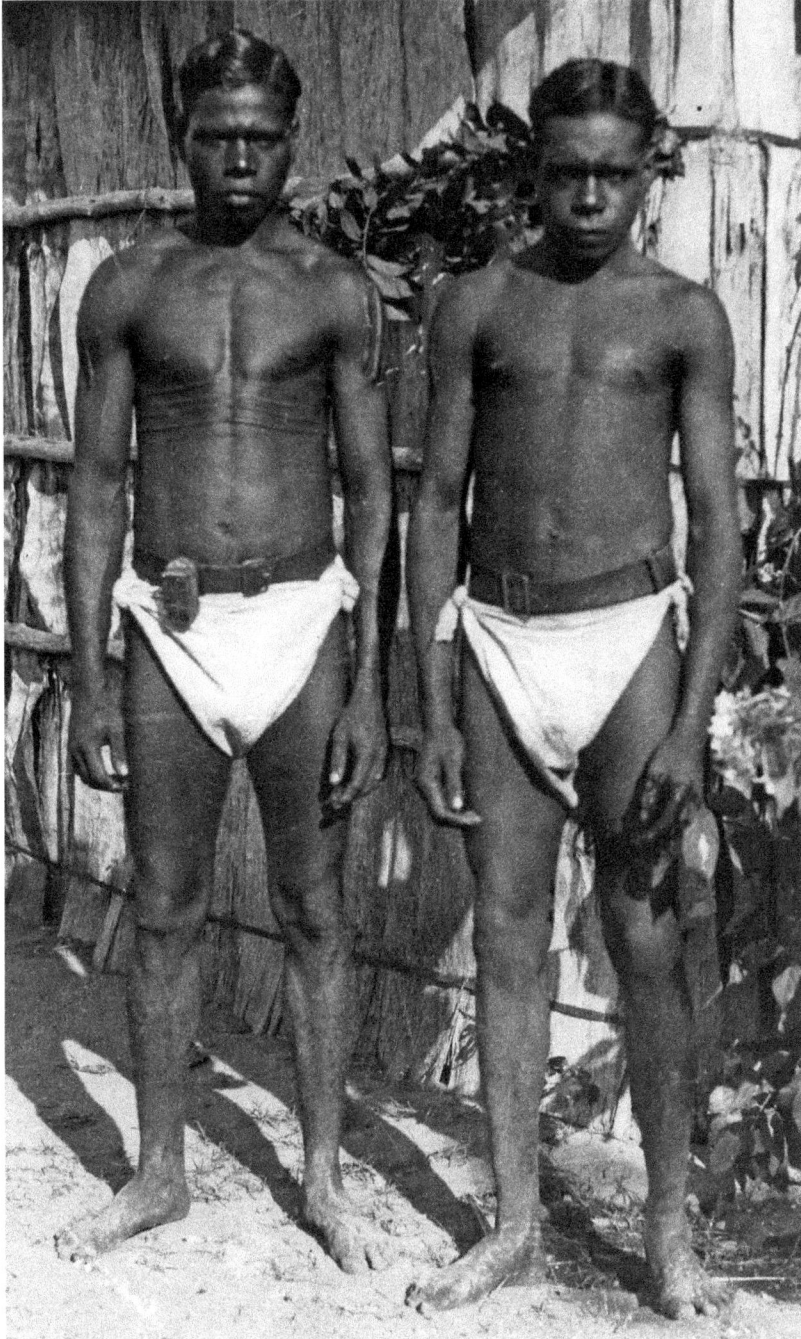

Figure 5.44: Nagal and Narlim, c. 1926.
Source: Northern Territory Archives Service (NTRS 694 P1 Box 4a Item 207).

Figure 5.45: 'Narlim, stock-worker, about 1929'.
Source: Northern Territory Archives Service (NTRS 694 P1 Box 4b Item 297).

* * *

OENPELLI REPORT APRIL 1928

The rainfall for the month was 105 points and things are now beginning to dry off, the kaffir corn and peanuts both give indications of being good crops.

Mr P.Taylor was off (from 22-3-28) until the 9th ins ~~although~~ and he is still suffering from the same complaint.

They continued on their room this month and moved into it one the 28th inst.

On the 30th inst we marked out the new meat house and they commenced the erection of same.

During the month we have planted the following:-

> Cabbage 3 lots failed
> app 1600 Cassava replacements and on new ground in far corner.
> "   200 Pumpkins coming up nicely. *(failed later...)*
> several lots of lettuce which failed.
> also we planted a further lot of Maize as an experiment.

Levels have been taken and drains prepared in readiness for irrigating, all available hands pulling put nut grass from the potato patch–clearing fire breaks round the fences and stock yards– general weeding and carting firewood.

On the 23rd inst we picked the Maize, which though a very fair crop did not turn out as well as expected as many cobs were only about half filled– the March rains being a bit too late for it.

On the 9th the school children gave a concert, which went very well with the parents, and the kids certainly enjoyed it.

We have broken in the available youngsters for this years work and rehandled one or two bad ones of last years lot, one filly reared over in the crush and injured herself internally and died the following day, we have also repaired the roof over the calf pen and repaired the Waterfall paddock fence and burnt off the grass along the same, the Horse paddock fence has also occupied a few days of repairing

I cut out a further three cancers which makes a total of thirty five cut this year.

We have had the following produce from the garden:-

Cassava	189 lbs
Pawpaws	73
Bananas	22doz.

Two new boys in the dormitory this month which brings the number of boys up to twenty seven.

All the pack saddles and pack bags etc have been overhauled and put in readiness for the mustering season

We started irrigating for the season on the 27th and also on the 28th and 30th. the pump and engine going well but the engine eating more wood than ever.

Mrs Thorne has been engaged as usual in Medical work, House-keeping and General supervision.

F.A. Thorne[44]

***

OENPELLI REPORT MAY 1928

Rainfall for month NIL.

The Taylor Bros were erecting the Meat house finishing same on the 19th inst and on the 21st to 23rd they were doing repairs to the Landing, on starting axx wheel came off the lorry and they had to make a new plate for the same, the old one having worn sufficiently to come right out over the collar. from the 24th to the 31st they were on small odd jobs.

The only plantings this month have been cabbage and lettuce and they are not showing up too well as yet.

We levelled and cemented the killing pen yard and this took 3½ bags of cement before we could get a good solid surface.

On the 7th I sent out a party of boys to burn off round the mustering yards and can only hope they did the job well , on the 8th I sent out another party to burn off round the bark stacks also.

---

44   NTRS 1099/P1 vol. 1.

Irrigating has occupied Mr Ivin and self 11 days during the month and we have had to get in 32 loads of wood to use in the engine[;] this latter in itself is a big job and it will be a great asset to the place when an up-to-date pumping plant can be procured

During the month, as well as her other many calls, Mrs Thorne has managed to get all the boys and girls blankets washed and repaired.

Several days were spent whitewashing the kitchen inside and out.

We have had the following produce from the garden:-

Cassava	205lbs
Pawpaw	73
Bananas	38doz
Sweet Potatoes	46lbs

On the 19th we started cutting the Kaffir corn but our inability to put on extra hands and later the putting off of those we had are making this a very protracted job.

One pair of pack bags falling to pieces during the burning off trip made it necessary to make a pair from raw hide for use during the coming season.

Once again no flour and so on the 31st I was reluctantly compelled to put off all outside workers and hope for the arrival of the boat within a few days ,but we are still keeping the children and carrying on with the School.

On the 31st Nipper was seriously injured in a fight in the camp (not his own fault) and got his skull fractured and the first finger of his right hand absolutely crushed to below the first joint. he put up he hand to ward off a blow from an iron bar about 3ft long of 1½ " x ¼ " material which was broken over his head.

The haed wound was fully 2½ " long and the fracture in the bone 2"[;] after necessary cleansing Mrs Thorne inserted seven stitches in the scalp wound and then repaired the finger, removing the splinters of bone and pulling it into shape as much as possible with nine stitches in various parts. He suffered a lot of pain and still requires a lot of nursing.

I have to report a death on the 5th inst[–] that of the woman Argawalmie who has been sick for some considerable time.

F.A. Thorne[45]

---

45   NTRS 1099/P1 vol. 1.

Figure 5.46: Nipper Marakarra Gumurdul standing behind seated man. Frank 'Naluwud' Girrabul on crutches (date unknown).

Source: Northern Territory Archives Service (NTRS 694 P1 Box 4b Item 276).

* * *

OENPELLI REPORT JUNE 1928.

Rainfall for the month, Nil.

The Taylor Bros during the month have made 14 stools for the school and spent three days fixing the bark on the Church and boring postsland [posts and] poisoning for White ants and other odd jobs.

The 1st & 4th Mr Ivin spent putting new handles into hoes and shovels etc.

On the 4th we had to put off more people and send the children out to hunt their dinners, keeping the nine smallest each day and occasionally some of the others in turns, I have insisted on their re-turning for school, and so far, have only had a few truants and have managed to keep school going without a break.

On the 9th a party of Goulburn Island boys arrived with 2 mail bags containing seven parcels and a note from Mr Dyer, but no letters[.] Mr Dyer[']s note stated they were waiting for the Air compressor which was on the Koolinda and that he was trying to get everything ready to get here for the tides on the 5th of June.

Also on the same day there arrived a party of 5 white men, a Mr Mackay of Sydney and Dr Basedow of South Australia, accompanied by a Cinematographer, a horsewrangler and a cook. who came round from the Katherine Via the Roper, Wilton ,Goyder, Liverpool and King rivers and went from here straight across to the Railway line.

From what I could gather they were out to see the country and the natives, Dr Basedow had, at one time, been Chief Protector of Aboriginals in the Northern Territory and is very interested in, and is working for the proposed Aboriginal State, and wanted to see the country.

They had been taking film pictures all the way across and took some panoramic views from the top of Umblanyon and Argolook, for which I accept no responsibility, as except for one of the natives taken round their camp they did not discuss the matter with me, though I hardly think it would be wise to refuse permission in any case.

Though Mrs Thorne was hard put to it to make up anything for meals, their arrival was most opportunate as they let us have four bags of Flour in return for beef etc, they moved on on Monday 11th inst.

Whilst here, Mrs Thorne took the opportunity of asking the Dr to look at Nippers head and finger and he O.K'd. what she had done and told Nipper he was lucky as it was what any Doctor would have done for him and particularly expressed astonishment at no complications arising during the after treatment. Nipper if still of, his head is now quite healed and the finger coming on really better than expected.

On the 15th seven boys were badly poisoned from eating Kaffir corn stalks and raw Cassava, necessitating first aid treatment, bowel washouts for all seven, emetics etc, it was an anxious time and Mrs Thorne was up practicallythe whole of two nights with them, two of them very nearly passed out, but all of them are now well again.

On the 25th & 27th Mr Ivin and self were busy repairing and re-constructing Guns from old parts.

Kaffir Corn :- Mt Ivin and self have spent nine whole days this month in cutting this crop and have had the boys cutting at all other available times, there is still about one third yet to be harvested.

It is beginning to fall out very rapidly now and I am afraid we are going to loose a lot of what is left

Peanuts :- We dug these up but only got about four bags, the heavy March rains had reshot them and kept the tops green, consequently the first crop of nuts formed were mostly rotted away and the majority of the second crop were only partly formed and did not ripen. hence the small net crop.

Irrigating has occupied Mr Ivin and self for six full days, on the 15th we had trouble with the Injector and tried to rectify it on the 16th, we also then discovered that the Engine had started to leak again from under the patch Mr Dyer put on last year, but with special care and precautions we managed to irrigate twice more with it, when I considered it too dangerous to try again, as the leak was so severe that the water in the boiler dropped at least 18 inches overnight, we therefore spent a day disconnecting everything, to be ready, when the boat comes with new bits etc, to see what can be done. Personally I am of opinion that it is only waste of time and that the only effective and by far the more economical remidy is a complete new pumping plant more suited to the job.

I .have had scouts out down the river since the 22 May and there being no sign of the Lugger on the 25th June I decided to send to Goulburn Island to try and borrow some flour and to send in by their boat a letter notifying Jolly's of the non-arrival of the Mary.

We are almost quite out of everything here now, only 5 small tins of Syrup, no Jam, some rice and some very small quantities of sago tapioca etc. The rice I am using for the children and remaining people for their midday meal also for breakfast and to thicken their evening stews.

Should we not get flour from Goulburn Island and miss their boat going in I do not know what we are going to do.

We have had the following out of the garden during the month:-

Cassava	274 lbs
Pawpaws	50
Bananas	28 doz
Sweet Potatoes	330lbs.

The Cassava has finished growing until the Wet comes and we are now just about at the end of it.

F.A. Thorne[46]

Figure 5.47: Stockyards with Arrkuluk Hill visible in the background (date unknown).
Source: Northern Territory Archives Service (NTRS 694 P1 Box 2 Item 536).

---

46 NTRS 1099/P1 vol. 1.

Figure 5.48: Children at the Oenpelli mission, 1928. Part of an album of photographs by J.W. Bleakley.
Source: National Archives of Australia (A263, 7873207).

* * *

OENPELLI REPORT JULY 1928.

Rainfall for the month ,Nil.

Up to the arrival of the boat on the 16th of the month our numbers were much the same as last month, but we managed to keep the school going all through and of course numbers are now beginning to increase again.

Mr P.F.Taylor went off sick again on the 10th and went into Darwin in th[e] boat on the 18th to consult the Doctor.

On the 6th we sent out for the first load of bark and the boys ran into the stump hidden in the grass and broke up the front carriage giving us a full days work on the 7th repairing same.

After the arrival of the boat on the 16thinst a week or more was spent by all hands carting things up.

On the 18th the boat returned to Darwin taking Mrs Thorne, Mr Ivin and Mr Taylor, the last named to visit the Doctor, Mr Dyer will have personally reported to you the cause of Mr Ivins return Southso there will be no need for me to say anything thereon.

On the 24th inst I got away on my first mustering trip for this year and was away for the rest of the month with fair success.

We finished harvesting the Kaffir corn on the 6th of the month and it has turned out a really good crop.

During the month we planted somemore Lettuce and Tomatoes and they are beginning to show up well.

We have had the following out of the garden during the month:-

Cassava	180lbs
Pawpaw	67
Bananas	21 doz
Sweet Potatoes	295 lbs

This will be the last report that I will be making as I am handing over to Mr Dyer on his return from Darwin.

F.A. Thorne[47]

***

Oenpelli Report August 1928

Mr Thorne & his boys have been busy mustering all the month. Mr Ion Taylor the general work about the station. The ladies their usual tasks with the addition of putting the store in order. Phil & myself away in Darwin repair the boat, engine over haul & altering the exhaust of the engine to the stern which ended the salt water trouble[;] a report on engine troubles was sent South.

The Govt asked me to take Mr Bleakley to Bathurst Is & to the Goulburn Is Miss[–] the latter part I did not promise to do but said we could leave him at Cape Don lighthouse on our way back. We called at Bathurst Is doing about 5 miles per hour no wind. The Fathers & Sisters gave us a warm welcome[;] one said he wanted to go bush when he saw so

---

many men coming. A lot of work has been done but they have to depend on wells for water so only grow food in the Wet. So the site has a big drawback. They hold fast to the girl, the boy comes & goes[,] so with the older people. We only stayed the one night & took away with us, new plants; goats & fowls. We left towing the St Francis out of the harbour as there was no wind[;] the day following reaching the Alligator & thence up the river in 4 hours which had taken us as long as 10 days on previous trips, it seemed like a dream flying up at 8 miles an hour, where we had tugged, pushed & stuck, so when the engine is right she should be fast.

Mr Bleakley seemed pleased with Oenpelli & enjoyed his visit. The future prospects of the station were duly put before him & he believed with us that with proper management can cater for all the needs of the blacks of Arnhem's Land as they are prepared to come in & leave their children; by out stations preparing the way. Caledon Bay being a needy spot. I told him what Lousada was trying to do. Since the recent murders he has been forbidden to go, he seems to be hindered at every turn. I only wish I had him here or a man like him with a keen love for the black, quick at learning his language who could travel away from the station among the many who still sit in darkness, & a keen gardener who could give his time there in the busy time when he could not travel owing to the Wet; that is what I want to see done. It can but so few are prepared to pay the price. Mr Bleakley suggested further Govt help[–] maybe or maybe not, the Govt cow is getting dry. Rather let us pray the Lord of the Harvest that more blood bought souls may pray & give we & ours shall likewise share in the blessing. Mr I & P Taylor then took Mr B onto Cape Don where the Maskee took him on to Gouburn Is. & they went on to Darwin.

Alf Dyer[48]

***

Oenpelli Report October 1928

The beginning of the month brought Holmes' buyer just at the time we had almost given him up. In two days Mr Thorne left with the 159-150 odd cattle purchased. The ladies have carried on their usual tasks. Miss Sherrin had a week's spell with the girls in Red Lily & enjoyed herself amongst the beauties. The boys had a camp near the station with Arawingi in charge of them.

---

48   NTRS 1099/P1 vol. 1.

Mail also arrived telling of the Mary's delay in Darwin & of engine troubles[;] a report was sent in reply to theirs. Have a lot of people grubbing & fencing in preparation for the Tractor. Mending wheels pumps & gardening impliments, & directing the labours of 50 people has kept me more than busy. More people about than I have seen before & over 20 children in their camps[–] only one has come in.

Made an inspection of the other boiler here, an engineer said the shell is in good order, but wants new tubes, only 5 spares here, there are 18 in all. I asked Mr Taylor if he could get any in Darwin & to wire Mr Ferrier about them. But one can only get an half hour or so here & there for such tasks, with the Taylors away for 3 months on end. With a fever stricken body it has been hard to trust that all things work together for good. Magnetic came with s[t]ores on the 31[st], we just got the boxes in before the rain[,] only one box got wet, with the Mary we could unload as we can take them. So lots of blessings & God rules over all through cloud and sunshine.

Alf Dyer[49]

Figure 5.49: 'Ship Mary on a reef' (date unknown).
Source: Northern Territory Archives Service (NTRS 694 P1 Box 4a Item 192).

---

49   NTRS 1099/P1 vol. 1.

Figure 5.50: Frank Naluwad and Lazarus Arawingi (date unknown).
Source: Northern Territory Archives Service (NTRS 694 P1 Box 4 Item 109).

***

Oenpelli Report November 1928

The early part of the month began by carting up the stores unpacking & putting away all the many stores & Xmas things. While we are doing this a big party of blacks come up all painted for fight, they say the trouble is over the boy who died suddenly in dormitory of heart failure, the uncle is blamed, there must be a cause for every effect. I go to see what I can do to stop it, when a mob is working themselves into a rage anything can happen & things did get lively at times, but the old men restrained them. I generally let them settle these troubles in their own way[,] standing by to act if it is necessary. Later two men were speared & so it blew over with a job for Mrs Dyer. Billabong is a low as I have seen it so made the new well 5 feet deeper. On 13th started a party on a new fence which will be about 7 miles long with about the same of Ranges this will be a breeding paddock for the best of the cattle also a horse paddock & will save a lot of time looking for them. I am only putting in good posts bored for barbed wire. It is necessary to get up about 3 miles of it before the rains come as this part will be in water then. Another party on grubbing & preparing the garden for the Wet, so we are over a hundred with the children so they keep me busy directing them & repairing their breakages so building is quite off till the boat returns. Others are carting in timber & bark have a lot in hand. Ladies their usual tasks, lots of dispensary cases, Miss Sherrin school sewing & general.

On the 16th boys return from taking in the cattle less 5 horses which they leave behind at various places, they say too tired. Mr Thorne reports 46 cattle got away, boys say they did not see them, but thought some were in Red Lily, so after a few days spell muster up the paddock, they pick 80 going through the race as returns, judged by the size so I should say they are all back[.] Put cattle through dip & brand 9 calves.[50]

***

---

50 NTRS 1099/P1 vol. 1.

Oenpelli Report December 1928

Large numbers of blacks about & children, whom they want to sell but I am not buying. Carrying on with the fence this will finish up the Govt barb wire much of it is rusty, & the posts in peaty ground made putting on the wire a long job, but we get across the plains to the hills on the 12th. Laying out the roadways in various places[,] put up gates flagpole & rockeries on central square[,] plant trees & flowers so things are beginning to look more shipshape. Working on the garden all the time planting out food stuffs. Take down the other boiler as Bill will only make a tank now. Put in what new tubes I have & put her through a water test but I want a few new tubes, these I hope the boat will bring. Net in the tennis court & finished it. On 16th down with fever a visitor tells me of a cow with a spear in so next day we find one killed that day, so we mustered up the camps & told them to come up to the station. I took all their shovelspears & break them & take the shovels amidst many black looks, this hurts them most, at the station I thrashed the two who killed it, the boys said they were afraid to do it. One of the dormitory girls who was always in trouble, 'better to marry than to burn', so arranged a marriage with consent of all, with a very plain talk on their conduct before all. Afterwards the parents repent of their consent the father & she have a fight he picks her up & runs away bush with her the black way of meeting trouble. After them next day with the willing husband we are parted & he finds them. On his gallant steed he must have struck terror into the heart of the father & they came back like drowned rats late at night in the rain. This is not like novels, but it is life, now they seem to be happy. Have our first lemons[–] 39 on small tree I budded. The large trees are 8 ft high but have not fruited, well pruned, perhaps too many roots. Fix up a rough jetty to land the tractor & piles to tie up the boat in the Wet, this elusive Mary, we hope she will mend her ways.

Xmas passed off well but was a very busy time, we had more people than ever before. 230 bags were given out, 30 odd were bush children. Mostly all at work now on the garden, many have gone back to the bush.

Our family of children have grown now to 17 girls, 12 babies & 30 boys. We have come to the stage when we three have as much as we can cope with & our stoves are too small to cook the food & I can patch them no more[–] they are done. So materially the work has grown beyond my expectations. We do thank God for all His many gifts, but there are some real wants I have mentioned from time to time to enable us to do many things left undone, I have tried to keep the costs as low as possible. Visitors are impressed with what they see, there are great changes since we came, & men will always judge the work by what they can see, but we long to see the deeper work of God's Spirit which is for eternity that God may get the glory of this work, then we & you at the Home Base will share in this with Him as co workers. Thanking you all for your many labours in the Lord

Yours in 'the blessed hope'
Alf Dyer[51]

Figure 5.51: 'Children Xmas receiving bags 1929'.
Source: Northern Territory Archives Service (NTRS 694 P1 Box 4 Item 62).

* * *

Report of the <u>Policy for Oenpelli 1929</u> as discussed by Staff

All these proposals have been discussed by staff in special meeting & afterwards read & agreed to by them.

<u>Reserve</u>

Now we have the increased area it is well to state in black & white a policy & our aim is to develop here now & plan to develop the seaboard. To make a real native station it is necessary to deal with seaboard & the saltwater blacks. Also there is marine wealth that can be worked & the Mary will be much better in use than lying idle in a river, but we have our hands

---

51   NTRS 1099/P1 vol. 1.

more full at present station. There is talk of Goulburn Is removing to their other station[;] if that is so that spot could be used as a station for Mary as it is a safe port. Mr Bleakley & self discussed this so if any new proposals are made by the Government it is well to know we have anticipated it & feel it is a move in the right direction. Nature has provided the materials to develop & in using of them an Arnheims Land State can be made in time self supporting. The first costs are too great for your present resources without special gifts. But with God all things are possible & as we step out He supplies. A road can easily be made between here & coast[;] a few weeks work would make a bush track & a motor lorry would soon do the rest.

People

More are coming in than we can cope with. We take the children, but naturally some parents do not wish to leave the children if they cannot work themselves. More gardens are the solution & we have the soil to do it. Therefore the garden is the principal t[h]ing[;] for even if we had 10000 cattle it only provides work for at most 20. There are many more people out beyond us wore or less hindered by our people from coming in. This can be overcome & a Native State is the only chance for these people. Also we are limited by cooking facilities as we have come to the stage when we cannot cook more food, so must remain at this level till it can be altered in the new kitchen with fittings etc. Dormitories are full as they can be with safety. And the store is too small.

Boat

Has been a worry over the engine but we hope for better things in the near future. There is no other way out so we have to face it. Short stays in Darwin will be the normal thing & stores from will cut out a lot of the big expense of the past year. A man on each trip has to be considered in the question of the staff as blacks could not be trusted alone.

Staff

We feel that three men & three women are the minimum to carry on with boat[,] garden & cattle. This leaves little chance to build which is most urgent. Then Miss Sherrin furlough is due next year, & Mr I. Taylor leaves at the end of the year, I do not know what Phil intends to do his brother does not know, so all these facts must be considered as you plan about staff. We think the time of service should be from 2½ to 3 years. So in the question of staff[,] allowance must be made for furloughs.

Cattle

We hope to complete new paddocks & select the cattle to improve the breed & practically keep in them, this will give a better chance to stop spearing, very hard otherwise to stop.

We do need a donkey to breed mules are they are most useful in our work here[–] all our carting & garden work is done by them now. We should be able then to pull through with the horses then.

Church & School

Daily services & school keep the most important side of our work to the front as the foundation of all our labour. Kindergarten is held in the morning so all the young children early[,] many of the older ones come rather late. Miss Sherrin gives a large part of the day to this.

Services

We have just about reached the full service on Sunday morning, with two Bible talks a day we seek to point them to Christ looking for the working of the Spirit within, before we suggest baptism. Have had no time to think of making Church furniture yet except what we have. These are wants if any opportunity offers.

Garden

Objective is to grow all we can, other reports tell of what done Irrigation is a necessity, you have expressed hope in this way. To make use of the tractors help, we must have Massey Harris No 12 Spring tooth 17 riding harrow, they gave me a small one while in Melbourne which is doing good work. M.H. No 43 Pony Plough with rolling coulter, many other real needs but we cannot do without these.

Buildings

Nothing has been done for 9 months[;] the garden & general will take most of my time. Mr Taylor has a big job to repair cattle yard & horse paddock, when the boat returns we will do our best to get on with Staff house & kitchen, store & girls dormitory, all most necessary as these place will not see another wet through[–] it is leaking everywhere & a blow will end it. Materials needed have already been sent on.

Expenditure

We cannot give you much guidance as the Annual report is the only statement I have seen of expenses, and as already report to Mr Ferrier Jolly's are most erratic in sending me copies of bills etc & with several months in between mails you are up against it. I do not know any items of Marys expenses in Darwin the last 5 months except the [...] mentioned in your letters. We will aim at keeping the stores account at present level, with the extra children we can do that & still carry on the works in hand. If the boat is normal[,] present stores may pull us through as we have more in hand with the smaller staff here.

The movements of staff new or old you have in the information[;] we cannot guide you in that, we have told you in this report all we can here.

We have done the best we can to give you the information you seek, trusting this will be a guide to you at the home base, we constantly seek to remember you all in this in our prayers.

Yours faithfully
Alf Dyer
Supt[52]

Figure 5.52: Group photo outside the new church (date unknown).
Source: Northern Territory Archives Service (NTRS 694 P1 Box 2 Item 545).

52   ML MSS 6040/12.

Figure 5.53: Young girl (date unknown).
Source: Northern Territory Archives Service (NTRS 694 P1 Box 4a Item 229).

* * *

Oenpelli Jan 14 1929

Dear Mr Ferrier

Only a few lines as I am sending off the packs to pick up Ion at Goulburn
Is .I cannot answer all yours yet as it is all rush getting them off . The
larger family makes our task bigger &we have had to work harder than
ever before to keep things going, so not much hope of pulling in a bit as
you suggest . He knows the need & will give more grace , the two reports
enclosed will show a good deal of trouble . Still we three have been very
happy. The last 3 weeks we have wondered much about the boat but we
are free now we know they are safe . I know no details till I see I Taylor
. It is very hard for me to cope with mail. Take an illustration . The only
letter I received from Jolly's was dated October which should have come
on the Magnetic , nothing in reply to my letter to him in Nov about
shorts etc or Darwin Accounts[;] yet I keep asking for them & asked Mr
Thorne to put in a personal word about them when in Darwin . He has
sent me Nobles invoices & asked to have them sent on to you which I will
do later . When you came[,] a saddle came for Paddy who died , we sent it
back , going through Darwin on my way South & saw Mr B & Dr Cook
about it , it had been there for some time then . When I came back after
furlough, one of men said to me I think there are some things of yours
in the shed[–] all had been forgotten so I tell them again they are full of
promises but I have heard nothing since . I have asked the Taylors to see
about it . everything has been such a mix up this year . when the Mary is
running normally things will I hope be better.

Fortunately we have everything we want but caustic soda for soap which
is rather low & salt[–] we only have one bag which at most will only do
two kills , what I will do I do not know .Will try the sun & smoke but do
not feel very hopeful in the Wet .

Had the boat arrived now we could not land the tractor .I went down on
the 11th to wire up the train & rails & had to walk a mile & a half to get
there in the slush up to my knees . We are ploughing with mules so must
be content with a smaller area, have 13000 potato plants out all growing
nicely ,a good deal more than ever before so if rains continue should have
a good crop .

Yes put Mrs Shaw's gift to irrigation plant which is the most pressing need. I will write & thank her & Mr Pretyman later today has been all rush & this may not go till after the Wet we do not know the McBride's movements.

Re Taylors yes that seems the best way & I am glad they have offered, buildings are off at present & the iron is at the mouth[.] Garden takes most of my time. The yards have to be repaired again. Re Thornes I have just left it in your hands . Many things happened which I only wanted to forget. It would take pages to tell of them & I have no desire to . I love peace & have always striven for it. May the Lord guide you into His will & whatever He sends or withholds will try to fit in with . I wrote for yourself to guide you in any decision you might have to make , my judgment is not a hasty one . Events may happen & nothing may be necessary. We can manage with two men here beside myself but I cannot do it alone. I liked what I saw of High but only saw him for a short time & did not paint a rosy picture to him . Men are willing to come & work , there is a certain amount of adventure in the life but it takes a very real devotion to Christ to go & sit with them in their dirt & try & love them & tell them of Him . We do not need great educational gifts but we do need practical Christianity with a love born of God's Spirit & men who are called of God, without that our work will produce only straw & it is a life work or the best of one's life . If he has some of this in him do as you are led.

We are thinking of Summer School. Too much statics for wireless now. Wishing you all every blessing for this New Year.

Yours sincerely
Alf Dyer

P.S.

Mr Thorne writes about some accounts at Roper. he was charged for ours. please adjust this he knows details.

Alf Dyer[53]

* * *

---

53   ML MSS 6040/12.

Our hearts were rejoiced yesterday when we knew that The Messrs Taylor our boys were safe & we know God makes no mistakes even when we cannot understand"

C.M.S
Oenpelli
Jan 14th 1929

Dear Mr Ferrier

Thank you for your letter perhaps it would have been wiser to tell you while South & yet I hoped there would be no need, I never mentioned the matter even to my own dear sister or to Mrs Harvey who is almost a life long friend – but when the news came that there was some talk of a hospital etc – I felt it was only right you should know somewhat of what I felt & you have been here & know something of conditions & oh we were so glad of your sympathy & that you saw things as they were – Mr Dyer's has always preferred to put things in God's hands & just leave them & I think he is right & we have prayed much about it & we are just leaving it to Him – So far the season has been a very trying one – prickly heat is dreadful as continually we are wet through but with it all we have been very happy & except for the wondering about where the boat was – had a very happy Christmas[.] Miss Sherrin is very keen on her kinders & helps me so lovingly in every way she can – I am trying to help Mr Dyer all I can & on the whole am very well but our family which all told at present is well over 100 – gives us all plenty to do-

Will you please remember me very kindly to Mrs Ferrier & Betty – With kindest remembrances & greetings pray much for us.

Yours in the same service
M.C. Dyer[54]

***

---

54   ML MSS 6040/12.

January Oenpelli Report 1929

Practically all our attention has been given to the garden.

Ploughing, harrowing, cultivating, weeding laying out new roadways pulling down old fences, planting out trees & shrubs, with the many repair jobs, & cancers to cut out of horses.

By the end of the month we had out & growing 3 ½ acres more than last year. The failure of the tractor to come delayed ploughing as I had the mules on fence jobs & getting timber till Xmas. It has been a good month for rains[–] nice showers & all the crops look well, we should have a large quantity of food if the season continues.

On the 22nd Mr. I. Taylor returned Via Goulburn Is[;] we were glad to get mail & to be relieved of care about them & the boat as we wondered if Davey had claimed them. He left within 24 hours to go to Charlie's landing to get salt before big rains set in, they returned on the 28th after a boggy trip with enough salt to see us through the Wet. He then repaired the horse paddock fence, he will relieve me now of that side of the work. The ladies have done their many tasks faithfully. I honestly think it is too much for two women to feed & clothe always now over an 100 people as well as school & medical[;] it is a day & night job without break only grace saves from breakdown. We are in that difficult stage when like Israel leaving Egypt, full of grumbles, they do not yet realised we seek to lead them to a higher state.

Alf Dyer[55]

---

55   NTRS 1099/P1 vol. 1.

Figure 5.54: 'Group at Oenpelli[,] Miss Sherren's [Sherrin's] room at the back 1929'. Rev. Dyer is standing at the back while his father is seated in the centre of the photo next to Mary Dyer. The other two *balanda* women are Miss Florence Sherrin and Mrs Thorne.
Source: Northern Territory Archives Service (NTRS 694 P1 Box 4 Item 71).

***

OENPELLI 1 Feb 1929
Port Darwin

R.H. Weddell, Esq,.
Government Resident, Darwin.

Sir,

Mission Station Annual Report.

In answer to request of yours of Dec 1928 please find as requested report on Oenpelli Mission .

(a). Receipts & expenditure for the year 1928.

For these figures I must refer you to C.M.S., 192 Castlereagh St Sydney, as all accounts are dealt by them direct .

(b). <u>Buildings & Assets.</u>

The buildings are as per last years report except a new beef house 10x 12 feet & one new house 15x15 ft with verandah. Buildings have been hung up by food shortage in May & June. Then Mr Ivin left & later both the Taylors went in the Mary for stores & the best engine which never ran properly was sent South & returned 2months later in much the same state, so they were away over six months . Mr Thorne left with cattle on his way South so I was alone 5 months when Mr I. Taylor returned via Goulburn Is. Mr P .Taylor is still in Darwin to see the engine trouble through. So all these hinderances must be kept in mind in the years report , so dreams of new buildings are still but castles in the air.

<u>Implements.</u> the only additions to last years list are two gifts given to me while South[–] a Single springtooth harrows & a Fordson tractor.

<u>Boat.</u> The lugger "Mary" was purchased for £400 & a Fairbanks Morse Diesel engine putt in,which with the installing, makes the cost well over a thousand pounds .

(c). <u>Area under cultivation.</u>

The area has increased to 13½ acres, 3½ being added in the past year, but 10 more were prepared for the tractor & fenced in. Waiting for the tractor delayed putting out next years crops .

During the year the garden produced :-

4000 lbs	Kaffir Corn.
2044 "	Cassava.
2275 "	Sweet potatoes.
382 doz	Bananas.
464 "	Paw Paws.
67	Pumpkins.
50	Pineapples.
2 cwt	Peanuts.
100	Cabbages.

Thousands of Mangoes.

Besides many small green vegetables.

300 Custard Apples.

All this has been used for food on the station

(d). <u>Stock.</u>

Goats dropped as low as 160 in July. I had to get them kept near the station & warn killers & kill some dogs & by the end of the year they had increased to 206.

Cattle & horses[–] Mr Bishop has the figures. Mr.Thorne took the books South with him & said he would give him the figures when in Darwin . A hundred odd cattle were sold in Darwin for the sum of £328 this being our first real income .

(e). <u>Aboriginals.</u>

(1) 1926   15 boys   7 girls
     1927   26 boys   11 girls.
     1928   32 boys   18 girls and   10 smaller children

The numbers in the dormitories are :

(2). 22 small boys.
      7 large boys.
      3 Leper boys.
      18 Girls.

15 smaller smaller children are being fed but live in the camp. All these are black except one child half Malay result of a boats visit .

(3) <u>Ablebodied natives.</u>

Numbers vary, this being controlled by the amount of stores. We average now 40 workers, some permanent others casual this brings us in touch with more people & there is no scarcity here generally of native food. Quite 100 to 200 would like to work, and with the tractor to help enable us to grow more food we should grow more with the help of a few more implements. A patch of rice in the swampy ground looks well at present . New South Wales Government gave me sample lots of wheat to grow but it has not been a success. More garden more people is the aim we have before us.

(4) <u>Infirm.</u>

Several old people died during the year leaving 5 at present, sick people are coming and going during the year . Xmas numbers give a fair number as a guide to those who come and go - this year we had 230 . We generally estimate the numbers around this area as about 500.

(f). <u>Technical & Education.</u>

We are young, and only have teacher who takes Kindergarten in the morning for the young ones and general school in the afternoon and sewing. All the young people work in the garden in the morning. We aim at the three Rs and to teach them agriculture, and a few boys stock work and the boat. The aim is to help them to help themselves in their own reserve. Those who have been in Darwin don't like it. Civilization spells their extinction, what a Native state offers remains to be proved. And since life is fleeting we seek to implant the hope of a better state..

(g). <u>Indistrial Activities.</u>

Several miles of fencing has been put up. Wire shipped from South 9 months ago is still not here. Next year we hope to complete paddocks, to begin to select the cattle and improve the breed. Most North Australia cattle are very inbred on these lines would be a great boon to the North. We can carry thousands of cattle here, this we hope to be one of the main sources of income as the herd grows.

The growth of fruit trees has been very good. Soursops from seeds are over 12 feet high bearing fruit. Lemons 8 feet, some fruiting, the growth of flowers and shrubs has been good and the place grows more beautiful as the plan of the Station grows.

Our steam boiler for irrigation and sawing has finished his course so irrigation ceased for the last six months[;] this has affected the results in the garden.

(H & I)

Timetable with give an idea of management

	Getup bell	6 o'clock.
	Start work	6.15 Sunrise.
	Breakfast	7
	Service	7.35
	Work	8 till 11.30
	Dinner	-
	Work	2 till ¼ to 5.
Staff	Rev. A.J. Dyer.	
	Mrs. M.S. Dyer	
	Mr. F.C. Thorne Stock Overseer	
	Mrs. " " Nurse.	
	Miss. G. Sherrin School Teacher.	
	Mr. I. Taylor Came to build.	
	Mr. P. Taylor do	

Generally we find most of the special problems with Aboriginals work are solving themselves. New tribes are coming in, a few fights ensue over past troubles but they settle down and become friends.

One man, one wife, one dog is the ideal set and all those who live on the station so agree. Those who cannot agree make their homes in the camp and come up for work. Most will fall into line as time goes on and the older ones die.

Things have grown beyond what I hoped in 1925, when many said our coming here would be a failure, we have all worked hard and now with the increased area D.V. [*Deo volente*] I feel we can make good for an Arnheim Land State. Many talk of leaving them to help themselves, but I believe it is too late, for the last 50 years many of these tribes have been going through to Roper River Maranboy and Katherine and still are, then they return with disease etc., North of the Roper I know of tribes almost wiped out with no station near them, then there is the lugger. The only hope I can see for these people is along the lines we aim at as this report gives evidence of. If we had an axe to grind we would not be here on our salary, and this report only speaks of facts, very far from ideal, but a beginning. If the Commonwealth was sincere in a desire to help the aboriginals she would see that we had the implements and tools we really need to make good. Problems that exist in other parts of Australia have not reached us yet as we have no neighbours & rocky walls, which took Leichhardt 2 months to get through[,] make good fences.

We have some trouble with cattle spearing but have to deal with it in our own way, and our own stock boys help a degree in this, and that help will grow as they realise it touches themselves as well.

Mr. Bleakley has been the only Government visitor since 1926, we have never had a Doctor this is a real outpost. Several blacks from other parts have caused some trouble lately, and when one has been the only man here with 200 odd natives about, one has had to rule with a firm hand, then an occasional visit of the powers that be does count.

(I). Medical work consists of a sick parade daily every morning and other cases are attended as necessary[–] much suffering has been relieved. An average of 26 per day for the last 6 months.

(J). Transport difficulties.

Failure of the new lugger engine has caused many setbacks this year, the boat has been in Darwin over seven months and we have had no news of her, so can only hope for the best. Once this trouble is overcome we should have no further troubles on this score, except accidents which are always liable to happen in uncharted waters.

Yours faithfully
Sgd. A.J. Dyer
Superintendent[56]

---

56 NTRS 1099/P1 vol. 1.

Figure 5.55: The lugger *Mary* with 'Ned Lilly' looking through life buoy and unidentified Aboriginal crew member, c. 1929.

We are unsure of this identification and suspect the man may actually be Alf Dyer's father who visited in 1929.

Source: Northern Territory Archives Service (NTRS 694 P1 Box 4 Item 111).

Figure 5.56: Steam boiler near the edge of the billabong (date unknown).
Source: Northern Territory Archives Service (NTRS 693 P1 Item 21).

* * *

Oenpelli Report February 1929

Other reports going with mail give most of the news, except to say that Mrs Dyer[,] Miss Sherrin & self have felt the strain of the of the past months & have each had a few days down with fever.

Mr Taylor has been able to relieve us by taking my duties & cutting up for Mrs Dyer some task when over a hundred come at you 3 times a day. Garden has occupied most of my time & a lot has b been put out.

Ladies usual tasks of house, school sewing dispensary etc. Mr Taylor is on the horse paddock, refencing[,] removing gates to more useful positions , also the usual cattle & horse work & repairs & making ropes etc

A lot of opposition over a little girl wife kept in the camp for a wife . She is now in the dormitory . Most of these tro troubles are being settled . I can act in ways I could not when we first came, when we were feeling our wa y.

Rain every day except 5 so we are having a good season no very heavy rain yet .

Yours sincerely
Alf Dyer[57]

***

Oenpelli, March 6th 1929
PORT DARWIN

Dear Mr Ferrier

When you are considering the question of staff & furloughs ; do not plan for us to come so soon as unless forced to for health reasons we would rather stay longer & we are climatized . I would never leave Mr Thorne in charge again . When I wrote on my return was only here a few hours & did not see much..Since formed the judgment which caused me to say what I did . I left the matter in God's hands as He knows all & it is very hard to write fairly of such matters . But if they are returning[,] feel you should know something of how matters are . In yours you speak of them being treated as missionaries , they were & with even more consideration , but they were always saying they were not missionaries . In Darwin Mr Thorne only went to the Methodist Church & told all their troubles & you know what that means in the Territoy .We never said a word not even to my own father , hoping the troubles would blow over , but found them much magnified when we returned . They tried to force me to do things or they would resign . I realize this is not likely to reach you in time to effect your decision & should they return will try & face it . And will do our best to help them as we did through all the constant assaults over trifles mostly imaginery. I still think Mrs Thorne should come as his wife & not on the staff at all . You need not worry about the cattle even if I am left with one man to carry on[.] Personally I would rather have a few whose hearts God has touched than many with other motives.

Yours sincerely
Alf Dyer[58]

***

---

57   NTRS 1099/P1 vol. 1.
58   ML MSS 6040/12.

WANTS

Dear Mr Ferrier

You know I have shop on Saturday when they come to buy with their monthly pocket money of 2/6 to 8/6 according to their work that is for permanent workers only .I do my best to use stuff sent in the boxes to keep down expenses , imagine my difficulties when I have not a thing in this list of articles here listed , of some none came in the last boxes, of others only a few which Xmas swallowed up hence my constant plea for that rouseabout to try & get the same.

Pocket knives, knives , But knives

Pipes

Small mirrows & ones in frames for their houses

Hatchets

Razors   need not be new any of these as long as they are not rubbish

Small beads

Shirts & trousers

Towels

Dresses

nagas

quilts   anything suitable for them to buy

Please for some of your old lantern slides , have a good set of life of Christ , old missionary ones they would love no matter how out of date , have a few of New Guinea which they have seen again & again or any subjects , there are always old ones being tossed out , I have repeatedly asked for these no luck yet . A small movie with suitable film would be a help if you strike one not wanted in some home .

Alf Dyer[59]

---

59   ML MSS 6040/12.

Figure 5.57: Mrs Dyer handing out dresses to the women (date unknown).

Source: Northern Territory Archives Service (NTRS 693 P1 Item 21).

* * *

Photographic Material

I have had bad luck in getting my supplies[.] I have not had a film for months[.] I asked Phil to order for last boat but none came & Ion does not know anything about them ,so it has happened the last three Wet seasons I have not had a film & it is the best time for snaps . The enclosed films are from Miss Sherrin so I would like you to post her a copy of them ,also a copy to my father & a copy to myself & charge to me . Mrs Thorne promised to send me a copy of them films Isent to you by her but none have come as I gave them all my snaps I have none here & you have all my films I would like a print of all of the good ones I have sent to you for my self & a copy also sent to my people please. Put the films into my collection[.] I hope you are guarding my trust as all these pictures are very valuable to me. You can use them as you will & if you can earn a few shillings from them so much the better as I have spent many in the cause.

Would you please arrange to come by each six monthly boat

1Doz Films in Tropical Tins No1 Brownie 117

1 Doz Pkts Nepera Paper 2¼ x 2¼

1Doz Films Tropical for Graflex camera

No 2 Brownie Size I think No 150

IDoz Pkts Nepera 3½ x 2½ Paper

so that I can have some quickly would you post on 6 each of both these size.of films extra please & charge to me .

Alf Dyer
Oenpelli
1929[60]

* * *

---

60   ML MSS 6040/12.

THE BIBLE IN BUFFALO COUNTRY

March 8ᵗʰ
1929

Miss Sherrin

Has just given me this report at the last minute she is down with fever or I would […] the last three on the list even Mrs D & self do not think they need that but I did not want to worry her with that today & I want Mrs Dyer to make some adjustments in school. The work here has been tremendous since return getting sewing in hand, stores etc most things were nil & had to be built up again it is too much for one woman she has them about in hand now. So she hopes to be able to help with the older ones being a teacher you will understand. Miss Sherrin tries to give them more than they are able to[;] it takes teachers a while to grasp the black mind but she is learning so you can send them if you like, if you forget the form work complain & time will give the adjustments necessary.

We have had a lot of stealing lately & a lot of punishments for the same. Last week I was not too well & did not count the goats just getting the boys to go, when I went this morning quite a number gone. It is hard to find out what most things we find out. It is so hard dealing with all these things when you would expect help from them[.] I tell you this to let you know we are up against lots of hard things we do long for the correction of sin. Remember us.

Cheerio AJ Dyer[61]

***

School Report [March 1929]

It has been a great privelege to teach these children. They respond so willingly to discipline, & are most eager to learn

At first I marvelled at their memories, & naturally thought they could be taught like little white children, but I soon learnt my mistake.

I also came to the conclusion that 30 children of different ages could not be taught properly as a whole; but rather in separate classes. To do this it was necessary to test them individually. This was not an easy task, because all needed occupation.

---

61   MLMSS 2040/12 Oenpelli Reports 1926–74.

However, I decided to give them Transcription for a while, thus enabling me to test some, whilst the others were writing. This served not only as a writing lesson but as a reading & a spelling lesson also. I wrote a simple copy on the board every day – sometimes it was taken from the Primer, sometimes from a simple Austral Geography, but it was always a lesson drawn up from their surroundings. I gradually introduced Tables, Arithmetic & Dictation.

At the end of 12 months I had my school divided into 5 Classes.

Class A consists of 10 children who are working on a proper foundation. Three of these children help to teach the Infant Classes reading. They have passed 1st Grade work & are now ready for 2nd Grade & they are up to that stage when books would be a great help to them, such as Geography, Arithmetic, & English Grammar.

In Class B there are 15 scholars doing 1st Grade work. There are 18 children learning to read & write, these have been put into Classes C & D.

We also have 12 tiny children, who do not need much attention yet. They are surrounded by pretty pictures, & they delight in drawing strange looking objects on their slates, with coloured chalks.

"Morning Kindergarten"

Kindergarten has increased wonderfully. We started with six tiny children. At the end of 9 months these were 19. Now there are 36 on the roll.

This is a happy centre. Ones heart cannot help swelling as one listens to the inspiring sounds, coming from these infant voices.

I am sure the best work will be done among them, because they have come to us at such an early age.

Florence Sherrin[62]

***

---

62   ML MSS 6040/12 Oenpelli Reports 1926–74.

Oenpelli Report March 1929

March has been a wonderful month for the garden. We have had 40" for the season in lovely showers & no heavy winds to knock down the crops. So we should have goodcrops, but in some things we miss the lack which irrigation would have started before the Wet.

Rice has grown well, but it is only in poor soil as I could not get the other ploughed without tractor help.

Garden[,] a new goat yard & repairs have occupied allmy time from the many general tasks. Mr Taylor likewise with yard repairs &new fencing & general with harness repairs. This place keeps one man repairing all the time with nothing else.

One girl & two more boys came in allwell but it takes us all our time just to keep things going Ido hope some help is coming on the ladies side I fear Mrs Dyer cant go on at the rate she has to go much longer.

We had nice Easter services & there seemed to be a deeper note of worship in them, one poor old blind soul was buried who has been with us since we came so we are constantly reminded of the brevity of life but the spiritual is not yet as we see the outward.

Yours sincerely
Alf Dyer[63]

---

63   NTRS 1099/P1 vol. 1.

Figure 5.58: Old woman living at the Oenpelli mission (date unknown).
Source: Northern Territory Archives Service (NTRS 694 P1 Box 4 Item 34).

Figure 5.59: Elderly couple living at Oenpelli mission, c. 1925.
Source: Northern Territory Archives Service (NTRS 694 P1 Box 4 Item 96).

* * *

Oenpelli, March 4 1929

Rev. Robert . Dey . D.D.

Dear Sir

Enclosed find a copy of an article I have written to educate the public on Aboriginal matters. I have sent a copy to the Sydney Morning Hearld , but they may not publish it . So I have just left the matter in yourown hands as my only wish is to help these dark people to whom I have given some 13 oddyears of my life . I am also sending a copy to our secretary in Sydney & you can get in touch with him about any questions that may arise should you wish to publish which I hope you will as it may help the cause of Aboriginal Missions generally.

Yours sincerely
Alf Dyer[64]

* * *

---

64   ML MSS 6040/12.

March 29

A statement of what has been done in three years may be more to the point in these days when Aboriginal questions & theories are before the public mind. Some say put them on a reserve & leave them to themselves. Some say that missions are a failure. Some say let them die out the quicker the better. But most fairminded Australians feel we owe them something, but they are perplexed about what should be done.

We are on the eastern side of Arnheim Land & the writer has had 14years experience at Roper River, Groote Eylandt, and the East Alligator River & has been round the coast of all its area several times & landed in many places, & has been inland on both sides on horse trips; from what I have seen in these years I feel it is too late of talking of leaving them to themselves, for the last 50 years many of these tribes have been going to work on station near Roper & Maranboy & about the line, & the red deseases are to be found right through all thes[e] parts that I have visited with the exception of Groote Eylandt which is 30 miles from the mainland. On the Southern side of Arnheim Land some tribes almost cease to exist so from purely national grounds, ought we to leave them alone & would a reserve to themselves stop them going out to what they think to better themselves which has always yet led to their extinction. Hence we seem forced to offer the inducement to stay in their own reserve or if they do go out to work for others they go under proper supervision from the government. The missionary has another motive The kingdom of God but surely that touches both body as well as soul, too often has the body been forgotten, hence the great gap between Church & Labour when both should work together.

The Church Missionary Society was asked by the Government to take over Oenpelli in 1925. It was then a Government cattle station on an Aboriginal reserve set apart by the advice of Sir Baldwin Spencer run by a stockoverseer & his wife with 6 boys & their wives, no other were wanted, so they wandered about, but not like Central Australian natives, because food abounds with a buffalo or a bullock as they got the chance from a herd of 3000.

We took over in Sept 1925 & sent out invitations to come in

By 1926 we had resident in dormitories

	15 boys	7 girls
1927	26 "	11, "
1928	37	23 afew of these are with parents

these figures indicate a willingnesss of the people to bring in their children. We could have many more if we could give the parents work. But we have come to a stage when present kitchen & store & what is in it will not carry a bigger family as we now employ about people, some come & go, some are permanent. I have noticed in the papers several times lately the statement that various tribes will not settle down together these children come from 7 tribes. When new tribes come in there is generally a fight over some old score. The last lot come in all painted up in white looking for trouble, but I was asked to go down to mediate between them. After a great deal of acting & biting of kidney fat bags it blows over. On this occasion some spears were thrown after I had gone away, but wounds were soon healed & they were working side by side

But some will say to feed them is to pauperise them too true unless they can be taught to work. Our aim is so to use their labour to make a home for themselves & by gardens to feed themselves, & if possible later to work out their own destiny, in my judgement that is only possible apart from civilization. When we came the Govt set apart 2000 sq miles of country with East Alligator River as the southern boundary, she enters the ranges above the tidal section, which are wall upon wall mostly unknown country which took Leichheardt 2 months to get through from the Roper to our lovely plains. So Nature has provided a good fence for this purpose. The Northern area ended about the 12th latitude, so last year I asked the government to increase the area to the coast to make the reserve as complete as natural causes can make it, this they have agreed to. A beginning has been made to put it on a basis whichI believe will very soon enable us to grow most of our food & meat.

Cattle

The government gave us 500, took off a large number, & we have since bought the balance 860 all the killers being taken off, this year we sold our first hundred in Darwin, our first income. The rate of increase given me by the Government overseer was that they double themselves in 3 years, we have notproved that yet as most of ours were old & the best taken away, but I think it is a fair estimate. We have no droughts[,] feed& water for a herd of 20,000, one feels he could safely on the increased area of 40,000. So that opens a field of industry for them & supply their needs in the North without making them paupers. But we need help to increase the herd to make this possible. Someone may cry what about the local market for private enterprise. Cattle are beingshipped to the East from Darwin that can be increased especially with a better class of cattle, which surely is a national project well worth taking in hand, or Vesty's works can be reopened rusting for the want of use. Darwin has too long been the taunt of the South; industry does not cease in the South because some men go on strike[,] men are willing enough to work generally speaking, & it is only on such lines that I can see much hope for the North. Britain believes in Darwin& is spending some millions as a naval base, has she not shown more vision than Australia,?

As this field of activity becomes a reality any income above the expenses can be used for their own wants. But stock work only provides work for a few, therefore the garden must be the means by which they can best help themselves.

Garden

Fortunately we have good soil, but that is not generally so in the North for it is mostly very poor country hence the stress on cattle industry generally for the North & that is so also on this reserve, but around the station we have a lot of good soil & a good Wet season rainfall average about 40 inches. Tropical foods & fruits grow well except such things as need water in the 6 dry months of the year.

When we came a small plough was given by some friends, then a gift of £10 enabled me to buy a 3 furrow plow stump jump new, but had waited an owner many years in Darwin[,] except for rust it was as good as new. Telling of this recently in a sermon in Melbourne led to an introduction to a manager of Massey Harris who on being told what was being done, gave a springwood harrows & a Sydney buisness man gave a tractor 9 months ago which is still in Darwin owing to transport difficulties. We have grown from less than an acre to 13 ½ acres this season, had the tractor been here the area would be 20 acres as this is already cleared & fenced. Aportion of this is naturally flooded, black soil, we are trying rice as an experiment which at the time of writing looks asif it will be a success, if so we have hundreds of such acres that can so be used. The Government asked to try wheat but this has been a failure. But we have grown thousands of lbs of Sweet potatoes, corn, cassava, besides fruit & vegetables. A soursop tree planted from seed is over 12 ft high in3 years. Lemons 8ft fruiting willgive indication of what can be grown, so I am speaking of facts when I say they can grow most of their own food under white instruction, already they are planting food around their own homes in their own time. Cotton has grown well in trial lots a bale was sent to Sydney & to England & both reports were good. Peanuts do well also, but our first object is to grow food, but we need implements we have made many homemade ones but they do not do the best work.

To overcome the dry time I erected an old boiler & steam pump from the butter plant on the billabong it did two seasons work, we have plenty of water, so it enabled us to grow in the dry time of the year which is our cool season when Southern vegetables grow well. Now the boiler is finished as it is easily over 25 years old.

Last Xmas 230 blacks came to visit us, most of whom would have liked to work. Out beyond the fringe we touch are many more still in their wild state, some whom we have seen willcome in when we can take them. My plea to the people of the Commonwealth is do you want to do the brotherly thing? Here at least is a real chance to make good, even if it should be a failure to save a remanant of the race. ManyAboriginal Missions have hard conditions to contend with hence what may seem failure as some judge, but not so counted by them who have helped many of these dark brothers, perhaps not always wisely. Need I make any apology that we do teach the gospel? That our children love their singing & their services, & are being taught to read & write & play our games, for they have helped also to make our race, thus their life is made fuller & richer. So the question in my mind which led to the penning of these lines, is shall we stop where we are & growslowly? or shall the help be forthcoming which would enable us to fulfil what I have planned in this venture & we become a native state? Take in also the saltwater blacks train them on luggers to help gather the marine wealth the Japenese are now coming in large number yearly to collect around the shores of Darwin, leaving behind them the bodies of natives whom they have poisoned with bad grog & worse. It can be done, but it must be done soon.

Alf Dyer
Superintendent
Oenpelli
March 1929[65]

---

65   NTRS 1099/P1 vol. 1.

* * *

Oenpelli Report April 1929

Most of April I had to give in, being in bed mostof the time the body refusing to work.

Mr Taylor had to carry on the general supervision of the Station. The construction of cattle yards & repairs to the same, mending harness[,] making ropes for mustering seasonhas taken all his spare time. We are removing the milking yard so as to be able to watch the milkers & milksuckers better. Also removing the killing yard to save a long carry to the beef house.

The few days I did work made anenclosed yard to the girls dormitory to give them more freedom at night. One very sad incident happened, we have a very deadly snake here and we have seen a horse die very quickly with the same kind since. On of these came into school & bit a little girl, one of the most promising ones, in the confusion Miss Sherrin did not know for a few minutes then she rushed her to the dispensary but the blood in the leg had congealed so after trying the usual we injected Strychnine & she rallied, & later we thought the worst was over but at midnight convulsions set in & we commended her to the Lord &she died. Next morning while the grave was being dug the mother took her to put her in a tree. I asked the father that she might be buried in the cementry & he had her brought back & we buried her singing Jesus loves me. Several of the children were taken away after this, but they were so happy we feel sure they will come back again later. The ladies usual task of school dispensary, household etc. Several cases of leprosy are very gruesome. Crops look well &rice is heading. We are using our own porridge 5 days a week, potatoes & cassava for dinner so we are on the way to growing our food

Alf Dyer[66]

---

66   NTRS 1099/P1 vol. 1.

Figure 5.60: Group of children (with onlooker in the background) (date unknown).

Source: Northern Territory Archives Service (NTRS 694 P1 Box 4a Item 189).

* * *

Report of the General Secretary's visit to Oenpelli
April to June 1929

Introduction:

It is proposed to give this report in narrative form and to make certain observations and recommendations.

A C.M.S. mission party comprising Mr and Mrs H .J. Mackaness and daughter, Miss F. A. Nevill and the General Secretary of the Branch left Sydney in the S. S. "MARELLA" on Wednesday April 10th. In addition to ordinary stores and luggage there were taken three goats, two crates of fowls (7 birds in all) and a lorry.

From the commencement of the voyage Mr Mackaness, whose statements as to his ability to succeed Mr Thorne as the cattle overseer at Oenpelli, supported by various papers and references[,] had been considered satisfactory by the General Secretary and the committees responsible, began to reveal himself more clearly, and it soon appeared doubtful whether he would be suitable for the post to which he had been appointed. One hoped there might have been improvement but subsequent events determined the question and his agreement was terminated on April 30th. (See special report)

We were met at Thursday Island by the Bishop of Carpentaria whom we expected would have been accompanied by William Williams, the man who was to sail the "MARY". Though the boat in which he was due to return from the island where he had left his family passed near the "MARELLA" he missed the ship. It transpired later that one of his children had died. He came on by the later steamer in May and is now engaged in his duties as master of the "MARY".

The "MARELLA" reached Darwin on April 20th where we found to our dismay that the Rector was up country and there was no one to meet us or to make arrangements for our hospitality. The hotels were all full and there are no private boarding places. After talking things over with Mr Beurteaux and others it was decided that the Mackanesses and Miss Nevill take possession of the Rectory while the Methodist minister, Rev. Stanley Jarvis, kindly offered hospitality for the General Secretary. This latter really meant that I was provided for for five weeks. I should like the Society to send an expression of appreciation to Mr and Mrs Jarvis. The Rector returned home that night and kindly approved the arrangement at the Rectory for the rest of the party, twelve days for Miss Nevill and nearly a month for the Mackanesses, that is until they returned to Sydney. The Victorian party by the "MALABAR", Mr Dyer Senior, and later the Rev. A. DYER also had the benefit of the Rector's hospitality and I would suggest that an official letter of appreciation be sent to him also.

I took the earliest opportunity of inspecting the "MARY" and found her beached high and dry at Carl's Beach, with no prospect of floating her until the top of the spring tides, a week later.

I was anxious to push on with all speed and put in an appearance night and morning in the hope that each tide would be enough to float the "MARY", and there was moreover the engine to be fitted in. When Friday came and there was no success[,] consulted with friends and decided to dig an 18 inch trench under the keel so that Saturday's opportunity would not be lost with the result that we should be delayed a further fortnight. This was done and we floated next morning, and we took delivery of the engine at the wharf that afternoon and proceeded to instal it. In the meantime the "MARY" had been copper painted, and the rigging all prepared, and I had had opportunity to notice the parlous condition of the rudder and of the stern generally. The false keel was also missing with the exception of a few feet from the stem of the vessel[,] of these more later. Except for the extreme end of the after part of the keel which was badly eaten by borer,,the hull was free of worm holes.

While the "MARY" was at the wharf I took the opportunity of loading her ready for the voyage. The engine was installed by the Tuesday. A broken pipe underneath was mended and a loose gudgeon pin was pointed out to me as a thing that would cause a knock. There was some trouble getting the air bottle filled as the small engine was not easy to start, but a pressure of 180 lbs was obtained and sufficed for three unsuccessful attempts to start. Failure might well have been due to faulty lighters. Under similar conditions on the following day, Thursday, at noon there was again failure and I decided to wait no longer but to proceed under sail, and this I did forthwith leaving with Miss Nevill that afternoon after obtaining supplies of fresh water for the journey, at 5 p. m. The crew was composed of three half castes of whom Herman Pon was master.

Sailing was slow and there was no doubt a drag of the screw, as well as the towing of a small launch that I thought it well to hire in case of emergency. We averaged about 25 miles each day and anchored for the night, and found ourselves about 5 miles off the mouth of the East Alligator on the afternoon of Wednesday the sixth day. The pump taken from Sydney at the advice of Mr P. Taylor was much in service. On the second day out I noticed water under the cabin floor and this was discovered to be due to the bilge outlet not having been closed when fitting the engine. We stopped the hole and pumped the vessel clear, but a little further leakage and water would have got into the engine, and certainly some of the stores in the hold would have been damaged.

I would like to pay a tribute to Miss Nevill who cheerfully endured the strange experiences of lugger travel. The food is all strange and is served in a primitive manner. There are not any conveniences. The cabin did not invite use for sleeping purposes and the deck, even with mattresses proved hard, and the early morning blows washed the deck occasionally. There was little or no shelter from the sun by day. The goats, fowls, and the boat and a drum of oil and other deck cargo allowed no facility for exercise, but there was no complaint only a cheerful acceptance of conditions. She and others like her who have made this journey should have a medaille de mer!

The first few days of the voyage are a time of settling in. There is cargo to be stowed, various bits of gear to be fixed and the duties of each one to be defined. One of the men was told off for the cooking, another acted as mate and the captain was at the head of all. I made myself responsible for the feeding of the fowls and goats, also for the pumping on the way out. When things were settled Herman Pon asked to look at the engine and very shortly I was glad to hear the air compressor engine humming away at its work. It stopped when it had passed the 200 lb mark. Next day he asked for the book of words for the Fairbanks Morse and looked the engine over[,] cleaning and oiling it. By the following afternoon he had it running, somewhat unsatisfactorily by reason of a leaking oil fue[l] pipe, but running. The pipe was mended, a neat soldering job, and the engine on starting ran well and until we returned to Darwin gave us all we asked of it.

That afternoon we ran about 15 miles on the high gear and anchored for the night about 10 miles up the river. We needed our mosquito nets and were awake at daylight. The tide was rising and we made a start and taking it at the flood carried it right through to the Oenpelli Landing which we reached about 10.30 full of praise to God for the blessing of the completed journey. The starting of the engine had been celebrated the night before in ginger ale!

After a little lunch Miss Nevill and I essayed the walk to the Station. There were several streams to wade and much long spear grass to negotiate. The heat was great and mosquitos worried us when we sat to rest, but the station was reached about 4 o'clock and though we were unexpected there was great joy and welcome refreshment. Miss Sherrin and the girls were at the Waterfall for a few days picnic and a number of the boys were out bush so the place was fairly quiet. One of the girls had died from snake bite the week before and that had made a scare in the school and Mr Dyer had been in indifferent health for some weeks. We spent the evening talking over various matters and appreciated the rest of a home after the week at sea.

Next day I had a look round and was impressed by the manifest development that had taken place since my previous visit, but was anxious to return to the boat by mid day. We had seen the cache of hardware on the river bank as we came up and I wished to have this at the station if possible as after 7 months, and most of that the wet season, it was likely to be damaged and would not improve. When Mr Ion Taylor and I reached the "MARY" the unloading was not completed so we missed a tide but we got away the next day. About 30 miles down we stuck in the mud and had to wait the fall and rise of the tide. Fortunately we bedded well and kept an even keel and when the tide came with a rush after dark we steamed against it to the cache by about 11 p.m. and anchored in deep water for the night. Early in the morning we moored at the bank and began to take in the cargo: galvanized iron, barbed wire, baths and tubs, 18 cases of kerosene and oils, half a ton of coarse salt, a 60 gallon drum of crude oil and some sundries. Most of the cases of kerosene when disturbed began to leak but we were able to put the worst of these into an empty oil drum. Some of the wire and iron was damaged by contact with the salt water. It was an arduous day's work for Mr Taylor, the boat's crew and the boys from the station as the tide was out and everything had to be carried through mud and slime up to the knees for about 20 yards. But at last it was all aboard and stowed and we waited for the tide. This came about 7 o'clock and we anchored in the channel for the night. We ascended the river by the rising tide next morning and reached the landing at noon where we speedily unloaded the goods we had brought. These with the cargo from Darwin were already being taken by pack horses to the foothills and thence by cart to the station. A dead horse on the river bank had died from snake bite the day before. Already the crocodiles had been at it and its appearance and smell were offensive so we towed it off into the stream. N. B. There are snakes in Oenpelli.

At the station during the next 36 hours I had opportunities of seeing in closer detail with Mr Dyer the various activities and plans of the Mission. These are dealt with in the report which Mr Dyer has sent to the office and will be considered in Sydney sooner or later. Our workers there in Oenpelli have to be praised for the use they are making of the opportunity they have for extending the Master's Kingdom, and it will be the responsibility of the officers and committees of the Society to give the most careful consideration and effect to the needs of the Mission. I appreciate the advance and improvements that have been made in the buildings the cultivation, the instruction of the children, the care of the sick and of the cattle, the spiritual welfare of the people, and in particular the happy relations of the present staff. Mr Dyer had nothing but praise and appreciation for his fellow workers and his remarks as to the quality of future reinforcements must not be disregarded.

As Mr Dyer intended returning with me to Darwin and I thought our opportunities of conference en route and while in Darwin would be ample I decided to hasten homewards, and arranged to depart from the landing on Wednesday forenoon. This we did, but found that the wear and tear on the bearings and stern tube had been such that the boat was leaking. Temporary repairs were effected and we started. We missed the channel by a few yards at the bad part of the river again and this time were not so fortunately placed as on the former occasion. But we were away again on the rising tide, and we did not lash the rudder. As the tide fell the boat slid in the inclined mud and the rudder broke away from its stem. This was a disaster of magnitude and as soon as the tide served we floated off and towed to the mouth of the river where we beached on sand and rigged a rough substitute. Off again at 10 p.m. we were forced to stop at 2 a.m. on account of the excessive leakage due to the faulty bearing. We kept afloat by pumping and at daylight effected the necessary repair and were able to start again at 10 a.m. It was a risky piece of work. The improvised rudder was not enough to sail the ship, but it sufficed for steering way for streaming and we made the non-stop run into Darwin doing in 24 hours what had taken six days sailing on the outward run. When we anchored at Darwin we were leaking at such a rate that we had to supplement the pump by bucket bailing. We therefore decided to put the "MARY" on the slip but owing to the small tides did not succeed in this till the following Saturday, just seven days after our arrival in Darwin, so it was necessary to take out the propeller and tube and plug the hole.

A careful survey made us realise that new and extra bearings would be necessary as well as a new rudder and false keel. These were put in hand and after a fortnight were practically completed.

I have brought pieces of the old bearings and shaft which shows the wear of less than one thousand miles of running and have reports from Mr Perriman and from Mr Kendrick which will bear out the urgent need for the work done. These will be discussed in detail in due course. An outstanding fact is that the mud of such a river as the East Alligator when it enters the bearings sets up a severe wezzing grind. The extra gland on the outside will minimise this to some extent. Another fact is that to have bought a vessel with a seven foot draught was a great mistake. A lesser draught by 24 inches would have made a great difference as the flat bottom of the lesser draught boat would have sat flat on grounding while the "MARY" when she grounds lies over with the deck at an angle of 45 degrees. This is bad enough on deck but a serious disadvantage in the engine room where oil tins if not hung up fall over and other such troubles. These matters have all been the subject of careful discussion with Mr Dyer and we are agreed that improvements are possible in these matters.

The long wait in Darwin owing to having missed the "MARELLA" was serious for me but was not altogether a disadvantage as certain important business matters connected with the cattle disposal and the Station generally were given attention. Apart from a good deal of anxiety there was the drawback of indifferent food and the broken rest during the journey to Oenpelli. During the 16 days' absence from Darwin I had 8 nights at sea, 5 nights on the river pestered with vicious mosquitos and two of these nights with the deck at an angle of 45 degrees. During one of the early morning storms on the run out I lost an artificial denture to my serious inconvenience, and during the journey back I was troubled with an attack of dyssentry, probably due to the use of the river water. I was quite a fortnight in Darwin before I approached normal and it is only now after a week on the "KYOGLE" in which I am travelli[n]g by the courtesy of the Government, that I am feeling happier again. I cannot speak too warmly of the kindness of my friends the Jarvis' during my stay in Darwin. Their unfailing sympathy and fellowship together with the rest and comfort of their home were invaluable to me and saved me from the worst effects of an evil depression.

Unfailing kindness has also been shown to our party and to our Society by Mrs Waters of our church in Darwin, and in this kindness she has been supported by her friends Mr and Mrs Normal Bell. Never a time does the Mission boat leave Darwin but a token of their love in the shape of a box of fruits and sweets is sent for the voyage, and such a hamper was also sent for me to the "KYOGLE". On our first Sunday in Darwin, after the service there were two envelopes one from Mrs Waters containing £10 and one from Mrs Bell of £5 and £3, making her total £10; and two later sums from Mrs Waters of £50 and £20, making her total £80. I am hoping the Committee will make special recognition of these gifts and at least indicate to Mrs Waters that she is a Life Governor of the Society. By the way[,] Mrs Waters Last gift of /~~WWP~~/ £20 was made to me personally, but I explained things to her satisfaction.

Any further comment on my journey can be made in person. I close this with an expression of my devout thankfulness to God for many tokens of His blessing and presence with us in our undertakings[.] I feel unworthy of the least of all His many mercies and take shame for many faults and failures which are so manifest to me in my part of the matter.

J.W. Ferrier
General Secretary
14th June 1929[67]

---

67   ML MSS 6040/12 Oenpelli Reports 1926–74.

Figure 5.61: Scene of activity, 1929.
Source: Northern Territory Archives Service (NTRS 694 P1 Box 4a Item 218).

***

Report for May, June, July. Oenpelli. 1929

May opened with self gradually getting stronger after my illness. Mrs Dyer & I went for a week's rest to the Waterfall where we saw more fish in shoals than we had ever seen before. Mr Taylor had carried on the previous month & nothing had been too much trouble to do to relieve me of any care. Miss Sherrin with girls came out on the 8th & we returned. The next day Mr Ferrier with Miss Nevill walked in to our great surprise. The boys had run away after being punished for stealing watermelon. When the goods had been collected from Smith's landing Mr Ferrier & I left for Darwin. The stern gland was very loose, shaft had been badly fitted, and came out & boat had to be beached in bad place when rudder broke off. The stern part of the boat was weak & we knew it had to be altered so put boat on slip & it took three weeks to complete. Mr Ferrier was in Darwin at the time & has no doubt given you details. Mr Perriman en route for Groote was able to give us valuable assistance in the three days he was with us. This meant I was away from the station for a month but the boat had a thorough overhaul & engine room all put in order & we need not be ashamed of her. In the three months three trips have been made with practically no wind to sail generally head winds. The cost for fuel & oil worked out at a little under £5 per trip.

While I was away Mr Taylor took ten heifers for Goulburn Is[land] he had two bulls but they broke away he tried to get two more but could not find them in the time. This was unfortunate as we may have to oblige later.

Ladies work has been carried on as usual. Household always involves a lot of work with a hundred odd people to cater for. A change was made in the school[:] Miss Sherrin taking the juniors in the morning & Miss Nevill taking the older ones in the afternoon to push them on as much as possible. A great number of sick cases have been treated

Two lepers died[,] a woman Garijala & a boy Denajong.

Mr Taylor has constructed new cow yards, killing yard, gates & repairs to old yards & fences to keep the horses on one section of the plains to be able to catch them quickly. While I was away general supervision, that always takes a lot of one mans time & in this he has been a great help to me.

On arrival of the boat we had the tractor to unload & assemble[;] also the Diesel engine. & all the cargo & goods to get away. Then mustering had to be commenced. We went out together & burnt round & mended yards & mustered 212 cattle practically all together[,] brought them in & branded 42, 20 of them were clean skins from two to five years old. The rest of the cattle are feeding quietly on plains & there is no problem with them. I can give no report on prospect of sale of cattle yet. There is only twelve in this lot for this year. Twenty five for next.

Many cattle have been speared, so I must get fence up to keep them near the station. Hope to start on that next week as the wire is here now. I may keep Williams & try him on this job as it is better to prevent this sort of thing & it will cut lots of mustering.

Pump arrived this trip but not all the parts. I may be able to make one, am on this job now. Report enclosed.

Garden, this has been a good year. We have already had over 2 tons of sweet potatoes. We sent seven hundred odd pounds to Darwin 4cwt were sold at 18/ per cwt. We have some tons left yet. Rice headed well a tin full of seed produced many bushels, but the soil needs working a bit to sweeten up.

The lorry sent is much too heavy for our horses. It bogged seven times coming from landing to station in the sand. Mr Taylor is cutting it down & shifting rear wheels nearer which will lighten it somewhat & I hope we will be able to use it.

New children are still coming & we have over 60 now & few come & go, mostly all stay. So the work has grown beyond us & we have not been able to pull in as suggested. The supervision makes it impossible.

We have had a good deal of trouble in many ways. One stock boy was sent away, others refused to take punishment for trouble with dormitory girls but I told them they must or go & they took it.

Constable Mc Nab is here & has been dealing with some men who tried to get into girl's dormitory & had also speared cattle. One has to rule with diligence otherwise they rule. The children are the bright spot but they are not easy to manage. However we press on[;] the Christian must not look behind be the earth never so unquiet.

Yours sincerely
Alf Dyer[68]

Figure 5.62: Two Aboriginal men from the Oenpelli mission (date unknown).
Source: Northern Territory Archives Service (NTRS 693 P1 Item 21).

---

68   NTRS 1099/P1 vol. 1.

Figure 5.63: Stockyards (date unknown).
Source: Northern Territory Archives Service (NTRS 693 P1 Item 21).

* * *

July

<u>*Private*</u>

Dear Mr Ferrier

From the tone of a few of your letters one has gathered the impression you are rather against the Taylors. During the past two months Ion has been all I could wish, no little extra is ever any trouble to run to do & the way he has done the cattle work does me. I had great trouble with boys on return they had just been spoilt we are getting them into working order again. He left the yards in very bad order. the last mustering trip instead of bringing the cattle in to brand he branded them with bits of fencing wire which is useless; Lately he did no work before breakfast. I just tell you that as you seem to think he is something out of the ordinary but the second year showed a very different man to the first. Ion will see the cattle work through this year. I found Phil a great help in the boat & I have every confidence in what they tried to do. They certainly did more than I could have done as they bumped on the jetty[,] most would have left her smashup & I do not know what I would have done without his help if he had not caught the McBride[,] could not be expected to await your reply so I felt they acted for the best in a difficult position. They are both clever with tools & have taught me many things so I felt I ought to say this for them & that I am satisfied in the way they have done their work & that they are loyal to my wishes.

*I notice a new address on Mr Beautreaux letters hope it is for a better position[.]
I suppose the Greeks would have something to do with it & I hope someone is
giving you a better rental anyrate whatever it is may the Lord bless & enlarge
you more than in the old site. Hope you are keeping well.*

Cheerio Alfred

*The boiler shell is in good order but the tubes are done we will be putting it
up in a few days to see if we can get a little work out of her at low pressure
as I have mended the worst valves but with the new ones she would do many
many years of service*

*15 valves 6 ft 3 inches long 2 ¾ inches diameter outside measurements[;] it
is a good thing to have it even with the other as engines always fail at times
& oil & we can then fall back on wood & water the cost would only be small*

AJ Dyer[69]

***

*C.M.S.
Oenpelli
Aug 4th 1929
Sunday.*

Dear Mr Ferrier

*Thank you for your letter. You were not here long enough really to do anything
much for you. It was a great joy to me to have you & also a great relief.
We have loved having Miss Nevill & she has been a great help to us. She had
made up her mind to go with Mr Dyer's father last night but this morning
feels as if she were acting Jonah. I think a great deal of it is that physically she
is not able to stand it in the morning & evening when it is cool she feels alright
but as soon as the heat comes her head gets muddled & she gets no rest much at
night. However she is going to try and stay & if anyone can reach these people
she should because it has cost her so much. She is so capable & spiritual & we
all love having her here. Poor old Garijala (Garreejarlar) the leper woman
died two days after you left & Denajong died very suddenly out in the camp
just after Mr Dyer and Mr Taylor had left for the King River. I am enclosing
copy of letters I sent to Dr Cook. he sent the medicines I asked for – it has been*

69   ML MSS 6040/12.

good having Mr Dyer's father with us & even in the short time he has taught them things they will not forget. I expect there will be a wailing when he leaves tomorrow – if he had been younger I think he would have wanted to take on the work. If Miss Nevill cannot stay eventually, we will really need another woman. For the woman's side the great essential is a personal knowledge of the Lord Jesus as Saviour & a real love for souls which will get over the fact that they are often very unlovable & unlovely. Then one able to turn to many things that come from specialists in anything & able to adapt themselves to quite different conditions – Mr Dyer is well but still has to work too hard[:] there seems no help for it if we are to do anything for the people who are coming to us & there are many more & we do need buildings. The room Miss Neville is in is too hot. however we must just go on doing the best we can till God sends us the helpers needed – Please remember me kindly to all the helpers in office & Depot.

With Christian love & greetings to Mrs Ferrier. Betty & yourself. We remember you constantly

Yours in the glad service of Christ
Mary C. Dyer[70]

Figure 5.64: Oenpelli mission (date unknown).
Source: Northern Territory Archives Service (NTRS 693 P1 Item 21).

---

70   ML MSS 6040/12.

Figure 5.65: Handing out bags or fabric (date unknown).
Source: Northern Territory Archives Service (NTRS 693 P1 Item 21).

Figure 5.66: Oenpelli mission (date unknown).
Source: Northern Territory Archives Service (NTRS 693 P1 Item 21).

* * *

OENPELLI October 25 1929
PORT DARWIN

Dear Mr Ferrier

This is a reply to some of your queries .

<u>Fencing</u> riding down with Miss Nevill made me think of the posts . I do not order such lines unless you have the money to buy them , we told you150posts[;] her request was only another reminder if you could, we had the wire here . We must try & get it up as the cattle are getting out all the time making our work harder as we are trying to get a count[,] so far we are a lot under last years figures . Please send on the figures you promised to send me, I wired you to get them here by the last mail for my yearly returns . We cannot use droppers as the blacks steal them . I am afraid I cannot get Fish Creek done as I am overtired trying to keep things going & Ion has kept going hard in spite of constant suffering with his eyes.

<u>Police Methods</u>

These men needed drastic punishment I have tried all methods they took no notice " arod for fools backs" seems to be the only thing they take any notice of , they laugh at Fanny Bay & I shall do my level best to keep out of Darwin Court House . Mc Nab wanted to take them in but I asked him to give them a public thrashing, but he took things into his own hands & punched them with his open hand next time I will insist that the strap only be used. One was back again in a few days so you can guess it was nothing very serious.

They were punished for breaking into the house & stealing ,killing cattle ,one killed a cow near the house came up to ask for a knife to skin it saying it had died ,they are paid then to bring in the hide[.] I was suspicious & asked Ion to go & see but they had bolted . For trying to get the girls out of the dormitory at night Mrs Dyer heard them ,then they went to the stock boys wives as we men were all away ,they gladly caught them for us when Mc Nab was here . Is is no use saying "be good boys & don't do it again", your note book stunt did not work ,the same women were at it again next day, & the strange thing about these people they seem to like you better after a good belting if it is just . We have a lot of wicked blacks about runaways from the police & we dare not be weak , but must rule with diligence ,or they would rule us. The children never get strap unless they needit[,] with some we find a dose of castor oil very effective . I am afraid the committee have no idea, what a tough ,difficult & thankless job it is . Let them imagine that tomorrow they are put in charge of one of the bad streets in Sydney to clean it up what they would be up against , a black's camp is much the same without the knowledge of something higher till it is shown to them , it takes time & above all the grace of God which is His to give[;] if it were mine like Moses I would wish them all Prophets of the Lord .

Mr Sunter Will enclose the correspondance

Please post it back when read. She has never turned up, but still is away in the bush[;] her father asked to go & get her but he has not returned.

Mr I Taylor will wait till the December boat, cattle work not finished.

Miss Sherrin's sister will not be offering for Oenpelli.

Williams is leaving this trip the bishop's letter enclosed gives his reason we will leave it there.

NORMAN BELL Letter enclosed re minerals at Oenpelli .I think it is hardly likely to be there , but it is a fact we may always have to face in such matters I am blind, yet have my eyes open.

Mr Warren did quite a lot of useful work for us in Darwin & did not spare himself to help us . He may mention to you a lathe for sale in Darwin they want £30 but he thinks £25 would buy it ,if C.M.S could buy it it would soon save it[s] cost on engineering jobs.

Mr Webb writes to say ,they were forced back with the cattle on board to Goulburn Is[land] 5 of the cows have since died ,he asks me to hold over the bulls till he returns from South .

Pump It is very unfair to blame me I never bought the pump ,nor ever had any description of what it was like ,how could I order the parts & I had to cut up my saw belts as no belting was sent.I asked Mr Warren to get me a piece in Darwin to carry on,but he could notget it ,he will be asking you about it .Since then I have made a belt out of buffalo hide which is still working , but the real test is now on; if it stands up to the strain in the drying; if this is a success we need buy no more belts. I ordered two lengths of 3=" pipe to lengthen the suction of the other pump & when that was ordered the other pump was only in the air as a possibility.Before Danks pump had done twoweeks works two valves were out of action, I complained of bad workmanship in another letter & this is further evidence within as I will post back the pieces,I have made others but would be glad of new parts ,they are breaks with normal work & very small lift . The spring in question seems very weak for such a task. They ought to replace these.

Since typing this the pin holding […] *will not hold the nute slates on the thread; came loose in 1ˢᵗ 24 rows. would hold, now slates loose all the* […] *that makes 4* […] *threads in one* […]

<u>Boat</u> I wired without saying much as no wire is secret in Darwin[:] go ahead if the way opens with the sale of the Mary if you can get a thousand for her as Mr Warren says . When I asked for a boat it seemed the best way out of many problems, which have only increased in other ways . My Roper experience had not led me to expect what we have since learned . We had four men on the staff & after the first trip we ran it largely ourselves ,the engine was anold one when it was bought & gave very little trouble & it solved Roper transport & they have never had a real shortage since 1921 but plenty before . The river is the greatest problem here[,] the new fittings in shaft caused no trouble at sea but as soon as she got into the river Hermon said she started to leak & the boat was full of mud when we unloaded so I suppose she is worn eccentric again . The knock in the engine which has been there since the beginning with the load on is getting worse & that means expense & Darwin is so dear & often unsatisfactory at that.

<u>Coloured crews</u> cost more money than a missionary & are unsatisfactory they can't manage the natives & lately there has been such a lot of sickness in Darwin the crews have not been allowed to land the last 3 trips & they are dead scared of Darwin, they are two boys short this trip[–] they ran away before she got out of the river . Then again 3 trips they have only brought part of a load[.] I have asked them & Mr Beurteaux but it does not alter ,the wharf people tried to bluff me last trip but I made them bring down two more trucks ,& we have to pay out for the extra loading .

<u>River</u> is badly silted up this year we cannot get near the landing. we rushed the cargo off the boat lying on her side in the middle of the river the day of fullmoon to give them the 5 big tides to get out[;] we put on 60 buffalo hides& told them to get off, 5 tides later they sent up word to say they were still there stuck till newmoon .

This would have meant no Willie for the next trip as November is near so we went down with two tanks to float the stern up & all the men. I was feeling far from well & prayed for a tide[;] they got off without our help I am thankful to say.

<u>Laying up boat</u> I had hoped to be able to put her in a creek near landing but there is no hope now we can't get there , she could be kept at Smiths or Field Is but I could not trust blacks to be always there in time of need[;] they have not come to that stage yet unless it was at a place like Goulburn IS where they could be under someone's eye . Darwin seems the safest thing for the present .

It seems fairly safe to expect boats to bring stores to Smiths & there are several now in Darwin it would cut out untold trouble . A small launch to tow a punt which we could make ,there was one here when I came but rotten evidently[.] P. Cahil used it for such a purpose . A small ships boat with outboard engine would cut out gland trouble ,but maybe that would not give best service , at anyrate in small shaft the trouble would not be so great . At need it could do to Darwin as C FReer uses a launch 14ft to go in & out to Darwin from Wildman river several times a year[–] he hugs the coast . A motor track to Smith's is the only other way out that would be as far as to the coast except for 3 months of the year when it could be done under 25 miles .

<u>Miss Nevill</u> she told us it was the people more than the heat ,&she said the same in Darwin[;] it is well youshould know this. Still Mrs Dyer does not think she would have stood the heat as it was only cool weather when she was here & she certainly felt it very much .

We are praying about the matter of the boat that you may be guided aright in any decisions you may have to make .

Yours Sincerely
Alf Dyer[71]

---

71   ML MSS 6040/12.

Figure 5.67: Caryl/Karil (later Rachel) caring for young child, Injalak Hill in background (date unknown).
Source: Northern Territory Archives Service (NTRS 694 P1 Box 4b Item 289).

* * *

Oenpelli Report for August. September. October.

Early in August got the boat off with my father & Miss Nevill. Willie stayed to help in the garden having expressed a wish to do this, it gave him a chance to see if he could handle the people as they are a difficult people to keep on the move. After a few trys he managed very well & was a great help to me as they always work much better if some one is with them. With the help of my father we have had hundreds of lettuce, cucumbers, cabbage, turnips, tomatoes, melons etc[.] The new irrigation plant completed what watercan had begun, & is also keeping the nurseries of young plants ready for the Wet, a good root start makes all the difference. We are fencing in a large area which will give us quite 50 acres of fair soil. A large part of this is for rice. The small patch put in late last season produced 80 lbs from a small tin of seeds, a beginning we hope of bigger things. I have a small party on grubbing but a lot of the people are away. We have had already over 4 tons of sweet potatoes & there are still more to dig, but they are beginning to go off now & we have not found a way of keeping them. The porridge crop has cut out rice 4 or 5 mornings a week but is finished now. Quantities of fruit as pawpaws etc.

Stock.

Mustering has been carried on all through these months. We have over 150 killers ready for market & are waiting for a decision from the buyers. When our neighbours arrived they reported that there were a number of cattle on the other side of river & some killers, evidently some of those lost en route for Darwin last year. It took four trips to clean these up, owing to jungle & they had been speared by natives. The result was 59 without calves. 16 were killers[,] the rest cows, some of them probably lost by government drovers, but we have a gain of 43. I could only guess what came back last year but should say ww have most of them now. This & other work on station which had to be done has hindered us in our general muster.

We have got a number of clean skins this year, final figures will be sent on later. To fit in with the new garden we have altered the approaches to the yard & also the race to the dip which has saved as much as two hours time putting through a fair sized mob.

Engineering jobs have taken a good deal of our time. Arranging shaft & pulleys to work the pump, sawbench, small dynamo (which was give[n to] me in Melbourne) we have used it for charging our batteries,. Also the power grist mill given me by a friend is all arranged so that the steam or diesel engine can drive it, as well as for future expansion[.] The boat's gear box & shafts had to be taken down[,] fortunately I had Mr Warren's help in this.

Carts have almost made us despair. Every cart, but the lorry which the mules cannot pull through the sand, was broken. In the last four months Ion & I have easily spent six weeks trying to fix these as firewood, timber & stores have to be carried. They are so bad we can at best only patch them up for awhile.

Three neighbours arrived with three motor trucks opposite the landing[.] We have taken in a few buffalo hides for them as loading. We had thought we might shoot a hundred ourselves but got word no sale for hides this season.

Ladies have carried on as usual. Miss Sherrin has school in the morning & Mrs Dyer has the older ones in the afternoon. Besides house, dispensary, sewing etc. This is far too much for them to carry on long without a breakdown. The average has been close on 60 children throughout the year.

Timber[.] have got a good lot carted in but have not been able to touch buildings which are one of our greatest needs. The people are here to work among. The garden can be made to supply most of our needs as the results of last year on prove, most of which was planted when I was alone. My greatest problem was to get the ploughing done & you can't do it till the rain comes & then it is go or you lose your season. This year we will D.V. have the help of tractor. I have gladly given every ounce I have to make this huge task a success but two men cannot do it, & the ladies would have a big overtime sheet if they were working for the Government.

People[.] We see progress in the school & in their knowledge of the Bible. Some are trying to do the right. Some customs are breaking down & there is less wife beating. Two dormitory girls have been married during the year, not given to old men who had other wives though they had a claim to them. This is one of our biggest problems. I got them to give consent. One afterwards tried tricks to take the girl but failed as I had the biggest pull & the girls do not want the older man & they do not get full privileges unless one man one wife & that counts also. So generally speaking we are getting on to right lines but this is not the work of a day.

We have a good deal of the spirit of unrest. We have heard of bad blacks wanted by the police being on the reserve. Red ideas spread only too quickly. Several times there have been whispers of things not being their job etc. On Saturday night they were rude to Mrs Dyer demanding more pay as they were doing big work, it was carrying the stores & some of the best men were in it. I thought I would try & reason with them & this is how I went about it. Sunday the usual services nothing said. Told all the staff no bell on Monday morning & not my job to get breakfast. Mr Taylor & I lifed copper of rice into store.. The first faithful one came to light fires, she started trying to open the kitchen door, we were nearly bursting in bed, soon more came & more, all talking, The uppermost thought was King Bing, who had stolen the rice? none of them used their brains to look for tracks, more late ones arrive, gr[e]at bedlam. It made me think of the time our Lord spoke of when two shall be in a bed one shall be in one taken & the other left, what a day for scofrers & what joy for believers.. Then they thought of us, a gentle tap at the door then louder & louder, the door pushed open they did not see us & went away great talking, the rice still uppermost, they were walking about everywhere & around our house. Then some of the bolder ones came right in & saw us & tried to wake us up. I told them I wanted a good sleep & they had better wake Mr Taylor up, he had been watching the fun from his window so sneaked into bed again. Knock: knock: & it happened to be one of the ringleaders. Mr Taylor said roughly not my job. We heard them come back very crestfallen, conscience was at work. Then I rang the bell, called them all up & talked to them quietly about what it was all about. They well knew we work much harder than they do. Then I reminded them what they had experienced when it was stock station & what had been done for them & their children & how that cheek & abuse might bring that back & far worse, which they are well aware of. I told them to talk it over among themselves & we would go & have our breakfast & then come & get their reply. So after breakfast we went out again & they said they were very sorry & wanted us to stay & help them. Then we had a prayer & then the rice walked out of the store & then they went to look out our tracks & they have been better since. I hope it lasts but that is hoping too much without the changed hearts. This will be the last report for this year, so I have made the report a little fuller.

Yours sincerely
Alf Dyer[72]

Figure 5.68: Buffalo hides (date unknown).
Source: Northern Territory Archives Service (NTRS 694 P1 Box 2 Item 549).

***

72   NTRS 1099/P1 vol. 1.

Report on engine & Boat trip to Oenpelli June 1929

We slipped off the slip on June 12[th] at a great rate & did not float for some time, but bumped about for some time & had an anxious time but finally sailed off. We had the engine going nicely on the slip but when we wanted it then an airvalve jam[m]ed & we could not get the air till we let all the air go &fix it & blow it up again when we went to the jetty &loaded the tractor & oil engine & other cargo & left on June 13 th a bearing was running hot before we reached the hospital[;] we anchored & cooled off & then went on to East Point & anchored for the night & tried again in the morning but too hot so go back under sail as the pump had also failed us twice already. On arriving at the jetty we took it down & found no trouble except that the new washers put in seemed too hard so replaced the old ones after regrinding them & since then have had no further trouble with the pump, the mud box worked well & kept the mud out.

We started off again on June 14th after putting in different packing in. We left at 5.30 & went right on, passed the first Vernon Light at midnight & then on to Field Island reaching it a 4.30 on the 15th which in a straight line is 138 miles but tides & winds always carry you North & South in the Gulf, so we averagedover 6 knots, wind against us all the way at times very strong & choppy sea. Everything went well[;] the engine doing up to 580 revolutions per minute at times not quite full out as a slower speed is better for our purpose. The stern bearing near the mast kept fairly the mast, I kept a wet bag over it for a margin of safety & towards the end of the trip was cooler. We anchored off Field Is[land] as it was fullneap tide & loaded up with turtle eggs & fresh meat & finished up my final touch on the boat two days later we tried the river & got up on the tide from Sod Bay sticking in the mud in a few bad places, being 13 hours doing from Field Is to the landing.

On opening up the engine we found a good deal of carbon dry in No1 cylinder & very sticky treacle in No2 lots of it but not so much as last trip.

The dirty oil pump worked all the way, the air device to blow it out to clean acted well when blocked. The engine was run at about 130 F.H. but there is a lot more carbon than I care to see so if Fairbanbs [Fairbanks] Morse have any advise to give to remedy this I shall be glad to have it.

Yours sincerely
Alf Dyer

P.S.
Got pump going.
Said the cogs will fit with a little work as one hole is too small for shaft.
Alf Dyer

Tractor & MacDonald at Station all O.K.
Sending in load of potatoes will write later.[73]

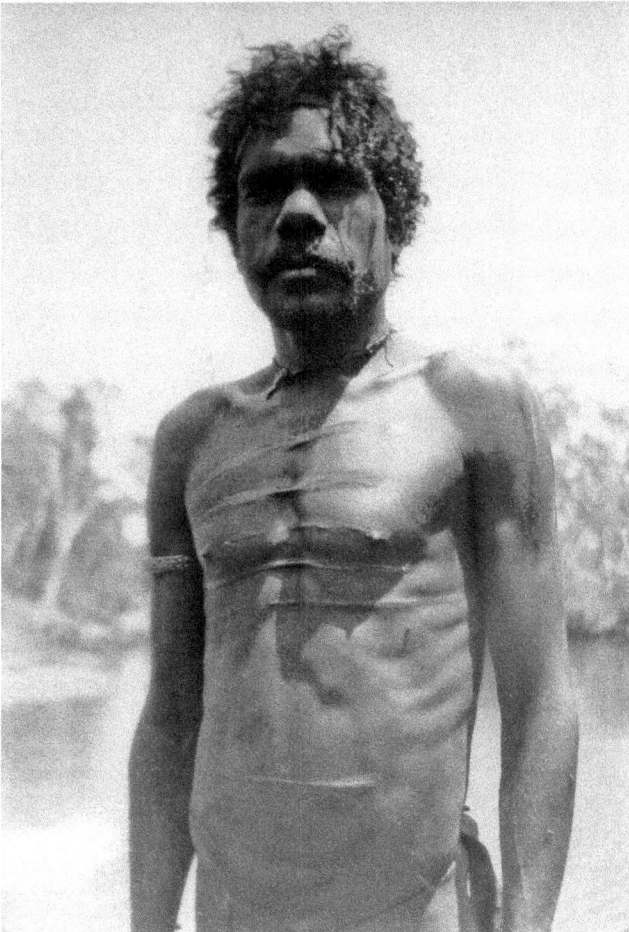

Figure 5.69: Worker on the mission (date unknown).
Source: Northern Territory Archives Service (NTRS 694 P1 Box 4a Item 162).

* * *

73   NTRS 1099/P1 vol. 1.

OENPELLI December 1929
PORT DARWIN

The General Secretary

Dear Mr Ferrier

All going well at Oenpelli, new party settling in a very happy company all hard at work . Very busy in the garden, thistime last year we had hardly begun ploughing , but this season with the help ofthe tractor we are well ahead with many new acres turned over .We have 4 acres of rice out & coming up ,2 acres of kaffir corn . 2 acres of Cotton. 1 acre of watermelons , & peanuts in single line 6 miles in length . 1 " of potatoes over 2000 sticks of cassava besides maize & beans sweet corn . We are still grubbing more ground so if the rains continue we shall D.V. have a bumper harvest. Large numbers of people are coming in for Xmas[.] There are over 70 children on the station now , & over 150 people on which has enabled me to geton with all this new garden[.] Mr Harris has been a tower of strength to me in this . Mr Clymo is busy building houses for the people & some natives are building theirs as I have pulled the old camp for garden site as the soil is wellenriched there.

Now we have to leave all these works to get ready for Xmas . Some Goulburn Is boys came over with a letter from Mr Bye & they say that the Mc Bride may go back to Darwin so I am sending on the chance of going to you in January. The staff are all well except little Audrey she has whooping cough ,but she is getting better now, she is a great attraction to the children .

All the staff send their greetings with many thanks for all the good things for Xmas ,we have to knock off other work now for it . Many sad cases in the dispensary at present . Trusting that the Lord has met all your needs .

Yours sincerely
Alf Dyer

P.S They say a boat is in at the docks tonight a neighbour I expect.
Alf Dyer[74]

***

---

74   ML MSS 6040/12.

OENPELLI Jan 29 1929
PORT DARWIN

Dear Mr Ferrier,

A reply to a few items in your last letters .

Manolios

I had the stern tube you me[n]tion cup up town & had a screw put on it[.] I can vouch for that for him .

Mary Allis over I trust[.] Mr Taylor did not write from Darwin , nor did Jolly so I have not heard any final news . We will have to arrange for a shed at Smiths when I know what the arrangements are , we have no means of getting iron there till the plains dry or the launch arrives . I do not know of any code of signals except keeping a blackfellow near a fixed date . The best would be wireless from Darwin , I believe Hugh Taylor made some arrangement about this, or as Groote Eylandt have arranged with 3 A.R. Melbourne to broad cast news every Friday night at 10 oclock . Our set is out of order[.] Ion knows what is wanted I will enclose a slip with a few needs to fix this .

Fences & Expenses

I will go into this matter in detail later . We should have a lot more food grown & boat costs should be much less .

Miss Sherrin I have not raised her hopes by telling her yet what you say[;] she is not well at present & it may be necessary so to act. Mrs Dyer is very run down also & the work is toolarge for two women now. Mrs Clymo is most willing & capable & the three are going all they know[.] Audrey brought whooping cough & all the family have it & are getting it[;] two children have died in 3 days & as I type they are going round the place with lights to chase the spirits away ,& they are saying we poison them etc .It is hard going in normal times for 3 with 70 odd children about , & I do not feel that I ought to lay such a burden on 2 & Mrs Dyer has done far more than she ought lately , & they are tasks that cannot be left undone. Hence if Miss Sherrin is well I will not say anything to Miss Sherrin as she expects to go just before the Wet . *WE NEED THREE WOMEN*

<u>Lathe</u> would be a great asset[–] the Darwin one dropped from £60 to £25. *I am told*

Mr Clymo has been 3 weeks today on a job a lathe would have done in a day & it is not finished yet , white metal wouldnot be safe on a sawbench job someone might get killed. So it was a scrapeing job & a very bad one[;] someone while I was South did not oil it & let it run hot ,it has never been run since as the boiler also went at the same time . You also know what a help it would have been on the Mary & such jobs are always turning up here . I will ask Mr Clymo to enclose his suggestions on lathe's Mr Warren would look about for you & give you good advise I would gladly leave it in his hands. He also knows the Darwin lathe[–] I do not .

<u>Log</u> I expect Mr Taylor took it down he knew you wanted a copy .

<u>Reports</u> You will get the years produce in annual report & number of people etc I try not to repeat myself too much

<u>Pump</u> is all O.K. now I hope for years of service .

<u>Launch</u> I have already written my views . Mr Clymo report of sea worthiness changed from Brisbane River to what he saw in the Gulf[:] cross waves influenced by big tides; & shallow; can be worse than the ocean . I do hope the days of mistakes are ended . Cheerio! With all good wishes

Yours sincerely.
Alf Dyer

PS
Mrs Dyer will write to Mrs Bragg re recipes[75]

---

75   ML MSS 6040/12.

Figure 5.70: Aboriginal man at the mission (date unknown).
Source: Northern Territory Archives Service (NTRS 693 P1 Item 21).

* * *

OENPELLI
February, 1, 1930

Report.

Re bearings on circular saw.

I very much regret to find it necessary to send in this report but do so to stress the need of the new bearings owing to the weakened state of the old ones just fitted. The saw will now be required a great deal for building work, and is absolutely essential to use for the next month or two ,and the cost of the bearings should not be great. £7/10/-

The trouble has been caused by not exercising proper care and attention running the saw till it was no longer possible,the bearings as a consequence being badly burnt.

The present bearings properly fitted as they are,are only 1/16th of an inch thick in the centre,which means that they will only last about four(4) months at the most,and should we not obtain the new brasses we so urgently need we will be forced to use white metal which will not be at all satisfactory and mean a great deal of attention.

To make the machine in good order has taken about ten(10) days since all the work has had to be done with file and scraper,but if we had had a lathe the work would have been completed in about a day and a half,time here just not being a very important factor.

we are enclosing a diagram with full measurements,and would esteem it a favour if you could give the matter your immediate attention and send us a new set as per attached diagram,sending the same as soon as possible.

If we could be so fortunate at a later date to possess a lathe we would be saved a great deal of time and worrybut of course it would haveto be fitted with a treadle as we have to consider the cost of running the engine.

Trusting you wil be able to see your way clear to assist us in this matter, and send us the new bearings at the earliest possible moment.[76]

***

---

76   ML MSS 6040/12.

OENPELLI Feb 5 1930
PORT DARWIN

Dear Friends

I[ ]do not know your names but I was asked to write and tell you how the billies got on, which Mr Ferrier brought up here . The worst of the hot weather is now over & they have come through & now look well, at first the heat & the mosquitoes troubled them very much & they got very thin but they seem well now & are with the mob and are not such pets as when they came,what results they will have on our herd is not yet evident but I expect it will be all to the good as we needed a change of blood .

The Rhode Island Reds did not stand up to the heat at all & were always sickly & miserable ,they eat their eggs so I was not able to get any chicks from them before they died . Mr Judson gave us some black orphingtons at the same time as yours ,they have done well[;] white leghorns do the best here . I am sorry I have not a good report to make of your kind gift ,but the goatswill be well worth while .

Our work is growing every hand we have about 80 o children about the place now & about 30 acres of foods & fruits now growing in our garden so I hope soon to be able to grow most of what we need with our own beef & goats ,many problems have yet to be overcome but with God's help we shall win through . Wishing you all every blessing from above from the Father of Lights .

Yours sincerely
Alf Dyer[77]

***

---

77   ML MSS 6040/12.

I have asked several times for a list of the names of those supported & by whom
please let me have it
Alf Dyer

February 5 30

Miss Barnes Long Gully

Dear Miss Barnes

Mr Ferrier has asked me to write to you about a child St Matthews have kindly sent in for the support of a child here. Narpyn was one of the first boys to come in ,he is reading & knows a good deal of the Old & New Testaments ,many of the songs of Zion & Psalms ,he is a son of the chief of the Oenpelli tribe about eleven years of age & learning to be useful in the garden with the harrows & plough ,they all love to work with horses but not much yet confessed with his lips, but the seed of the word of God has been faithfully sown in his heart & you must join with us in your prayers that the work of grace may be completed . Most black children are very deceitful & he is no exception to the rule as lying to them is rather a code of honour , & much that we call darkness , all these things are not put away in a day ,only prayer & God's grace changes these things so we are always glad to know that our hands are being strengthened by others in God to destroy the work of the devil . Wishing you & all that labour with you in this work every blessing .

Yours sincerely
Alf Dyer[78]

***

---

78   ML MSS 6040/12.

Feby 10 1930

R.H. Weddell Esq
Government Resident Darwin

Sir

Mission Station Report

Your usual request for annual report on Oenpelli Mission has no come to hand but I am sending it on as usual .

(A) Receipts & expenditure for the year 1929

For these figures I must again refer you to C.M.S 242 Castlereagh St Sydney as all accounts are dealt by them direct .

(B) Buildings & Assets

Buildingsare as per last years report with the exception of two native houses 12feet x 12 ft the reason for this is that 2 men can only just carry on all the general work of the station & these two were put up by the arrival of a new man in December .

An engine workshop was also started.

Implements

The following have been added to past lists

2 Sections of springtooth harrows
1 Single furrow plough
1 Lorry & many small items

Boat

The Mary has been sold as we found the running costs to heavy. The mud also in the river ground out the shaft nearly every trip causing costly repairs . We hope to charter a boat to the mouth of the river & then launch up the goods with a launch to arrive soon.

(C) Area under cultivation

This has been increased to about 30 acres with hope of getting a little income from peanuts & cotton also to increase our food supply . 15 acres were grubbed & cleaned up this year .

Stock

Goats   180
Horses   110
Cattle   1407 bangtail muster

These figures as less than the last report for reasons Captain Bishop can give you details if you wish .

(E) Aboriginals.

1. 1926   15 boys   7 girls
    1927   26 "   11 "
    1928   32 "   18 "
2. Number inDormitory
    1929   36 boys   22girls

These numbers fluctuate as will be understood with Aboriginals

(3) Ablebodied

Since growing more of our own foods we have been able to increase the number have had up to 80 working at a time for weeks but the average for the year would be 50.

4 Infirm several have died leaving us 6 who come & go more about.

(F) Technical Education.

All the small children have morning Kinderarten. In the afternoon school is held to give them a simple education, a knowledge of the 3R's. Farming, cattle work, boat work & household work, harness repairs & assisting in building & engine work, is all we are able to cope with at present.

Industrial activities.

Garden work all through the year. One new cattle yard & repairs to the old ones. 5 miles of new fencing has been put up & repairs. New diesel irrigation plant & pump has been put up, which will help in the growing of food, also, cutting timber for new buildings on the saw bench. Boat repairs.

(H)

Staff,   Rev. A. J. Dyer

Mrs. Dyer

Miss F. Sherrin

Mr. G. R. Harris

Mr. E. J. Clymo

Mrs. Clymo.

Enclosed is a seperate report which deals in a more general way with the years doings.

Yours sincerely,
Alf Dyer[79]

* * *

OENPELLI. North Australia. Feb '30

The last few months have brought to us a good number of new children[.] There has been resident on the station between 70 & 80 children straining our accommodation to its limits. For a greater part of the year two men carried on the work of the station. Agricultural, cattle, repairs, also helping in the shipping at Darwin, so building work had to be left undone till a new man arrived in December, when two people's houses were put up, it takes tow men to keep things going as all the work has to have our help, we cannot leave any task wholly to them yet. The ladies have had more than they could do feeding this big family, with sewing, school & dispensary, the latter has been a very busy place. This year there has been much sickness, each time the boat came it brought colds or flu, that means all the people get it besides all the gruesome sores of the bush & leprosy, many needing much grace to attend to. Then Xmas brings many extras, boxes to be unpacked, bags to be got ready for the day, then the writing of letters to thank friends who have sent gifts with a photo of the people, these are done at night after one has been going for 14 hours on general work, which often means at the end, to get mail, reports & orders done one has to take a couple of days off to get the task finished, before the mail leaves on its 60 mile's walk on two legs to the coast to Goulburn Is. Mission who kindly take it for us to Darwin in their lugger.

---

79   NTRS 1099/P1 vol. 1.

Generally we see progress, we have increased our garden this year by 15 acres which means we have about 30 acres under cultivation largely food stuffs, also some cotton & peanuts for sale, 5 acres of this is rice, representing a lot of labour to get heavy speargrass land ready, early rains bogged the tractor so the ploughing could not be done thoroughly & poor seed only about 35% coming up, but it will be all to the good, as we have learned what to do, & the ploughing will be easier. Also we shall have our own seed as my trial lot from last year came up well this year. So with the prospect of plenty of corn potatoes, cassava & some rice, our food bill will not be increased though we have so many more people. We have about 200. 5 year old bullocks ready for the market in good condition, if we get a sale which should mean a fair income, it would be at Sydney prices as they are big beasts & fat.

A lot of work has been done, grubbing, weeding, fencing in new paddocks about 5 miles in all, repairing cattle yards & making new ones. Setting up a new diesel irrigation plant, a small lighting plant besides numerous small tasks, such as helping to put in new shafting into the boat, refitting the engine room when the builders were putting a new keel on her with rudder & stern post.

The place looks very pretty now with the growing trees, shrubs & flower[.] We have gathered large quantities of fruits & vegetables here are some of them, tomatoes, cucumbers, melons, pumpkins, cabbage, turnips, kohlrabi, lettice & numbers of small things. The fruit has been thousands of mangoes, 771 pawpaws, 75 doz. bananas, pineapples, custard apples, soursops, bullocks hearts, lemons, cocoanuts, rockmelons, and now with irrigation, we shall be able to do better, & the tractor gave us a big pull up as horses cannot stand much work here.

People_ We have had up to 150 all told, being fed & working, the average has been well over the 100 daily for the year. Some do a fair day[']s work, most are very lazy & take a lot of pushing, but we keep on with the stir up & get a little out of them, they have their children with them with whom we hope to do better things. They have a Kindergarten in the morning, the older ones work in the morning & have school in the afternoon, we see many improvements, but they are not easy people to help, because they are not keen to help themselves.

They sing well and remember easily & some are reading, but it is very hard to get them to use their brains, this falls on the teacher to make them, but they are getting a knowledge of the 3Rs.

In the daily services they are learning to know their Old & New Testament[,] a book that has made & unmade nations. They are not a grateful people they soon forget their benefits & demand more than we are able to give them, for £ s d. plays a large factor in developing the white child's activities,we do to the extent, we are able by a small pocket money allowance for those who work well, by this means, they are able to buy mosquito nets & other things, but human like they want more, but the spirit of cheerfulness would lighten our burdens, that joy is a gift from God not yet come to them. Our task is to go on as those who do not look back but up. There are plenty of problems yet to solve, such as, some with 4 & 5 wives, & some with none, a number have agreed to have only one. Old men taking young girls for wives, are largely being solved by feeding the old people. Cattle spearing is hard to stop on 2000 sq. miles of country & no fences beyond, but they are learning there are consequences, as we often find out & they are dealt with when caught. The latest arrivals to our staff brought a little girl 4 years old who had the germ of whooping cough which developed here, we knew too late to isolate her, all the family got it, many would have died without medical attention, this is another factor why black races need help against white man's diseases. 3 babies have died & the ladies have been run off their legs. The people got wind up properly & have been going round the place with fires to chase the devils away.

The new garden as made on the old camp site, & they blamed that also for the sickness, & many have gone bush till the trouble is over.

So mixed up is truth & untruth in human hearts, but truth always wins in the end, so we press on knowing that the light will dispel the darkness as the sun does the night.[80]

***

---

80   NTRS 1099/P1 vol. 1.

Oenpelli Report for December, January, March. 1930

During December Mr Harris & I were largely occupied with the new garden: grubbing & preparing about 15 acres. Also ploughing the old garden & planting out etc. Mr Clymo put up two new houses for the people. Early rains in November had blocked us getting any more timber across the plains. Ladies were busy putting away stores & Xmas things in between the usual tasks. Mrs Clymo took over the afternoon school[;] Miss Sherrin still continued the morning school. Other reports cover the balance of this month's doings & the event of Xmas. The numbers were not as large as last year but still enough to tax our Xmas supplies to the full. Before Xmas we had as many as 150 people including the children who with the babies numbered just on 80.

About this time Audrey Clymo developed whooping cough & it soon spre[a]d to the people who developed it, in many cases, with serious symptoms, malaria was bad also. One baby whom they treated in the black way died, another child had dysentery with it & the mother did not tell us till too late, also died, & Carabumba's baby only a few days old. She herself has been very ill with it & fever.

February it rained every day & with floods there has been much fever. Many were frightened especially after a little boy was drowned in the billabong, so they went bush, we have fewer children in the dormitories than since the early days. School had to be stopped as all were sick, & Miss Sherrin had it, Mrs Dyer & Mrs Clymo had their hands more than full looking after the sick day & night, both were very tired after it all. We would have had to send some away ere this to ease the flour supply as it would not have lasted out among so many. We have killed two cows nearly every week, we have lots of old ones that will breed no more calves & would go off & die out bush later & we would lose the hide. We have only killed one bullock so far this year.

January & February the garden claimed most of my attention & Mr Harris's also. Then leeches & cancer became so bad that we had to put all the men on horse paddock fences, under Mr Harris's supervision this was completed in Feb. using mostly the old wire in pieces & there is a mile or so of it still left. Mr Clymo was busy on engineering jobs connected with the saw bench, pulleys etc. & putting tools in order.

We experienced severe floods which lasted all through February, covering the rice & up into the mangoes. Then on March 6th we had a flood that rose higher than ever before in the history of Oenpelli as far back as the blacks know. Once in Cahill's time it came to the front verandah but this rose right into the blacksmith's shop. When the water reached the dispensary we started to put things higher up on shelves in case it rose, but it stayed there till evening. While we were having our prayer meeting it rained heavily 3 inches in a very short time. As we rose from prayer it was coming into the dining room & soon after it was right round the house. After putting things up on tables there were goats to be got out of the paddock, we lost some forty through the floods then the salt & cement had to be raised up on boxes & it was well into the morning ere all was safe. The people were very excited rushing up for the children, but they were all safe, the girls were with Miss Sherrin. The waters went down a little through[ou]t the night but rose again on Saturday, remaining in the house most of Sunday[,] gradually receded by the 12[th]. No stores were damaged, only the mess & unpleasentness & the extra work clearing up. In the garden the loss is great. We averaged nearly an inch a day for over a month. We could not walk on the garden nor nor work to fight the weeds; things got waterlogged & did not grow, so there is very little food left on the area not covered by the water. On the flood area it is nearly all dead loss. A number of trees 7 shrub died, all the pawpaws, & we must have had over 1000 fruit showing & a lot almost ripe, lots of the cassava & potatoes too. The rice was well covered for over a month, a number seeded through the water, but the geese came in hundreds & ate them off, I cannot find one head, many of the plants are still growing, the hand planted ones showing best. Crows finished the maize when it was only half formed. I planted several acres of Kaffir corn, but this also suffered, hundreds of pigeons, crows & cockatoos would have finished it for us, they would not be driven away, we tried to poison them but not much success & we could not spare the cartridges to shoot them, so we were forced to cut it green & only a little at that with twice as much in as ever before. The floods have made the birds so much worse this year as all their usual feeding grounds were covered. Cotton was a complete failure, the soil in the new garden is too poor for it but will be all right for peanuts in a normal season; this year they rotted in the ground 6ft above flood level. We have also now a plague of rats. It is all very sad as most of our hard work has failed this season & our food supply will be limited. Actual results will follow later.

The sickness is about finished, we have heard of 3 more deaths in the bush. Very few children remained here which was a mercy during the floods, also from a store point of view as we could not have kept on the large family we had at the end of the year. General routine has been al[l] upset, no school was possible they were all so sick; the people too with the sickness & the rains were difficult, we have had to drive many to save their lives as they clung to the black Dr. who did plenty of sucking & they can feel that & he generally has something to show. When some of the children came back towards the end of the month & we had got over the flood mess we thought school ought to be started, but all were tired & Miss Sherrin had fever with the cough & I thought it would be good for the staff to have a few days spell away before starting afresh.

Thousands of fish about & the people were asking to go fishing, so we let them go & tucker themselves for 10 days. Mr & Mrs Clymo with Miss Sherrin went camping. Mr Harris went to visit some neighbours to see if he could help in any way. We carried on here with a few, so I hope we will soon be normal again now. We had hoped with more food supply to have increased the family, buildings restrict us in this as yet.

This is not a very cheerful report but in spite of hindrances we believe, as it is promised, "All things work together for good."

Yours sincerely
Alf Dyer[81]

Figure 5.71: Group of children and men with Audrey Clymo seated in centre at front, 1930.
Source: Northern Territory Archives Service (NTRS 694 P1 Box 4b Item 291).

81   NTRS 1099/P1 vol. 1.

Figure 5.72: Elizabeth Garabbunba ('Carabumba') (date unknown).
Source: Northern Territory Archives Service (NTRS 694 P1 Box 4a Item 223).

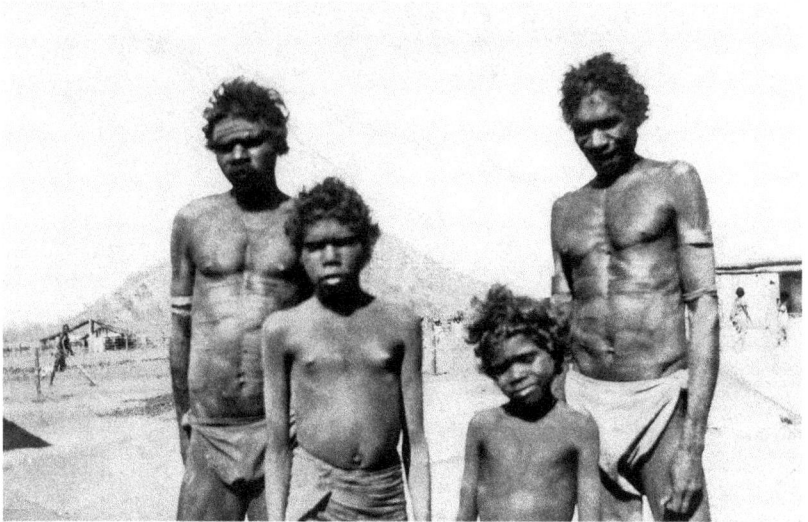

Figure 5.73: 'Black Dr who threatened to kill me brings his 2 children in[.] Notice heathen faces' (date unknown).
Source: Northern Territory Archives Service (NTRS 694 P1 Box 4a Item 172).

* * *

OENPELLI APRIL 8 1930
PORT DARWIN

General Secretary
Sydney

Dear Mr Ferrier

Enclosed you will find a report giving details of our doings here . Rev Jarvis sent word over from Goulburn Is early in March saying we might expect a mail anyday but it has not arrived yet . He came out with a Dr to operate on Mrs Bye who had been for weeks at death's door ,the Mc Bride went in for them but met bad weather & was damaged so they came in the Mareebut forgot our mail, the new folk are all pretty hungry for theirs. The Maree took the Bye's into Darwin & Mr Jarvis stayed . Mrs Bye's sickness was brought on by attending to sickness among their people severn [seven] of whom died .

A most unusual flood has destroyed the garden , so most of our food has been destroyed , I will regulate the family so as to carry on with what is coming . But I will have to increase the order for flour & rice for the Wet Season if we are to take in the children as they come back . If for any reason you are not able to do this we will just have to carry on as a small family . You will let me know at your earliest what I am to do & I can also advise the people what to do . It will mean that we shall need 6 tons of flour & 2 tons of rice to do this . With the smaller family we have at present we have sufficient to last till the end of July, but in the order coming [...] ordering we made allowance for a good supply from the garden so it will mean there will be very little left when the Wet season supplies come,with the extra ton you brought we had a ton & a half to carry over on to the Wet stores last year .

April 11th mail has just arrived the only note we have from C.M.S is dated December 16th[;] we have mail from Melb written in March ,Ion has not written, nor Mr Beurteaux, so like Topsy I know nothing,being a letter mail only we have no Gleaner also so it is all so dark . In this letter you mention Miss Sherrin she is well again and she has agreed to stay on till the Wet season boat arrives about October, unless anything happens to cause another decision .

Miss Nevil[l] has also written to me asking about returning ,we have no objections if she thinks she can face the heat[–] she was here in the best time of the year, & aboriginal work is always difficult & not to[o] many bright sides , the issue remains with herself & the C.M.S.

Allis going on happily here ,except the response of the people towards the spiritual, we are having special prayer to that end this week.Trusting that your many needs are being supplied.

Yours in 'The blessed hope'
Alf Dyer[82]

***

82   ML MSS 6040/12, p. 28.

Oenpelli

So far 1930. has brought to us many troubles, 15 acres of new garden has been grubbed & some trees that were on the old camp sites were sacred trees in which spirits lived, I was not informed of this till they were down & about to be burnt, then they asked me not to burn them there as some would die, I respected their wishes & burnt them further away. At Xmas whooping cough developed & they all got it & it lasted till April, the ladies had a very anxious time & several babies died, also others out bush, the camp people were most difficult to help.

The fault generally was their own ideas about sickness & some said our medicines were poisonous, & refused to come for them, they had firmly fixed in their minds that the trees chopped down would cause death, one night they went out with fires to chase the spirits away, – these people lie down o[n] things quickly & will not move to help themselves. Some of the dormitory girls were very sick with malaria & other troubles, they were most difficulty to help & not a smile only whine all the time, & did not seem to care if they lived or died, they were deep down in the valley of the shadow. Carabumba who was married last year had a bonny baby just before she took it whooping cough, the baby died.

I was coming back from burying one child & she died in our house before my return, we had prayer with them & tried to comfort them.

I told them to get her ready for burial in the afternoon, the grandfather took her & wanted to put her up a tree with native rites.

We waited half an hour at the grave, no sign of them coming, so guessing a hitch I went to see what could be done & plead for a decent burial for the little one, like Michael, over the body of Moses won.

Then the big floods came right through the house & practically destroying all the food in our gardens, all our hard work to grow plenty all gone. Great excitement happened the night of the big waters, the blacks rushed up to carry away their children, we had them all safe, it was very funny to see them peering into the empty dormitories, they were in Miss Sherrin's house which was higher, some were carried to the camps, Carabumba among them & there she wanted to stay so she could dodge taking medicine. I went & brought her back, but again she went to camp, by this time she had lost over two stone & had to be brought back again & forced to eat & be cared for, at times before this there had been indications of a desire for a higher life, but seemed lost. At last the whoops weakened & she grew stronger, & now she has come to ask for baptism[;] a very real change has come over her, with her came 6 others. Elwyndiwyndi, a little tartar, the ladies were almost in despair with the cheek & disobedience, constant punishing seems to make no difference, at times it seemed real demon possession, I told them all publicly that we would not take cheek from anyone, it either meant obedience or go & cheek the trees as much as they liked, one or two women paid the penalty, but the grace of God is the only real remedy.

To this end we decided to spend Good Friday after the people's service as a day of prayer and meditation on the Cross, our prayers to be definitely confined to our people, women & girls in the morning, men & boys in the afternoon, all being mentioned by name, & before we had all met together fo[r] our weekly prayer meeting again, which was because we were separated, the answer had come. This child since coming to ask for baptism had been like an angel, most willing & faithful, others too, some of the others are younger & probably come because of the others, but time proves all things, there names are–

Carabumba, Elwyndiwyndi, Elmynjalinmag, Garijala, Galinower, Jaragalgal, Garynjulu.

We see many changes in the older ones, but these young ones may help them to come out especially if they remain faithful.

Will you help them & us in your prayer.
Alf Dyer[83]

---

83 NTRS 1099/P1 vol. 1.

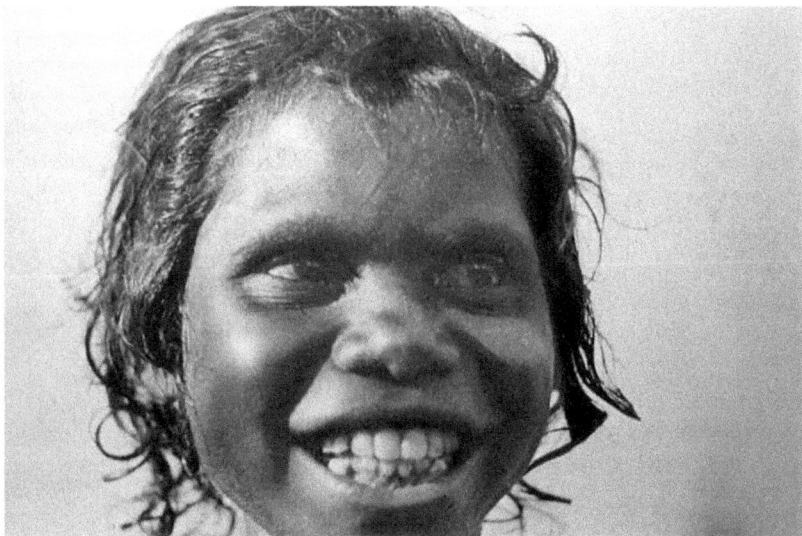

Figure 5.74: Elwyndiwyndi, 1926.
Source: Northern Territory Archives Service (NTRS 694 P1 Box 4a Item 235).

Figure 5.75: Garijala one of the first pupils helping to teach a class (date unknown).
Source: Northern Territory Archives Service (NTRS 694 P1 Box 4 Item 66).

Figures 5.76a and 5.76b: Joseph and Elizabeth Garabbunba ('Carabumba') (date unknown).
Source: Northern Territory Archives Service (Left: NTRS 693 P1 Item 21; Right: NTRS 694 P1 Box 4a Item 217).

* * *

C.M.S.
Oenpelli
May 20th 1930

Dear friends & co-workers,

There will probably be a mail in a few days so I am trying to get delayed mail ready. The last few months have been, I think, the most trying I have spent in the Territory. We commenced the New Year with an epidemic of whooping cough which lasted till the middle of April. Some were very ill with it & fever, some also showed symptoms of pneumonia, with a few I was really afraid of T B. but most of them seem to be really getting stronger again & putting on flesh.

February & March were very wet months, rain almost every day for six weeks. While the cloudy weather certainly kept temperature down, everything was damp & moist, the odour of decaying vegetation was very disagreeable. During March we had a flood; the waters rose higher than ever before in the history of Oenpelli & for several days were through the main mission house, girl's dormitory & other buildings, those on the new site were quite alright. Of course that did not improve the health of the sick ones. As most of the natives were ill in varying degrees we were short handed in the kitchen & for almost all the work, school of course was suspended. The flood ruined the garden & we had hoped to have more food this year for people, had planted such a lot of potatoes, last year a row produced 200lbs. this year two rows are only producing 25lbs. & very stringy ones. Kaffir corn is a failure, also maize, rice was under water for weeks but now seems to be looking up a bit. The wet season came to a very abrupt end about March 20th only a couple of showers after that & nothing in April which is rather unusual.

During the flood most of the casual workers who were able went bush taking their children with them, partly from fear of what was going to happen, so Mr & Mrs Clymo with Miss Sherrin took all the girls in the dormitory for a camp & after Easter Mr Dyer & I went away for 12 days & camped only a couple of miles away, but it was out of sight & sound of mission & we both felt better for it. Mr Harris went out with stock boys to burn around yards & pick up parcel & paper mail at Goulburn Is. the letters came just before, the first for the year, & with them came another epidemic, influenza, & almost all the family have or have had severe colds, some nearly as bad as when they had whooping cough, they are recovering now.

After Easter Mrs Clymo & Miss Sherrin started school again, the former has the older children in the afternoon & Miss Sherrin kindergarten for the younger ones, there are not nearly as many as we had, but we have 11 in the girls dormitory & 12 in the boy's & 6 who come to kinder who are not in the dormitoties yet. Three girls who were in the dormitory have married during the last year. Elmareri, Carabumba, & Jaragalgal[.] Carabumba married a dormitory boy Gamarad, Jaragalgal married the youngest of the stock boys, he has been with us ever since we came here, they seem very happy. The other children will no doubt come back later. We feel the people going was really overruled as it would have been impossible to have kept so many with the failure of the garden; we have some 70 now & we had between 140 & 150. We still have enough flour with the family we have, to last till the end of June.

We have had many trials & sorrows during the year, but the week before last we had great joy when seven girls came to Mr Dyer & said they wanted to be baptized & to follow Jesus, they really seem as if they mean it. They have at various times seemed near the Kingdom, but we never like to force things as it would be easy for them to say it, just to please us. Then during the sickness they were trying & so difficult to help & it almost seemed as if it was in vain trying to. There is a very marked change in some of them; we feel that it is in answer to prayer many are praying for us & our people. On Good Friday we spent the day in prayer especially for our people & each was remembered by name & within 3 weeks the answer came with the first fruits & we do praise God for it & you who help us I am sure will rejoice & praise Him too. Elwyndiwyndi is one that we notice a great change in & she is the making of a fine character, if she allows God to have His way in her, Caramumba, Elwyndiwyndi, Garynjulu, Jaragalgal, Garijala, Galinower, & Elmynjalilmag, are those who have come. Please continue to pray for them, also for the others & for us, that we may be faithful sowers of the Seed & not grow weary.

With loving greetings to all & praying you too may have abundant joy in Christ Jesus.

Yours in His glad service.
M. C. Dyer[84]

---

84   ML MSS 6040/12.

Figure 5.77: Aboriginal man at mission (date unknown).
Source: Northern Territory Archives Service (NTRS 694 P1 Box 4a Item 157).

* * *

C.M.S.
Oenpelli
May 22nd 1930

Dear Miss Harper,

There will not be time when boat comes to write & I have nothing to answer, so just a wee note to go with the circular. You will rejoice I am sure at its news – Some how I felt before we came back we had trials awaiting us & it has just seemed all through as if we had been attacked by Satan. Just before the girls came or rather before we went for our camp Mr Dyer was not well & he was very despondant & said it did not seem any use trying to help people who did not want to be helped & is it not often just like that? The Lord's opportunity just when all seems failure & so we take courage & press on. He is able to do exceeding abundantly above all we can ask or think. The weather is pleasant now though of course in the middle of day it is often 100° but mornings & evenings are perfect & it is dry heat. The mosquitoes are very troublesome though Mr Harris & Mrs Clymo have quite settled in & are happy in the work, I think – Miss Sherrin is well & looking forward to going South before next Wet. While the [...] is with us am trying to get all the extra things that are impossible with only two women done. Some of the girls have begun to learn to machine & will be able to help in that later[.] Please give my love & greetings to all in office & depot. With love

yours in Him
M. C. Dyer[85]

***

---

85   ML MSS 6040/12.

Oenpelli
via Darwin
May 24th 1930

Rev. J W Ferrier
C M S.
Sydney.

Dear Mr Ferrier,

A second mail has just come from Goulburn Is. & still nothing from the office, only Darwin letters came last mail but in April we had letters from Melbourne. Jan, Feb, March Mr Taylor did not write so I know nothing since he left, fortunately Mr Beurteaux enclosed your wire re-cattle, launch & Mr Taylor. One mail I know you have with annual reports, another large mail for you has been waiting at G.I. for 2 months, owing to McBride being held up over court cases. In that you will have reports which are sad reading, March brought big floods twice right through the houses & into the sheds. The only real damage is that our crops were destroyed, so instead of having large quantities of food we have practically none, for even the parts above flood level were so sodden with water that nothing grew. I am keeping the family small at present. I will keep it so to make the stores coming see us through till the wet stores come. There are numbers of children [out] bush but the parents like to work while they are here, still we shall endeavour to get them & leave them with us, but it means more stores of rice & flour for the wet if we are to invite them in again; if this is not possible we must just go on in a small way. In a normal season we can grow rice, since the floods, which covered the rice for a month, but I would also like a sack of seed rice for next season. Peanuts will do well on the old camp site but not cotton. Such a flood as this has not been known before, so next season's crop should be normal & what I have been aiming should succeed, as an act if God frustrated it this year. In the other letter I have asked for 6 tons of flour instead of 4 or 5 as in other years, & two of rice as we have very little corn instead of one. that is for the coming order, let me know if this is possible at your earliest, if not I will just regulate here as we are able.

All is going on well except that mail brought a very bad flu & all got it, yards are reconstructed, garden being restored, engine house & machinery put in order, floods upset some foundations. The ladies are catching up on tasks waiting long to be done, Red Lily fence is done & now it is the cattle work, put up new fence & get on to buildings, we are doing engine house in between many jobs, enclosed you will find a report on the pump.

I asked for this coming boat to come to the landing[.] I cannot see how we shall get heavy stuff into a small launch it means a punt, the Mac Donald will not work saw enough H P. and kero. was used in ploughing besides floods hindered doing this if we had the time or the material; all Mr Clymo's time has been spent in repairs, mine in the garden, so buildings seem doomed, & this place is not dry or safe lots of things have to be done & I am not as strong as I was. There has been sickness amongst horses & some 20 have died.

Cattle – you have a copy of Mr Beurteax enclosed, it might be better to cut the price in Darwin if shipping fails, or some outlet might be found Catherine way to be drove overland with others, you & Mr Beurteaux must act & let me know promptly.

You will be gladdened as we were after a time of many sets back to know seven girls have sought after baptism, we are most thankful to God for this, as work here has been extremely difficult, with the unrest of the times. Trusting to hear from you soon.

Give our greetings to all & we pray that the many needs may be supplied.

Yours sincerely
Alf Dyer[86]

---

86   ML MSS 6040/12.

Figure 5.78: Aboriginal man from mission (date unknown).
Source: Northern Territory Archives Service (NTRS 693 P1 Item 21).

***

OENPELLI MAY 29 1930
PORT DARWIN

Rev J .W Ferrier
C.M.S Sydney

Dear Mr Ferrier

Your air mail letter arrived last night . Our reports of floods herein March
& the destruction of the crops , Have been at Goulburn Is since March so
have typed another copy as Mr Rilstone is very anxious about it missing
as she is 17days overdue between the other station. a sweep carried on her
deck has been picked up on the beach .

Mr Warren Glad to hear he was able to return , I fear he was misjudged in
some things , strange I hear from two sources in this mail ,that soon he is
coming to bump me out here , queer what little birds tell.

Launch Trust that she shall fulfil,all we expect of her .I am wondering if
you made any provision for the mud wear on the shaft[.] I hope so . And
I was hoping she would be coppered the borer is so bad on a stationary
ship . Other problems now commence & cannot anchor her on the banks
of the river at Smiths[−] you know the dangerous tide[;] so we ought
to have a ding[h]y to get in & out to her so it looks like a dingy, then
there is the making of a dinghy-punt cutting trees getting in sawing up
& making it[;] looks like 2 months for one man ,then the shed at Smiths
& a landing! can see another month gone with that & the carting up the
stores from there this time with launch only this time .

Mr Harris will be on cattle all the time,& one man to run the station it
means we remain where we are for buildings and they are so important

Mr Taylor Has not written to me but sent a wire re Dr saying letter
following .

Miss Nevill I have already written you but it is at G. Is . saying we are
agreeable if you are,only be sure on health grounds .

Miss Dove We also heard that she was coming ,but she tells she is going
to England & her future was not clear ,she felt when trying to come here
God was leading her here time will show .

Tractor I knew nothing of tractors when we bought , she slips a bit but does the work , the catorpillar will be useful in boggey ground but we will manage without (I do need if you can a motor truck,) she is too expensive for drawing timber & we have not got the kero ,doing Red lily fence 4 mules could only pull 15 posts , they are poor ,have sore shoulders .one has cancer another is dead ,so we are in a bad way for haulage & we have only have about 2 months we can get building timber across the plains . There are two Ford motor trucks lying idle on the other side of the river, both men are poorly off with no buffalo hidesales . I have never mentioned the matter to them . It might be a way out ,I have mail this time saying no mules for sale at present , I quite realise the £ & d factor but the problem is a real one .

Cattle I advise a cut price in Darwin if other ways do not open , still they will keep till next year . We will bangtail again this year & check figures ,there are none near Mr Sunters camp ,all the usual grounds were covered butit is easy to miss on 4000sq miles .

Buildings The question of buildings your suggested plan will not suit the requirements , but we will drawup a new plan much reduced in size , I will send plans next mail. These buildings[,] the timbers are rotten & could only be renewed by practically rebuilding & that in dry weather. it would be a big job & only like putting a new patch on an old garment & spoil new iron, as the holes are in various places all over. Buildings are most important & yet we cannot seem to get at them, & tasks already mentioned seem to engulf the next months.

Stores. Note re various items will await arrival. 10 coils of wire will complete the fish creek fence, Red Lily is finished & we hope to start the other fence now, other items ought to right.

Lathe Hope you can get it , have had such a lot of lathe work lately.

Wireless We only asked for a battery, I wish now I had ordered one myself, then we might have had the pleasure now, there is too much static during the wet.

Saw Bearings Will be glad to have them they seem to be very costly still such things are.

Mary Yes, sails & things were rotten they were never renewed, I thought he would be buying with his eyes open, Mr Warren knew her condition.

Children supported I do not favour such, but requests, still they seem to keep coming.

Estimate Will be cut down, by 2nd class fares, Mr Taylor's allowance roofing iron, but owing to floods we need more flour & rice still can reduce family, to suit with no real hardship to them, as they have plenty of food in the bush, you must be guided by your finances.

Will close now as G Is boys are waiting to go ,no sign of the boat & it may go that way first ,have another copy for the other way . Cheerio!

May the Lord supply all yours needs , remembrances to all the staff

Yours sincerely
Alf Dyer[87]

---

87   ML MSS 6040/12.

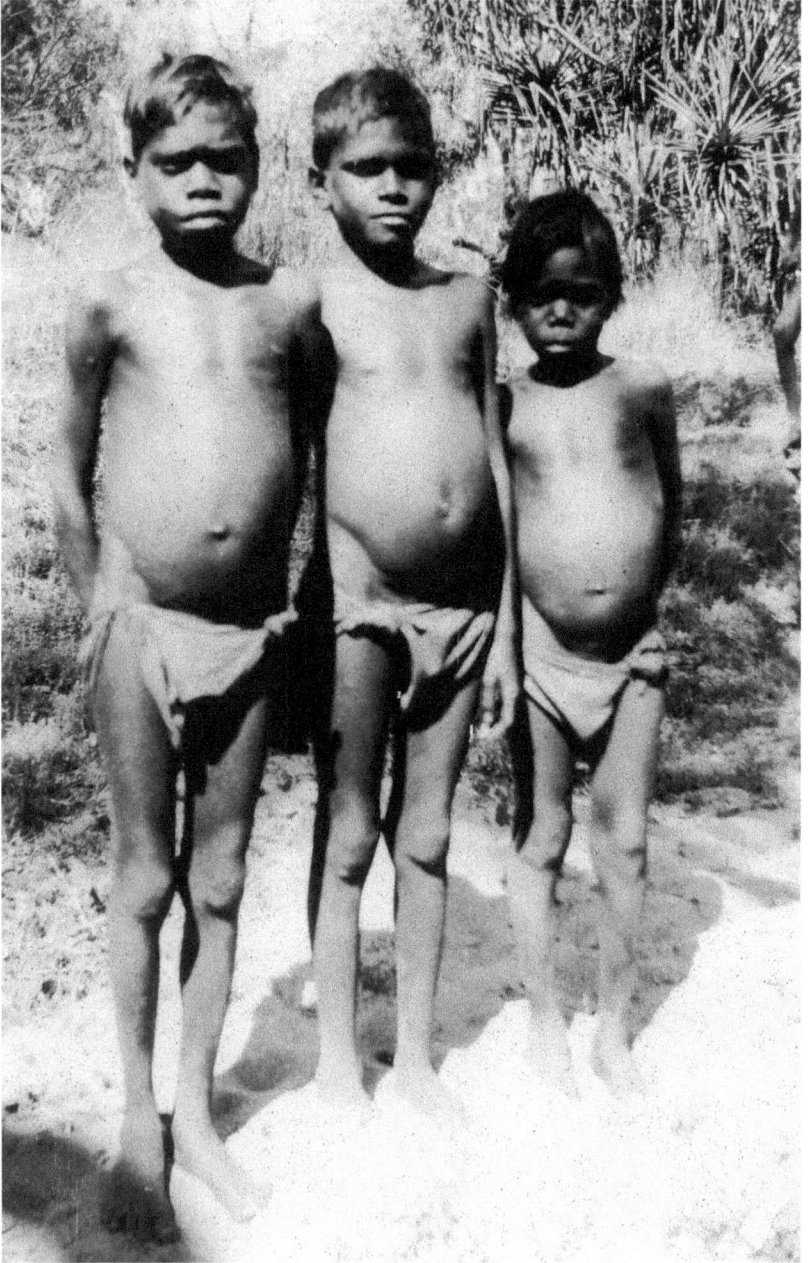

Figure 5.79: Three young boys (date unknown).
Source: Northern Territory Archives Service (NTRS 694 P1 Box 4a Item 161).

***

OENPELLI JUNE 17 1930
PORT DARWIN

Arthur Yates & CO
Sydney

Dear Mr Yates .

We had big floods here this year. which destroyed practically all our hard work in the garden. Such a flood had never been known before as far as the blacks remember . The rice seed you gave me did not come up very well ,it was covered nearly a month with water ,but some pulled through & seeded again after the flood , my own seed did much better growing again & seeding well so I have seed for next year . It headed through 2 ft of water but the geese skinned it & I could not find a grain left ,but was rejoiced when it grew again. So now I know I can grow rice in a flood or normal year.

The vegetable seeds I put in a milk can for the Wet sprayed it with Flytox inside & sealed & the seed came up quite well . so I am asking you for some more for next season if you would kindly send them into C.M.S . offices to be packed in the boxes in September next . We have not had a boat since December & when it comes with your fresh seed I have missed the best part of the cool time[,] our best time for seeds, it is hard luck the boat was promised for last month ,but still we wait ,& I made arrangements with Darwin & C.M.S to get them through in first mail & I could or had them in March & like Topsy I sow nothing ,anyrate brother one or the old Government milk cans will best help to overcome this difficulty or isolation , & moisture . Thanking you for many past favours , I supposemwe beggars are a bit of a pest , but I can assure you I did not approach your father as a beggar but God send him to me . Cheerio! Trust this finds you prospering .

Yours sincerely
Alf Dyer[88]

***

---

88   NTRS 1099/P1 vol. 1.

Seeds for Oenpelli Sept 1930

To be sent in to Church Missionary Society 242 Castlereagh St

2 ozs cabbage or packets
2 " carrot
2 " Cucumber
2 Pkt apple cucumber
Few Cranadailla
2ozs Kohl Rabi
2ozs Lettice
2ozs Rock Melons
2 " Water "
2 Pkts Parsley
2 Raddish
θ 1 Pkt Rosella
1 oz Squash
1 " Pumpkin Queens Blue
1 " Iron bark & 1oz Triamble
θ 1 = Assorted
2 oz "" Tomato's
8lbs 2 Canadian Wonder Beans
1lb Epicure beans
Some climbing beans   Snake   Severn [Seven] Year   Tongan
2 lbs Cow peas
8 packet Bush Marrows
1 lb Shallots
Is there an onion suitable for tropics have not had any luck yet .
4 oz Sweet Corn
2oz Turnips & Swede turnip
1 Pkt Passion Fruit   1 pkts Petunias   2 Zinnias   Gal llardia

Alf Dyer[89]

---

89   ML MSS 6040/12.

Figure 5.80: Bark paintings at Oenpelli mission (date unknown).
Source: Northern Territory Archives Service (NTRS 694 P1 Box 4b Item 278).

***

Von Arnheim's Land

Vioissitudes at Oenpelli.

----J.W. Ferrier.---

About four years ago a member of the Herald Staff visited Von Arnheim's Land, and called at Oenpelli, the Church Missionary Society's Aboriginal Station on the East Alligator River. It is a journey necessitating special transport either overland or by sea, and involves considerable hardship. Oenpelli is actually more difficult of access and of regular communications than Africa or Asia.

There are six white missionaries and a child – the furthest north white girl in that part of Australia. Effective wireless facilities for transmission and reception would be a godsend both to the isolated missionaries and to the responsible society. Contacts are entirely lost and outside resources cannot be tapped for several months of the year. We always seem to be on the verge of tragedy. A message just received – practically the first news for six months – is one long story of trouble on trouble – superstition, sickness, fatalities, floods and famine.

Superstition:

An interesting coincidence occurs in the fact that in the early part of this year an extension of the acreage for growing food-stuffs necessitated the cutting down of some trees. While these trees were being prepared for burning, information was given to the missionary by some of the old men of the tribe that the trees were on an old camp site and were sacred, and that spirits lived in them. The blacks earnestly begged that the trees should not be burned or disaster would surely result, and some would die. They had it firmly fixed in their minds that troubles would come to them because their grove had been destroyed. They spent one night parading with fires to drive the spirits away.

Whooping Cough and Malaria:

At Christmas time whooping cough developed, a sickness apparently not generally known among the blacks, though this year it has practically spread throughout the North of Australia. Nearly everybody took the sickness, and it lasted for several months, giving the ladies a very anxious time, nursing day and night. Three members of the camp died; there were several other deaths out bush, and the people were most difficult to help, owing generally to their own ideas about sickness. Some of them said our medicines were poisonous, and refused to come for them. Their own remedy was sucking at the bodies of the sick. In addition to the whooping cough there was a good deal of malaria, and even the dormitory girls were mo[s]t difficult to help and would not smile, but kept whining all the time, and di[d] not seem to care whether they lived or died. One of our girls who was married last year had a baby just before she took the whooping cough. The baby also contracted it, and died. The missionary told her and her family to get the child ready for burial in the afternoon, but the grandfather took the body and wanted it put up a tree, with native rites. After waiting for an hour at the grave, Rev.A.J. Dyer seeing no sign of anyone coming thought there was a hitch and went to see what was being done, pleading for a decent burial for the little one.

Floods:

The next great trouble was a series of big floods, the result of constant rain for the greater part of a month; over an inch a day fell. One small boy fell into the billabong and was drowned in the flood waters. Practically all the food in the gardens was destroyed, and the hard work put in for months to grow plenty of food-stuffs was brought to nothing. There was great excitement the night of the "big waters," when the blacks rushed up to carry away their children. They were all safe in one of the houses which was on slightly higher ground.

Early in March the flood waters gradually subsided . The mud and unpleasantness was very disagreeable, and there was a lot of extra work clearing up. The whole of the houses in the vicinity were in a hopelessly muddy condition. It then became evident that the losses in the garden were very great; many of the crops had got water-logged, and there was very little food left on the area not covered by the water. On the flood area it was found that practically everything was lost. Large numbers of trees and shrubs died, including all the paw paw trees, which were just fruiting. An experimental plot of rice was well covered for over a month, and a number of plants seeded through the water, but the geese came in hundreds and ate off the heads. Black Cockatoos and Crows in great flocks attacked the maize when it was only half formed, and several acres of the staple meal, kaffir corn, also suffered. Hundreds of pigeons, crows and cockatoos stormed the place; it was impossible to drive them away. Poison was tried, but with very little success, and cartridges could not be spared to shoot them. It has been necessary to cut the stuff green, and only a little of that, though twice as much was under cultivation as ever before. The floods have made the birds so much worse this year as all their feeding grounds were covered. There is also now a plague of rats, which is all very sad, as a great deal of very hard work has failed this season, and food supplies will be limited. Cotton has been a complete failure, and the peanuts which previously have done very well, rotted in the ground six feet above the flood level.

Staff:

The present mission staff at Oenpelli consists of Rev. & Mrs. A.J. Dyer, who are the pioneers of the Mission; Miss Florence Sherrin, who has done splendid work teaching the boys and girls; Mr.G.R.Harris, who is helping with the farming work and the stock; Mr.& Mrs.E.J.Clymo, the latest recruits, who are helping with the general and practical work of the Mission, Mrs.Clymo being especially helpful to Mrs.Dyer in the care and attendance of the sick people.

Specially urgent needs at the present are two tons of flour and one ton of rice as emergency rations in place of the food-stuffs destroyed, and the replacing of the old residence and cookinghouse, now over forty years old. The provision of immediately necessary buildings will cost £500. for material alone – the work will be done by the staff, helped by the blacks. A small dinghy is also needed for use with the launch in the River. Sooner or later efficient wireless apparatus must be provided, but the Society is unable at present to afford this, and the Postmaster General has not yet made provisions for such facilities. The Headquarters of the Church Missionary Society are at 242 Castlereagh St., Sydney[90]

Figure 5.81: Men dancing for ceremony (possibly as part of burial ceremony). Nipper Marakarra Gumurdul holding spearthrower (date unknown).

Source: Northern Territory Archives Service (NTRS 693 P1 Item 21).

90　ML MSS 6040/12.

Figure 5.82: Women dancing for ceremony (date unknown).
Source: Northern Territory Archives Service (NTRS 693 P1 Item 21).

Figure 5.83: Women dancing for ceremony (date unknown).
Source: Northern Territory Archives Service (NTRS 693 P1 Item 21).

* * *

C.M.S
Oenpelli
June 18th 1930

Dear Mr Ferrier

Am enclosing in this a copy of my letter to the Health Officer Darwin & things I have asked for. We are sending a big medical order this time as we are right out of everything almost, in the nature of cold medicines & drugs for making them, quinine, asperin, etc I have not put any tabloids on order as Mrs Langley asked me if there was anything we would like to let her know & am sending that list to be forwarded to her as they can get it from Burroughs. Welcome at reduction for missionaries –

You will be glad to know that we are almost normal now. As the weather is helping people all to cheer up. Staff generally are well Mr Dyer is not very strong & I still have the remains of cold hanging round. I am not getting younger & have felt the strain a good deal, however, have proved over & over. "As thy days so shall thy strength be". I hope some one is coming to relieve Miss Sherrin because we will certainly need her during the Wet. You have all the reports etc that give details of work. So will not burden you with anymore. We have been a very happy family in spite of the strenuous times & except that there does not seem much prospect of buildings[,] things are going well & the people seem more responsive & the girls who asked for baptism are very bright.

Please remember me very kindly to Mrs Ferrier Hope you are all well. With kindest regards remembering you constantly in our prayers

Yours in glad service -
M. C. Dyer.

P.S. I think you know that the quan[t]ities of things sent by Dr Cook were so small, we were right out when I arrived here from furlough & what we received from south has kept us well supplied. Last year they sent the list of things kept in stock to replenish First Aid Kits & suggested I kept as near as possible to those amounts – If we are entitled to the things on list I thought we ought to have the additional ones & so am trying for them & they certainly will lessen our medical order in future if we can get them.
M.C.D.[91]

***

---

91   ML MSS 6040/12.

C.M.S
Oenpelli
June 20th 1930

Medical Officer
Health Dept.
Darwin.

Dear Sir.

This past twelve months has been a very strenuous one in the dispensary & nursing part of our work. Several times during the latter part of last year, we had more or less severe influenza outbreaks – Just at Xmas whooping cough developed & practically the whole of our people over 150 had it, some very severely with fever too, running temperatures of 105. & in some cases 105.8[.] Several had symptoms of Pneumonia. It was the Wet& during Feb. & March continuous rains were not conducive to quick recovery, the sick parade took two of us two hours every morning & about 1 ¾ hours each evening. With the exception of 3 infants we had no deaths, one was 3 weeks old, another 18 months & had not been treated, the third had dysentry as well when his Mother brought him in, though we have heard of deaths out bush. The Wet closed with a big flood here & quite a number who were convalescent went bush; it was April before we were clear. then we had another very severe outbreak of influenza & we are just about normal now. It was impossible to keep record of numbers each day, cases treated include – burns, yaws, snake bites, sore eyes, & several cases from bush literally covered in sores, which have completely healed after a few month's treatment.

Leprosy patients—Garijala (woman) died & Denajong (boy)[;] two others left the station & went right away before I received instructions re Challmoogra. The son of Garijala came back here recently, he is about 9 years old & shows symptoms of it so will treat him.

In spite of epidemics we have only had since May 1st. 1929. 10deaths 2 leprosy, 3 whooping cough, 1little boy drowning, 2 other infants, & 2 old age.

Dr. Cook promised Rev. J.W. Ferrier secretary of the C. M. S. we could have quantities of the following– Tr. Iodine Fortis, Tr. Iodine Mitis, Friars Balsam, Calomol, Zinc Sulphate, Iod. Potass Crystals. I have a fair amount of most of these at present so am only asking for the amount allowed to replenish first aid kit, Zinc Sulphate not needed. Are we entitled free of charge to the things on the list, sent last year, for first aid? If so will be glad of the additional things on the order if you would kindly send them.

Thanking you in anticipation
Yours faithfully
M. C. Dyer.[92]

Figure 5.84: Men, women and children crowded around a tractor at Oenpelli mission (date unknown).
Source: Northern Territory Archives Service (NTRS 693 P1 Item 21).

* * *

List of things wanted for Oenpelli Mission.

8oz. Tr Iodi Fort
8oz. Tr Iodi Mitis
12 Doz. Friars Balsam
½ lb. Calomel Powder for ointment
8oz. Iod. Pot. Crystals

If we are entitled to these things to replenish first aid kit, will you please send these additional things.

12oz. Glycerine
8oz. Lysol

---

92   NTRS 1099/P1 vol. 1.

1lb. Lint
8oz. Ipecaouanha
4oz. Laudanum
12oz. Eucalyptus
1/2lb. Asperin
8oz. Sal Volatile
1Tin 100 Quinine Capsules
12oz [...]⁹³

* * *

"As thy days so shalt thy strength be"

C.M.S.

Oenpelli

June 21ˢᵗ 1930

Dear Miss Harper.

We are waiting in daily expectation of the boat. & now Goulburn Is. boat is wrecked we are not certain of getting mails through that way so our orders have to go before the next one arrives which always makes it a little difficult. Sometimes things are mixed etc. I am enclosing in this the order for Burroughs. Melbourne. I asked Mrs Langley if we might get the friends there to get it & of course have not her reply so will you find out please & if they are willing let them have list. They would be able to get missionary reduction I think. We are right out of quinine tabloids & only a little bisulf of gum I use that in making up fever mixture; there has been such a lot of sickness this year our stock has got very low. Eucalyptus we are out of but I put some on special order to go Goulburn Is. I hope it got down in time. June 22ⁿᵈ we were having staff service this evening when great commotion in the dormitories. The boat is at Smith's landing & they are coming up in launch tonight as Mr Dyer and Mr Clymo will be leaving at daybreak. So letters must be finished. You will get a big budget this time; the delayed Goulburn Is mail, the boat is going straight there now, & also the mail be sent to the line cart Monday – I have tried to think of everything we need this order that goes now is our Wet season supply & we always try to have a reserve so that if anything happens we are able to hold out for 3 months. We had 16 days of flour in tank yesterday but we got

---

93   ML MSS 6040/12.

rather a shock as during the floods the water had leaked in round the tap &
8 of them were spoilt so we were letting children get their dinners[;] however
there is no need now.

I am very tired & cannot think of anything else. It seems a long time since we
heard from you & do hope you are well. Please remember me lovingly to all the
staff & also Mrs Biggs & depot workers – with love.

Yours lovingly in glad service
Mary. C. Dyer.[94]

***

C.M.S.
Oenpelli
July 10th 1930

Dear Mr Ferrier

Mr Dyer asked me to write you about the drapery. Most of the things are
fairly good but the print is very poor quality– I can get better quality cheaper
retail than what is sent & we do need strong materials for dresses & nagas –
then the shorts are really rubbish I thought when the boys brought them in
after about 3 weeks wear they were bringing old ones; one has to be watchful of
these things; however Mr Dyer has taken to wearing them & I put some of his
long ones into store & took a couple of pairs out as he only had 2 pairs. In three
washes they were in pieces – I have been wondering if someone could not do
that part of shopping for us I am sure it would save money & we would have
more satisfaction & it would save much mending – We will go back to dungaree
trousers for stock boys the last ones bought at Lowe's were 3/9- & the khaki are
7/- & the former really wear best & were what they had in Government days –

Re the tea. I am the culprit but we all like the tea & it is really economical
I could not drink the tea I got in Darwin except No1… even then prefer ours
– twice we had other ration tea but it was dreadful stuff & once the box was
all broken it did not last the six months fortunately we had a reserve – I like
our ration tea better than Bushells – tea is my one & only drink but I do like
the nice […] flavour – very weak -----

About the houses I would like you to know just what we feel here about them.
The plan is our present one & except that the roof is very low & passage way
much to narrow for our purposes & there are no verandahs, in some ways it is

---

94   ML MSS 6040/12.

about ideal – my suggestion was that our two rooms should be put where the store & bedroom are – with a 4 ft passage between to make the current of air in the room but all area agreed it is too noisy & especially in case of sickness & so that meant these must be two houses – our present house is 15+18 -& for a single person's house is ideal with a verandah say 9 ft round it – but we really need two rooms & yet I would rather have one big one than two small ones; even ours on stormy nights when it is shut up is very hot, the temperature is often 90°; but wide verandahs make all the difference it stops the sun & can be up unless storm is very bad. In walls – my suggestion now is that we have two rooms at least 16 + 13– with passage way between & I would like that 10 ft wide & mosquito proof; while I am writing Mr Dyer has a class of 17 in our room & has to shut it to keep family clear of mosquitos, (also if ever there should be a superintendant with children it would be safe to put them in.) the space I suggest would just take them in nicely & they would be able to listen in comfort. The other room would be really like a study as bookshelves would be there but it would also be available in case of need to put any one sick in[;] for instance the week Miss Sherrin was sick we had to tramp up & down several times a day – & Mrs Clymo had to sleep up there at night but such a room would do away with that also if the Bishop or any other visitors come we could fit it up for their use—made with bush timbers at least 1ft each way length & breadth comes off size of rooms ____

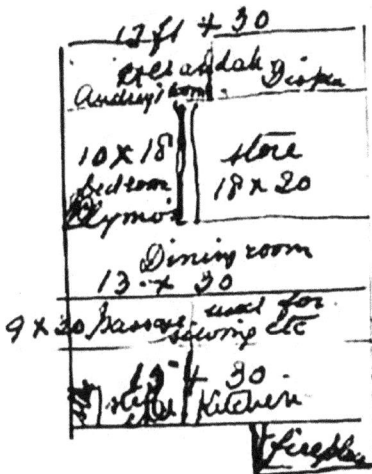

Figure 5.85: Sketch of proposed changes to home, from Mary C. Dyer's letter to Mr J.W. Ferrier, dated 10 July 1930.

Source: Mitchell Library (ML MSS 6040/12).

Our dining room may seem big but it is a common room & is only 1 ft wider than the present one. & when we are all in with work etc there is no room to spare. It has two tables in, one is 9ft 6 in & has been full at meal time more than once. The other is at present in use with type writer etc. It is only wired wall on two sides & the new one will only have one iron wall on front side.

The passage way was put up as an afterthought in this place. It is the most used place during the day but is much too narrow. The walls will have big cupboards to take materials, sewing etc & people's clothing. With cutting out table.. machines etc & 2 ft will not be too wide __

The kitchen is really a double room one end is for staff about 10 x 15 the other the cooking for as many as 150 is done & 8 bags of flour made into bread in a week sometimes; the stove space included, baker's oven & verandah on that side has coppers planned to cook soup etc – By putting stove back on verandah it makes kitchen much cooler – the rest of verandah space will be for men & boys to stand in when they come for meals out of heat & rain as at present they have to ____ Practically all the verandah space except the two sides & front of dining room is utilised. We will find that very useful for instance on Sunday 3 classes have to go out[:] one into Miss Sherrin's room & two crouched outside wherever they can find a bit of shade. Mr Dyer will be sending plans but this may give you some idea of just what we want. Nothing but the necessary iron.

I do hope all this will not weary you I have just read it to Mr Dyer & he says he is very glad I have written it because it gives details he could not give. We are all well at present & very happy about the children & people who are showing some desire after spiritual things some are really seeking to follow the Lord Jesus & there is a marked change in them & we praise Him.

With loving greetings to all in Offices & Depot & all who so continually remember us in prayer. Praying always for you all that God will abundantly bless you in your part of His being and in Him yours

Mary C. Dyer

List for Burroughs Welcome

2. 200 – Bisulphate of Quinine 5 gr.
3. 100 – Bihydropclorate of Quinine 5 gr.
1- 100. Bisulphate of Quinine 2 grs.
10 – 100. Asperin 5 grs.
2. 100 – Asperin Phenaciltin & Caffeine or Phenacutin Comp –
1 – 100. Sodi Bromide Comp-
2. 100. Salicylate of Soda 5 grs
1 – 100 Chlorate of Potash

In the medical supplies that came from C.M.S. Also some bottles of Heenjo or any concentrated cough mixture.

½ doz tins of Coupland's Eradied ____
*Cotton wool not needed this time but we are right out of lint_*

M.C. Dyer[95]

---

95   ML MSS 6040/12.

Figure 5.86: Stockmen (date unknown).
Source: Northern Territory Archives Service (NTRS 693 P1 Item 21).

Figure 5.87: Stockman and horse (date unknown).
Source: Northern Territory Archives Service (NTRS 693 P1 Item 21).

* * *

Oenpelli July 11th 1930
PORT DARWIN

Rev. J.W. Ferrier
C.M.S.

Dear Mr. Ferrier.

Most of the stores opened up well , Mrs Dyer will have something to say about the drapery, some of which is very poor in quality. My films were posted & I expect walked in Darwin things do there, but if they are put in the boxes they are as safe then as possible. Would you put 1doz. No 2 Brownie films on the Wet order if I have not got them on No 116.

Buildings, hope to get more time now, Mr Clymo has had a lot of engine jobs & the new bearings do not anywhere fit, this means days of work. The pump is wearing to pieces & we can only patch, it was a shocking job the only fair thing is they ought to give us a new pump.

Then the launch engine will take some time to put in order & the boat re-ribbed, punt, etc. I can see the year nearly gone. At anyrate I will get what I can done & await your reply re other buildings

Aboriginal Ordinance.

I would not worry about this, if it did effect us I expect we could overcome it by paying stock drovers to take delivery from our plant.

Mr Clymo's cartridges are 1000. 22 extra long cartridges, the rest are for station use, you asked to notify you re this so as to arrange the charges which are private.

[…]

5 copies come here under separate postage, 2 copies & a Round World would be sufficient all are agreed. Re Air mail. the air mail & the copies all came together, generally the ordinary mail suits our irregular mails, but there are times near boat sailings, & the March & April trips of Methodist boat when it might be advisable, for instanc if you had not sent your first mail for this year written near the end of April air mail, I would not have heard from you for 6 months.

I am enclosing a plan of kitchen & general workrooms & store, we have iron for that here, & will go on with that, we will try & patch up this to hold out for another Wet. the others we will await your reply & more iron, the iron in the old buildings will do for sides etc. but not for roofs except a few, & we have a new store if a blow comes, the stores will not suffer.

Cattle.

You will note what I suggest to Mr Beurteaux for next year, if no sale of cattle arrises mobs are always going overland, & if we get on our new fence up they will be ready near station for a start in May.

Accounts.

I have run over the accounts with interest you sent last year, what a terrible year it was with all the Mary's pranks, it is good to have no more of her expenses. This year will show a big drop even with the launch cost & freight.

Smiths Landing

At present I am not building as the stores were brought this time nearly to Ebenbow, which is the last rocks. Our neighbour's goods are landed there & the skipper says he will come so far which is 15 miles or so beyond Smith's old landing. We can shift the stores in a week with the launch, so I think the best thing is to wait & see what really happens, as we have two neighbours on that side & the boat has […] ing their stores. Two good tarpaulins to cover the goods as though sometimes there are no showers, then at times there are heavy ones, but they do not last long. This will be the best arrangement for the present; so would you put them on the next shipment please, they will be much cheaper than iron for a shed which might go in a flood like we had this year.

Launch

At present she is anchored in the river, we have to build some cover for her or bring her to the billabong no cover on river will last a Wet so we are going to try & cart it up when the saw is going to make a cradle.

Prayer Books

Now the children are reading we need Prayer books & Hymn books Hymnal Companion 3rd edition, they need not be new if in good order. Also some copies of Catechism for baptismal classes, a set of numbers for hymn board in Church. (An organ for the Church if anyone likes to give it)

Engines.

The pump has cost Mr Clymo days, all the arms had to be drilled & bushed.he will report on this. We will want new casting for launch engine plugs etc. as per separate list.

The Mc Donald is not pulling well, has no compression, would you order a new set of piston rings as per list. *I took her down again she is good now but would be wise to send the spares.*

We have taken the boiler in the shed to pieces & find she is quite sound & will give us a lot of work with 14 new tubes 6ft 6" 2 ¾ external 2 ¾" internal measurement, the lot should cost under £40, There is going to be a lot of sawing from now on to do, the Mac. wont look at it[.] The tractor is very expensive to run & the scraps of wood from the saw will almost keep the boiler going & steam is the best sawing power, the £10 cost is much the best as it is the only cost for some years, except […]. oil which is very small. The engine is set up & we have all the fittings for the boiler & pulleys etc.

Wheels.

I have asked Mr Harris to write & tell you what he knows about farm wheels, you will remember how sick the wheels were last year, we are still patching them up, & the day of doom is coming fast. Mr Warren sent two wheels cast iron a weight in themselves, they are too short & useless as they do not fit the axle even if we could use them, he said they could be sent back, but I have no details & you will notice I have asked Mr Beurteaux about caps for them, nothing came on them, so I am as far off as ever. We cannot use the lorry last sent even reduced in size, the wheels I made last year out of old bits & new bits are still hanging, & bringing in our building timber, but I am far from being a wheel wright. The set of 4 good wheels & 2 axles I asked for 2 years ago so we could build one ourselves would have saved months of labour which does not last & the freight on the lorry would have brought them, I think. It is unfortunate but I stress this point to guard against such things occurring again. Since writing this I have found statement in the journal concerning wheels,

Steel lorry wheels cost £5.5. each, renewal hubs. 17/6 (not come) if not suitable to be returned, £4 allowed if suitable, ,2 others to be purchased.

The renewal hubs will make it fit the axle, but they are in Darwin or lost, as they were there all through the Wet which makes it more hopeless. I have not the firm's name so I do not know what to advise, we do not want the 2 other wheels, we may use these for launch cradle.

Yours sincerely
Alf Dyer[96]

Figure 5.88: 'Launching the JW Ferrier' (date unknown).
Source: Northern Territory Archives Service (NTRS 694 P1 Box 4 Item 133).

96   ML MSS 6040/12.

Figure 5.89: Group of girls (date unknown).

Source: Northern Territory Archives Service (NTRS 693 P1 Item 2).

Figure 5.90: Boat moored on the East Alligator River (date unknown).

Source: Northern Territory Archives Service (NTRS 694 P1 Box 4a Item 154).

✳ ✳ ✳

C.M.S.
Oenpelli
Via Darwin
July 28th 1930

Dear Miss Harper.

We heard definitely that our neighbour will be going to Darwin on 30th & will take mail & so I am sending this the enclosure is from Miss Barnett & is part of the offering of the Burra Bee Dee. Sunday school it is a mission mostly ½ & ¼ caste native children & 6/- is for the Oenpelli girls & other 6/- to help the poor lepers here. I have written Miss Barnett suggesting she sends the money direct to C.M.S & writes to me as they are anxious for the children to have a personal interest in the work. I sent a letter to you via G.I. [Goulburn Island] but in all probability this will reach you first – If the boxes are not already packed – please do not send balls we have quantities for the next twelve months & we have also a pretty good supply of bandages. & fortunately we had a very good supply of cotton wool for we have the worst case of burning I have ever seen Waranbiyga (Biddy) one of our most useful women was standing with her back to fire & her dress caught fire & she was literally burnt from shoulders to knees one leg below knee & both hands & by far the most extensive burns I have ever treated . Only one packed of lint came in boxes last year & I kept it in case of accident & I used two thirds of it in the first two dressings so you can imagine what she was like & a 6 oz pot of ointment each time. She was shocked of course but quickly got over it; though she said one day when I was doing her if she had been in camp she would have been finished. She is making a wonderful recovery each day there is new skin coming & fortunately most of the burns were not deep. Though one leg is right into flesh. I am sure it is in answer to prayer. She was the woman who used to interpret for me when I first had school & is always ready to help & likes us to pray with her but she has not expressed any wish to follow the Lord Jesus, yet her life would put many white Christians to shame. I had only put 2 lbs of Vaseline in order as we had 20 lb tins & there is generally a good lot of boxes. We have had a good many cases needing ointment this last year & especially lately. I had only made up 5 lb of various […] – boracic, zinc, calomel & 3 in 1 – a fortnight before Biddy's accident & I had to make up another 8 lbs the other day – So would you please if there is not plenty in boxes – get 2-5 lbs tins Vaseline also the eye dropper almost all that come up on order are perished I got it out of my last dozen to get one I could use & yet I am still using one *in my room bought in Sydney one day – so Mr Dyer said to ask you please to get 1doz for us – if there is not <u>lint a couple of packets please</u> too – I cannot think of anything else that is not on order – you will be glad to know that Mrs Clymo has fitted into the work splendidly she does it, when the epidemics were on she was such a help in the dispensary & since she carries on doing all the ordinary dressings at sick parade I just prescribe for sick ones & do any special cases. She is very good in school. I know by the way the children are improving in reading she has also done Mrs Dyers typing. & she is so observant & ready to help anywhere, she plays the organ too & that is an asset in this work. Miss Sherrin has the kinders for 1 ½ hours every morning looks after staff cooking, childrens clothes etc etc I do not do as much of general routine as I used but all the odd jobs fall to my share – men & women's clothes, soap, store (I am store woman), laundry, teaching sewing & machining, superintendency such things as ant bedding – we have just about finished the last of the six monthly renewal of that & it has been a lengthy job this year with flood damage etc. The rubberoid I put in our dining room floor when we came back saved that, we have not touched it for two years & though the water was 6 in on it for 3 days it did not seem damaged in any way – you can see we do not have many idle moments but generally it is a very happy life & especially so when we see people responding to the message. It seems such a long time since I heard from the office or of the Depot.*

Give my loving greetings to all. Trusting you are well. Continue in prayer for us & we remember you constantly with love. Yours in the happiest service Mary C. Dyer

P.S letters are all sealed so would you please ask Mr Ferrier to put 12 lbs Borat – on order. I am out for soap – & last order boracic came instead, M.C.D.[97]

---

97   ML MSS 6040/12.

Figure 5.91: Elderly couple and their son (date unknown).
Source: Northern Territory Archives Service (NTRS 694 P1 Box 4a Item 181).

* * *

REV.A.DYER'S REPORT ON LAUNCH – OENPELLI.

The first thing that caught my eye on the launch was one of the stanchions holding up the roof was full of dry rot. I took my knife out and it went right through it. This naturally broke coming up and took one of the side windows with it – there are three pieces of such timber in the boat which are all gone to pieces, but can be replaced.

The rudder was broken, the borer had settled that – the wood was eaten right away, and the pins had fallen out. We had to use an oar on first trips. I have not had the launch out of the water to inspect for borer in the hull, but she seems sound as far as the inside shows, and the timbers seem sound to the knife, except that the engine bed seems very loose.

These are not serious, but what is serious is that nearly every [side] – is pulled away from the keel; one side is nearly 2"– the other side has all pulled away from the one little nail holding the rib on to the keel; that means she will not last long, and will I fear prove too weak in Alligator River experiences.

The only thing we can see to do is to put a strap across the keel and rivet to the rib on each side, and that is a fairly big job, but will have to be done to save her. Otherwise she is very suitable; comfy if one had to go to Darwin at pinch, very bonny, but hardly a sea-boat, but by picking the weather could get there.

By putting the exhaust through the roof we can load over two ton of flour, and got our stores up in five trips, but before we did this got water in the engine on the first trip, which was well we did, for the big ends well all loose with a ¼ inch play, when we tightened her up you can take the fly-wheel and rock the shaft in each of the main bearings in the engine, they are in a very bad state and will take days of scraping to get them anything like again, without proper tools. One of the manifold studs was missing and the hole was filled up with putty.

The plugs were very old and full of rust, which gave us a lot of trouble, and we wished a shop was near by, we had no spare plugs as they are a special size, nor any right kind of lub. oil, ours is tractor oil.

The propeller shaft was very wobbly and had a good settle and a few hours in the mud soon made things worse, the mud was pouring into the boat, but we have not had it out yet to see the state it is in, but it is very sick. Mr. Clymo and self started off with our first load, got past the rocks and had to put out our cargo. It took two days and two nights before she was a going concern, as she had to be taken right down and repaired before we could go on, and that was only to patchup, but there is two or three weeks in the work-shop to put her in order, which is very unfortunate for us with all the work we have in hand. The great pity is that Wilsons, the makers in Brisbane did not put her in order for us, the cost would not have been great.

I am sorry to have to write in such a strain, but they are just the plain facts. Mr. Clymo says the ribs were not like that when he saw the boat, but he did not have time to inspect the inward parts of the engine, nor did he realise what conditions a launch has to face up to in our harbour, but when these repairs are effected I hope we will get some years of service out of her.

Later on going down to inspect the launch we find she is leaking badly under the engine bed, the rivets are all loose and the planks cracked. She was filled with pitch or marine glue along the cracks, this is rather serious, and very difficult to make a job of it. Also the stern gland bearing is all worn right away and the propeller shaft is wearing away, the wood of the stern post, we will have to try and make a new one if we can find any material, that is the query? If we can make a job of this, the launch is the best way out of our shipping problem.[98]

August, 1930.[99]

* * *

C.M.S.
Oenpelli
C/o Jolly & Co.
Darwin
Aug 24th 1930

Dear Miss Harper.

We are in the throes of a double mail though G.I. [Goulburn Island] arrived last night just as service at tea with July mail. Then as we came from S.S. we found Mr Hall from boat had walked up to station he had left the mail bags at landing so we only have Mr Beuxteaup's letter – but gather there is quite a lot of building material so our wants in that way are supplied even before our letters went down. In my last I think I told you about Biddy's burns they have healed most wonderfully & she says it is God who has made her better & today though she has only been out of bed since Thursday she came up to service to specially thank Him[.] I am sure if she is not already in the Kingdom she is very near & she has been so patient with all the pain – We all felt it would be well for Miss Sherrin not to miss this opportunity of getting away rather than wait until October or November the weather just now is better for travelling – on the whole her health has been good since she came, but last year she has a nasty throat cough for some months. & again this year it seems

---

98   NTRS 1099/P1 vol. 1.
99   ML MSS 6040/12.

to be wearing off now – In the last two months she has had two attacks of pain, in the lower part of abdomen. on right side. & since with it she had a nasty giddy turn & looked very bad - but it only lasted an hour or two. I could not detect any symptoms of appendix trouble & the spot she complained of was rather lower. Still I thought better to mention the matter she gets headaches sometimes but says not so badly as she did south – she has been a great help to us in many ways & we have had some very happy fellowship she is very bright & never thinks anything a trouble to do for any one – she loved her school & is very good with the kinders just my [...] but with these people her deafness prevents her from being a teacher as even with good hearing it is not easy to get sounds.

Mrs Clymo has settled in well she does all the casuals at sick parade - has charge of poultry does the cutting up for people & has school in the afternoon besides many numerous tasks & she is very happy & at home & I am sure she is a growing soul. She is very keen, not to give addresses, but trying to help the individuals - lately things have been much more normal & I have been trying to get things well in hand & so we feel that she can manage for a little while with the two of us if we keep well. The last three Sundays our hearts have just been full of praise as we gathered for services. attendances have varied from 82 to 92 but I am sure you would rejoice if you could see & hear how they join in the rejoices & try God's praises & it is not quite 6 years since we took over here & they did not know the name of Jesus. "What hath God wrought" we do praise Him there are 23 in the catechumen's classes of course it does not mean they are all out & out but there is certainly a work of the spirit going on & a chance in their lives.

Please convey to all our helpers by prayer & gift our thanks. They who stay by the staff divide the spoil & I am sure it is in the answer to the many prayers that have gone up we are getting the blessings. With loving greeting to all in offices & depot fam. Yours in Him Mary C. Dyer.[100]

---

100 ML MSS 6040/12.

Figure 5.92: Group photo (date unknown).
Source: Northern Territory Archives Service (NTRS 693 P1 Item 21).

* * *

Report for July, August, & September [1930].

All through these months mustering work was carried on & the bullocks were ready if word came of a sale to go at any moment. the mustering is almost completed & 1400 are in Red Lily of which 223 are calves branded this year, & some 100 odd on the plains. The new fence has been a great asset as not a beast has gone through it to our knowledge, nor have buffaloes broken it, this has saved us lots of work. Before the Wet we are aiming at trying to complete the new fence to keep the cattle in for the Wet, if this succeeds, the bullocks will be ready to get away early next year. We have made the boys more responsable this year & Mr. Harris has not had to go out so much & has been able to help on many station tasks. Quilp has tried hard to help us, he is not far from the Kingdom. Nagal, Nalyn & Abandali who are in baptism class have backed him up in this.

The garden always takes a certain amount of my time to irrigate twice a week, we have had a nice lot of vegetables, pumpkins, cabbage, tomatos cucumbers, melons, potatoes, sweet corn, turnips etc. Some hundreds of new paw-paws are growing again & showing fruit net growth since the flo[o]d Got a nice lot of rice for seed next year & some to spare, also a new corn some seeds originally from Egypt, were under the flood waters only one survived, this was watered & one head produced nearly 2000 seeds a large white clean grain. These I replanted & have the new seed for the Wet, the seed is different to that I planted & looks like a cross, I am sending some to Yates for identification, if new, will call it "Oenpelli["] we believe it is going to be a very good food. Other things are being planted out for the Wet nurseries.

Mr. Clymo started on saw bench bearings & then had to do pump arms with new sleeves, then he did a for repairs on launch engines & took launch down to Mr. Yates to inspect this motor lorry, he found the engine in fair order & Mr. Yates practically gave it to us, so we decided to go ahead & bring it over the river. Mr. Harris went out on a big mustering trip to Coomoodah [Goomadeer] River, Mr. Clymo & self went to fetch up the truck with lorry too, we made a punt with six crude oil drums, the [...] was put on top, but when the tide came up a drum shifted & she turned turtle in the soft mud, we righted her & tied the drums on the lorry & after many adventures floated her over & took to station under two mule power; Mr. Clymo took her down, overhauled & put the engine in order, & I made a hood for shade over her, & remade all the wood work of the body, you have a snap of her. With some spares & tyres which I ordered we shall have a serviceable lorry.

A near neighbour whose blacks were dying of whooping cough asked for help, as I went to see what could be done & had some nice talks to them & to him re some aboriginal problem & himself. In between these jobs with Mr. Harris help we finished off the reef of the engine house, it will be a nice cool place to work in & saw timber, also set up old Bill again, Mr. Warren told me how to fill it with cement, it was quite a simple task, made a new grate it did not take long so now we have the stern pump, a steam engine for the saw bench.

(Miss Sherrin) Then the surprise boat came with angle iron buildings, the best thing for this country, no ant worries & timber going rotten in a few years, it ought to solve the buildingworries for this generation, then we might have one man free for itinerstion which someone ought to be doing.

Miss Sherrin had not been too well so we all thought she had better go[–] we miss her help very much, she was always ready & willing to do any task cheerfully & did the best she knew in the school. One black man said to me "We big fellow sorry along Miss Sherrin she gone away, she look after our children good way."

Both Mrs. Clymo & Mrs. Dyer are facing bravely up to the extra tasks, but it is telling on them & the cool has gone. I cannot write up their work of pots & pens, washing & sewing, what could we men do without all that which is so lovingly given.

The dispensary is always busy & Mrs. Clymo is helping Mrs. Dyer here learning to fill her place, several lepers have died & new ones have come in poor creatures. One is listening very hard to the good news of Him who put forth His hand & touched the lepers. The worst case this quarter was a burn almost 2/3 of the body, she recovered, & has gone bush for a while, she told us she had fellowship with Him who never sleeps & found comfort in His presence. The children are reading well under Mrs. Clymo's teaching & are brightening up in arithmetic & mental work as well, this is all to the good.

Not being able to use the launch we had to cart the stores, the motor lorry brought up two loads, but the old tyres gave out, she would have done it in a few days but I had to fall back on the carts, I am writing this on the 9th Oct. the boat came on the 24th August, they may bring its last load to day, (Why so long for so little[)] every day except Sunday the little word = "wheels" & losing the mules. I sent you a snap of the crocks, the wheels on the lorry had to be mended, then the buck-board, boxes brokenfellows & spokes, & the buggy, the best part of Sept. it took me to repair, but they will not last. I made one like a Chinese wheel, it seems to be standing up to it. The launch repairs had to be faced. she started to sink in the river & had before we got her up. Mr. Harris & Mr. Clymo said they would try with motor lorry to bring her up, but she was too heavy, they brought up the engine & shafts etc. for repairs, the engine was full of water & had to be taken down & the boat was left in the river. After Mr. Clymo had cleaned her up he started to build his house, putting another room on to Miss Sherrin's & a verandah all round, he is doing this now & they will go in in a few days. Later Mr Harris & self went down to pain[t] the bottom of the launch & see if we could arrange some shade for her, we found her sunken on the bank, & I felt we must try to get her to the station for repairs as soon as we could, so we took the tractor & big lorry, after 4 days of hard work & breaking all our old & new ropes, we finally got to work with Mary's old anchor chain, & succeeded with the tractor digging into the soft ground to her axles. We had to block & tackle her the first ¼ mile then got on to hard ground round the end of the plains, & got her home to shade till we can attend to her, as the buildings come first.

We have 19 boys, 14 girls & babies, about 80 people in all, others are coming back again who went away in the time of sickness, all are well again except the chronic cases. Generally, with many ups and downs, those asked for baptism are moving upwards & small beginnings have to be encouraged. Cheerio.

Yours sincerely,
Alf Dyer[101]

Figure 5.93: Quilp, a head stockman at Oenpelli (date unknown).
Source: Northern Territory Archives Service (NTRS 694 P1 Box 4a Item 170).

* * *

---

101 ML MSS 6040/12.

Oenpelli Mission
C/O Jolly & Co
Darwin
N.T.
23-10-30

Rev J.W. Ferrier
General Secretary
C.M.S.
242 Castlereagh St
Sydney

Dear Sir.

I am writing to let you know that we are all right here, our health is good, and of work we find plenty to do. Mrs Clymo, Audrey & self are installed in our new house, having added another room, verandahs etc to Miss Sherrins house; we are very comfortable in it, and are grateful for the help of Mrs Dyer in the making of many things, also for Mr Dyer's placing of things at our disposal, they have both been very kind to us.

With regard to things mechanically we are getting straightened out a bit, but a number of improvements have yet to be carried out. The launch is going to cause us a little concern but Mr Dyer will tell you what he proposes to do, he will do, of course, what he thinks but I must just fit in

The Ford ton truck is in good running order mechanically our only holdup being tyres, no doubt they will reach us eventually.

The Fordson Tractor is O.K. and other machinery in good running order.

Mr Dyer & Mr Harris have been erecting the garage and laying the foundations & bed of kitchen. The garage being practically finished. They will be excellent buildings for here and are ant proof etc so will last well.

One thing I feel I must draw your attention to is the suggestion that the launch engine be sent to Brisbane (Wilson's) for overhaul. It can be done just as well here, hence, why pay freight etc to get it done elsewhere. However a new circulating pump is really required, I may say necessary, but those details Mr Dyer will deal with in his own way.

I have written to Mr Beusteaux of Jolly & Co sending back (per new boat) 4 pounds (weight) of Dark Tobacco asking him to credit me the same to my account. It was sent on owing to a slight misunderstanding of my letters, or if you could see that the above is dealt with I would be very much obliged.

With regards to things spiritual we have a hard uphill task, but Praise God we are winning though. Many of these people do not want Christ, all they want is tobbacco & tucker, but some are showing changes for the better. We thank God for His many blessings and especially for the young people who have expressed their desire to serve Christ, of course at times they allow the power of darkness to get the better of them but their lives do show that they really are trying, and conquering, and I feel that God will use them as His Messengers. The stock boys also show a marked deepening of the spiritual influence and we trust they will not backslide.

We need all the prayers of faithfull Christians that God will add His seal of Blessing to our labours. That the people may respond to financial side of Missionary work that the C.M.S may meet all its obligations, also that more labourers may be sent into the fields already while unto harvest. The C.M.S and all its staff are ever before us in our prayers, and we feel that your prayers for us are all answered.

Mrs Clymo joins with me in kindest regards to all, and as this is our last mail (as far as we know) this year we sent to you and all the staff the greetings of the Christmas Season. May it indeed be a Happy Christmas and the New Year a Prosperous one.

I remain
Yours in the Masters' service
Edgar J. Clymo[102]

---

102 ML MSS 6040/12.

Figure 5.94: 'Dormitory girls outside new dormitory. Mt Agarluk [Arrkuluk] in background. Mrs Clymo's daughter [Audrey] with hat and Hazel (halfcaste just in front of her)' (date unknown).
Source: Northern Territory Archives Service (NTRS 694 P1 Box 4 Item 58).

Figure 5.95: Stockmen with sheds in the background (date unknown).
Source: Northern Territory Archives Service (NTRS 693 P1 Item 21).

* * *

C.M.S. Oenpelli, C/O Jolly's & Co
Darwin, Nth Aus.
5.11.30

Rev. J.W. Ferrier
Gen. Sec. C.M.S.
242 Castlereagh St.,
Sydney

Dear Mr Ferrier.

In reply to your note dated 14 Aug. 30. With regard to people not under the influence of the Mission: I was on a long mustering trip early in August & came in contact with people on the Goomadair [Goomadeer] River come forty to fifty miles to the N.E. of here. Their condition of living and circumstances generally were enough to make ones heart bleed. They, of course, knew of the Mission here & also of the Mission at Goulburn Is. Some of them had been in here, even since my arrival. I talked to some of them & invited them in: some of them are now on the Stat[ion]. & others, I understand, are coming along for Christmas.

Mr Dyer is anxious to reach these people & plans to get out amongst them "as soon as the rush of work is over". Meanwhile we remember them continually in prayer.

With regard to your communication of 15th Sept. Thank you very much for all you have done on my behalf. The £1 is, of course in addition to the 5/- a month.

Mr Dyer received one dozen films No 120 in the boxes that have just arrived; as they are the wrong size for his camera & the right size for mine I have taken them over. Will you kindly charge them to my account? Miss Harper I thinks made the purchase for Mr Dyer.

Will you also have a copy of 'the Practice of the Love of Christ' by L. Harrington Lees sent to Miss E. Tandey, 18 Durham St, Carlton N.S.W & a copy of the same book to my father Mr G. Harris "Weerona" Wee Waa N.S.W, a copy of "the transforming friendship" by Leslie D. Weatherhead to Miss E. Collett, 11 Mullers Rd, Chatswood. & a "Keswick Calendar" to Mrs C.J. Collett 63 Adelaide St., West Ryde N.S.W.

Again thanking you & wishing you the compliments of the season

Yours Sincerely,
G.R. Harris[103]

---

103 ML MSS 6040/12.

* * *

OENPELLI Nov. 7 1930

General Secretary.

Dear Sir.

Mr Ferrier asked for a report about Miss Sherrin. We all like her very much she was always so cheerful & willing in her work nothing was any bother to her and we would be glad to welcome her back. Towards the end of her term we were anxious about her health, but it was only a few days in bed at the worst. He wondered if there were internal troubles[;] we did not like her cough but you have exact medical reports to go upon & should know the facts. there maybe nothing in our fears, & we hope to hear this is so.

Her deafness is a great impediment & it is wonderful how she strives to overcome it. With white children who would speak up it would be easier for her, but these people are hard to reach even with one who has perfect hearing, with Miss Sherrin they moved the lips and she lip reads & asks Mrs Dyer. Miss Nevil[l] & Mrs Clymo found that they only knew things as pictures were shown them she did a wonderful lot of work at night preparing charts with pictures, but after two years reading they had advanced very little. We tried to tell her, but some are very harsh to continue against their pet ideas so when Miss Nevil[l] came we let her just have the kinders then Mrs Dyer carried on till Mrs Clymo came. & now they are making rapid progress, she was very grieved over this as she loved her 'teaching' but facts are facts & one has to act for the best good of all. even if it is unpleasant to another. If you are quite satisfied on health grounds we shall be glad to have her help again to help generally & take the kinders, but I could not honestly recommend her as general teacher unless she should at any time recover her hearing which she still hopes that would make a big difference.

I am not sending any Blue Prints this mail as they might get wet the garage is up. but not the store. we have had many other calls see the stores are up safely some got wet but not much damage done. Trusting this finds all your work prospering & needs being met

Yours in 'the blessed hope'
Alf Dyer[104]

* * *

---

104 ML MSS 6040/12.

Report for Oct. Nov. & Dec. 1930.

Mr. Clymo on his house most of the month of Oct. put new room on & verandah all round the house which makes it very comfortable for them. Mr. Harris & boys were finishing off the mustering of the cattle branding etc. & put them into Red Lily, but in November we had to let a lot out as feed was scarce, we put most of them back when rain came at the end of November as we hope to have paddock finished by Xmas to keep in the best cattle & bullocks in case of early sale. Between whiles Mr. Harris was on the garage, which we are using at present for a store & then got on to the new store & kitchen. I helped him when I could & Mr. Clymo came on when his house was finished.

Made a new jetty on site where the boat people said they would come to, & just had it finished a day or so when the boat came, this proved a great asset as we unloaded at midnight, the boat was delayed owing to the black failing to come & tell us, we worked all night, Mr. Clymo & I & two boys, after riding down on horses 12 miles after sunset, so Mr Clymo & self fell in again to unload all the cargo[;] one was thankful for the jetty. Then we got to the carting, 3 carts & the motor lorry[,] little over a week it was all up. Then when other tasks gave us a chance we got on to the building, but as the launch was sinking in the river & the repair being a big job we carted the launch up to the station,,first tried motor lorry then the tractor & after a lot of hard work got her to the station under the shade of the mango trees to await repairs, which is a very big task as she will need new ribs & engine bed renewing. Other tasks, the buildings, the new fence & the garden are essential, the other can be done without while boats come to the new landing.

By the end of November we had the roof on the angle iron stores & kitchen. Mr. Clymo continued on putting up the spouting & other tasks about the house. Mr. Harris left with a party of boys to put up a fence about 4 miles long from one hill to the range which makes one side of the fence.

We hope to keep all the cattle here during the Wet to save mustering & control spearing, & later to improve the herd when we can get our new bulls. I helped the boys repair the other mile across the plains & revive it, this will use up all Mr. Lee Nails wire & some C.M.C. have sent it was finished by New Year, two wires on another to go.

All this month ploughing, harrowing, & planting potatoes & cassava, self directed, this as well as general. We have also made two new wells[:] one for the peoples houses, we get good permanent water in the dry at about 18ft[,] a rock like clay makes good sides; the other is by new houses 12ft.

in diameter, as I hope to make underground tank of it later & then sank a small shaft to the water for the pump for the new kitchen & bathroom. We have 6 wells in all now. These tasks have hindered us in our garden work, but managed to get 4 acres of rice out to finish the year with as the boys were then able to finish the fence when the posts were up & some wire on, this releasing Mr. Harris for tractor, as I had to keep the six mules going daily for timber before the plains are covered with water, so we have a fine heap of timber in. Mr Clymo went up to the ranges & got some of the Cyprus pine logs, & now is putting a new fence around the back of the station which is enclosing some 6 acres of garden & more as we are able to clear it. Mr. Harris cut the Cyprus pine to float down last Wet but the rain stopped. We wanted some for dining room roof, the rest will float down later.

During these 3 months the family steadily increased until we had over 150 with practically all the children back & some new ones, over 70 at Xmas, & over 200 in all come for Xmas & enjoyed themselves, they listened well to the message of God's love in English & their own tongue; we had several lantern lactures. Two lepers come some time before Xmas, one died soon after, we felt he died in the faith, the other was more or less healed for a season, but just as indifferent to things divine as many prove.

All sorts of sick ones come in the crowd, hence the dispensary was a very busy place, the feeding, the making of nagas & dresses meant late work, I wondered if the ladies would not break down, it is too much for two, but after Xmas many want to go walk about so the numbers reduce again or I fear we would break down with the strain. We are very glad to see them come to hear & many leave their children.

So ends a year of many activities, some set-backs which do not look very large as we see the station growing up around us, from the hill top it looks quite a little settlement, but there is unrest in many hearts, they want more,& cannot see that they are working to make a settlement for themselves, with many real problems in agriculture which make the task no light one.

Of those who have asked for baptism, some have slipped back, but may come again, we feel that they do believe but when they come in numbers the motives are mixed, & the pull of their world is strong, however, we will go on seeking to bring them in.

Yours sincerely,
Alf Dyer[105]

---

105 ML MSS 6040/12.

Figure 5.96: 'Staff of Oenpelli Mission – 1931'.
Source: Northern Territory Archives Service (NTRS 694 P1 Box 4b Item 290).

Figure 5.97: Visit to Red Lily (date unknown).
Source: Northern Territory Archives Service (NTRS 693 P1 Item 21 Red Lily).

* * *

General Secretary

Dear Mr Secretary.

We have 200 people here for Xmas and are in the midst of many activities that such times make. We are all well but tired as the going has been heavy lately with all the things we have been trying to do. But more of that later as 3 boys are going to Goulburn Island in the morning I just pen these lines to let you know all is well here all the children came back and new ones. Your November mail came last night it was good to get news after a long wait & now the Methodists have a boat we will get more regular mails I expect and more chances of sending as we have been shut off since October & began to think it might be April of next year. The orders & reports will follow later. Trusting all is well & that your needs have been supplied[.] All send loving greetings. 'The Lord reigneth'

Yours in 'the blessed Role'
Alf Dyer[106]

Figure 5.98: Christmas Day games (date unknown).
Source: Northern Territory Archives Service (NTRS 694 P1 Box 4a Item 269).

***

106 NTRS 1099/P1 vol. 1.

Oenpelli Report. July, August, September. 1931

The police party was with us for 4 days after their return from Goulburn Is. Three men were punished for spearing cattle; this evidently has had a very wholesome effect, as since then only one cause of spearing has been reported. The people were examined & it was found that 5 men were suffering from a form of V.D. Mr. Kennett had had experience in the treatment of such cases during the war, & was able to advise us as to the proper treatment, which, with the care of Sister Grieve, has effected the recovery of 3 of the cases: 2 cases are still undergoing treatment. One of the recovered cases was that of a boy who had just taken Elwyndiwyndi as his wife & this caused us some concern: we trust, however, that there will be no after effects. The Lord used Mr. Dyer to lead Mr. Kennett into the Way of Light & Life: this rejoiced [us] greatly; Praise the Lord: In his position Mr. Kennett could be greatly used of our Father, & we pray that He may "make him a channel of blessing."

The "Maskee" arrived with our stores on the 8th of July. Miss Nevill & Sister Grieve did not come by this boat (as was expected) & it gave us some concern that it would require the chartering of another boat to bring them from Darwin. We were very thankful that the "Maskee" was able to come right up to Cahills Landing, as it is much easier to cart the stores from there, than from the new landing. We had been expecting a boat for some time: once it had actually been seen in the river: Mr. & Mrs Dyer were packed up & ready to go – but it all proved groundless "black feller dream him I think." There were many false alarms; you can imagine the tension – & the relief when the boat did come.

The "Maroubra" brought the ladies on the 23rd of July & Mr. & Mrs. Dyer left the same day. I still hear the boys repeating the text of Mr. Dyer's last message to them.

The next event of any importance was our moving into the new Mission House. The new building is a great boon to all concerned & especially the ladies. We sing the Doxology.

The first lot of cattle came into the yards the day Mr. Dyer left us & after that the boys were kept busy right up till the end of August when about 1300 were mustered: 248 calves branded, all being dipped. This is not a complete muster, but the best [we] were able to do under the circumstances. I was out on one trip only, the rest being entrusted to the boys who did their work very well. I miss Quilp very much, Nipper is not his equal in stock work, although perhaps a better leader of men. the bullocks were drafted off & put into Red Lily, the balance kept in our new paddock near the station. I have since had to let this lot go as the feed got short, I merely opened the frnce [fence] & let them go or stay, just as they pleased: a big mob stayed– perhaps brcouse [because] they had not the bullocks to lead them. While in Darwin, Mr. Dyer obtained an offer from the Ice & Cold Storage Co to purchase a hundred (100) fat bullocks @ 14/- a hundred pounds dressed weight. We accepted this offer, believing it better to sell them at that price than leave them to waste, as many of the older bullocks would be unsaleable if kept any longer. The bullocks are ready & we hope to get them away in charge of Mr. Yates, a neighbour, about the 1ˢᵗ Nov. The cattle generally are very quiet, just now they are not being disturbed by the natives: one can ride through them in the open & they are only mildly interested.

The sale of bullocks was made possible by Mr. K. Langford Smith who brought our mail in July, together with the offer to purchase, on the 16ᵗʰ Aug. Everyone was excited by the arrivalof the aeroplane, I was rather concerned,as the landing ground was not yet in order.

Mr. Langford Smith landed safely however, & we could do nothing less than sing "Praise God from whom all blessings flow." Mr. Langford Smith stayed a few days & then continued his journey to Roper River. The following two weeks most of the family was engaged in clearing the landing ground, & it was much improved when the "Sky Pilot" retutned to us at the end of that time; having flown from Groote Is. to here via Millingimbe [Milingimbi Island] On the occasion of this visit, I went with Mr. Langford Smith to investigate a reported salt pan on Field Is. The salt was there all right & we bagged approx.. 24 cwt. This flight to Field Is. was very interesting & gave me a very good idea of the country. The mobs of buffalo were particularly interesting, as at this time we had in mind the shooting of about 100 bulls for the hides. To get the salt it would be necessary to repair the launch: to repair the launch we would need copper nails etc. Mr. Langford Smith offered to bring the nails from Darwin, so after discussion, it was decided that that was the best thing to do, that the benifit to the Work would warrant his making the trip.

So the "Sky Pilot" went on his way to Darwin, returning in two day's time. In making a landing this tiem, the undercarriage of the plane bumped into a heap of roots which had been dug up by those who were engaged in clearing the ground, & for some unaccountable reason placed right in the run way. Mr. Langford Smith narrowly escaped serious accident, but, with the assistance of Mr. Clymo, was able to repair the damaged part sufficiently to enable him to take off for Darwin after 3 days. We all enjoyed Mr. Langford Smith's visits very much, & having visited & studied the methods of many Mission Stations, his advise & hints were very helpful.

Mr. Clymo immediately got to work on the launch & has made very satisfactory progress with repairs.

It was getting toward the end of Sep. when I had the horses mustered & we were able to get away after the buffalo. We had hoped to get about 100 hides, but at the end of 2 weeks had only 59. The condition of the horses made it necessary for them to have a spell, before putting them on the road to Darwin with the bullocks, so decided to be content with what we had; came home & turned them out. The horses have had a strenuous time: we have not very many & they have had to work "double shift". There are about 10 young foals, but there is usually a very heavy mortality among them during the Wet. We branded 7 yearlings[–] 4 over 2 years, & gelded 1.

During these months we have enjoyed a bountiful supply of fresh vegetable & fruit, sweet potatoes, cassava, pumpkins, tomatoes, beans, cow-peas, pawpaws, & bananas. We found that gristed cow-peas make an excellent soup thickening, & as they are easily grown, we need not want for "thickening". Have also been giving the people Kiffir corn for breakfast on alternate days, tried it as a porridge at first & then simply boiled: they seem to likr [like] it all right– only one boy complained that it made him "sick along bingy". Also had a good supply of eggs & milk.

Started the erection of new Girl's dormitory, Dispensary, & Shelter house: they are not yet completed, as we had to leave them to get on with more urgent work.

Have kept the heavy lorry going carting bush timber, & the buck-board carting bark. The light lorry is out of action– the wheels are about finished. Mr. Clymo repaired the buck-board wheels, but they are a continual source of worry & steal away a lot of our time. The heavy lorry is in good order, but it is a "four mule pull". Some time ago I had some horses broken to harness, but these people cannot drive horses, & soon had them so that they were useless, the same collar is never put on the same horse twice, nor are the chains hooked up evenly. Mules seem to stand up to the wear & tear, but horses break down under the strain.

The school work seems to be making progress. Neither Mrs. Clymo nor Miss Nevill spare themselves in their efforts. There are now 19 girls & 18 boys in the dormitories: 6 younger children who live with their parents. The facilities in the new kitchen has enabled Mrs. Clymo to place more responsibility on the girls with regard to house-work, cooking etc. & has thus set herself free to take classes both morning & afternoon. There are 8 young men here who are able to read "just a little" so we thought it would be good if they could be brought up to a standard of efficiency: a standard which would enable them to read the scriptures; so 4 of them attended the afternoon class alternately. With the increase in the number of young children Miss Nevill too, now has classes morning & afternoon.

We have made the attendance at Sunday School "voluntary" for non reading adults. There are a lot of Goulburn Is. & bush people about, who have come in to reap the harvest of fish from our billabong: Either Mr. Clymo or I take some of the boys & go to the camp on Sunday afternoons & with the aid of picture rolls, try to tell them the Glad Tidings of Great Joy.

After the Sunday morning service Mrs. Clymo started teaching some of the older boys to sing the Canticles etc. closing with voluntary prayer. This has developed into a service of their own: it is good to see the number of men, women, girls & boys who attend– one to lead in the service, some to sing, one to read a passage of Scripture, one to give the address, & nearly all to pray.

The numbers attending the classes for preparation for baptism are increasing– 12 women, 13 men, (2 others not here) 9 boys, 6 girls: they are all learning to pray: of the 12 who attended my last class, 10 of them offered prayer. There is a new Spirit among us; a wonderful Spirit of helpfulness: we (the staff) feel the people are with us.

They are learning to know what it is to walk in the Way of Light & Life. We feel that the work is established, that the pioneering work is over. We remember always that the work is supported by the "prayers of the Saints" that we are now reaping the harvest of the good Seed sown by Mr. & Mrs. Dyer, Miss Sherrin & others who have laboured here in the past, & we say "Thanks to God who giveth us the Victory through our Lord Jesus Christ".

Sister Grieve has attended very well the medical side of the work there have been no very serious "new" cases: but there are always a large number of yaws, sick bingy, burns, sore eyes, etc. that require constant attention.

The weather has been pleasantly cool with more wind, I think, than is usual.

Yours sincerely,
G.R. Harris[107]

Figure 5.99: Keith Langford Smith, first flight to arrive in Oenpelli (heading to Roper River), 1931. Aboriginal housing can be seen in the background.
Source: Northern Territory Archives Service (NTRS 694 P1 Box 4 Item 57).

---

107 NTRS 1099/P1 vol. 1.

Figure 5.100: 'Keith Langford Smith's plane in peanut patch', chapel can be seen on the right-hand side (date unknown).

Source: Northern Territory Archives Service (NTRS 694 P1 Box 4a Item 244).

Figure 5.101: Keith Langford Smith lands in Oenpelli, 1931.

Source: Northern Territory Archives Service (NTRS 694 P1 Box 4 Item 64).

6

MEMORIES OF THE MISSION DAYS – ESTHER MANAKGU

Figure 6.1: Esther Manakgu, 2012.
Source: Sally K. May.

In 2012, Esther Manakgu sat down with Sally K. May and talked about her memories of the mission as a little girl. What follows are selected words from her oral history.

Esther's story

Gunbalanya that is this country name. Oenpelli. That *balanda* English, they say Oenpelli name. Gunbalanya. All the *balanda* mob they call the name Oenpelli but all the *bininj* they call Gunbalanya, in our language.

My father used to be named Nowenyako, that's native name. My mother used to be named Wayaliba.

My country name Wajapin Pujapin. That my country, where I been born… My father's country. My mother's country's name Kunburray.

Kunwinjku is my language, our language.

They used to call my name Jessie, out in the bush… They been call my name Jessie – they used to call my name Jessie for a while [laughs] out in the bush. Esther, that Oenpelli name, Christian name from Bible.

No, the white people was here when I was little girl. When all that people, the white people came here, but they went back, Paddy Cahill and Mr Campbell they went back…

My father and my mother, my grandmother, they used to live in bush. My father he brought me here because my father said, 'Come on children I'll take you. You got to learn for school so you can go to school so you can speak and understand little English, so you speak'. That was what my father say when he was alive.

I was born in bush with my father, my mother and my grandmother. And my father, he brought me here when I was a little girl, little bit, he brought me here at Oenpelli.

They were starving for smoke and my father said, 'Oh children we go down and you can go to school at Oenpelli'.

We came down from bush and my father used to brought me here not only myself – my brother too, all my brothers, but they died.

We used to camp here, just near that Arrkuluk Hill. But bottom part on the hill, we used to live there, they have little humpie. They used to build that humpie, we didn't have more house. Now we used to live there father and mother, not only my father but more people, they were coming from Liverpool [River] and some from Tin Camp, some people and some people from every country. They used to come and live with us. From Maningrida people they used to come walking. They used to come and visit us.

We didn't have any house here. We used to live in a cave, on Injalak, they got nice cave there. And Arrkuluk, bottom part, you got cave other side, bottom part you got cave, we used to live there, with my father. They used to make little humpie. We didn't have any house and after that when all the white people they came.

The beginning of the mission

Mr Dyer he came and brought Bible. No. Paddy Cahill, Mr Campbell they went back. Gone back to their country.

Reverend Dyer [he was the] Minister. He came here and brought the Bible here. And everyone came Christian to church, minister here. And all the Mandjurlngunj people, some they died and some people they was still alive when I came and I saw them.

Mr Dyer, after he brought the Bible. Reverend Dyer used to be minister, but he put the cross on that hill there. Arrkuluk, he put a cross there, another cross he put at Injalak. Mr Dyer used to be minister. Mr Dyer and this way Nimbabirr. Only two hills they had a cross, but we used to walk there, all there walk there on top of that hill there, and all the people, the first people their own country here.

The dormitory

We used to live in dormitory. They locked up door with a key until six o'clock. Seven o'clock they didn't opened the door for us. Some children … my brother and my sister and some boys they used to live there, other dormitory, they will lock them up. Because missionary people they save the people, the children, they save us, children walking alone. They wouldn't let us go walking alone. We sleep safe. We got a bucket inside dormitory. We used to sleep until six o'clock, then they opened the door and let us out go to school. We had our breakfast and go to school. They wouldn't let us to get running around for anything. First missionary came they wouldn't let us go walking around: go to church, good, go to school. We couldn't get baby early. We got to baby little bit later! They wouldn't let us smoking too. No.

Figure 6.2: Girls outside dormitory (date unknown).
Source: NTRS 693 P1 Item 21.

Mummy and Daddy they been staying outside camping. Out in the camp, but all this we are children, used to camp inside the dormitory.

Some people they let children out they can stay with their mother and father, they take us out. And leave the dormitory... And they said 'Alright'. 'If you take your children, I can't give you smoke. If you leave all children, stay in the dormitory, alright! If you take them out you won't get any smoke!'

Some girls they were smoking, starving for a smoke. I didn't smoke. That was what *balanda* say, 'I can't give you any smoke if you taking your child out into camp. I can leave it for you. You boss. You can looking up to them'. Alright other, I don't know who that man came and say, 'You don't lock them up – let them out and stay with mother and father', and they say, 'Alright, we will let them out'. They went to mother and father [laughs].

We used to sleep alright, say the prayer, and we sleep at night. We had a prayer. We sleep. We had a nice sister. We had a prayer and good. We wouldn't worry. We just sleep. Some big girls, some little girls, like some big boys and little boys, other dormitory, staying other house away from girls. But no smoking! They can starve people. They wouldn't let us meet with girls and boys now. We just went to the school that's all, and come back and stay in the dormitory and some of the people might be all sorry to us and they say, might be they say to the missionary, 'Alright, you can let the children out and stay with their mother and father' and they said, 'Alright, we will stay with our father and mother' and everybody was happy and some children, they got big and they got married in the church like me. I got married in the church.

Signs from heaven

When I used to [be a] little girl I got lost I went out to school and I been walking. I was walking along on that Red Lily road. I ran away. I was thinking [about] my mother and my father. They went hunting on that rock there what you call Nambatu waterfall [the small waterfall near the road]. I went there. Just walking along there. I was thinking myself 'Ah I have to go after my mother and father. Where they gone?' I been walking along there and I climbed up big tree on Red Lily road and I was yell out there calling to my father and my mother. I said, 'MUMMY! DADDY! Where are you?' And no one answer my voice. And this one I saw dingo. One dingo he was sitting down there with the eyeglass [glasses]. Big dog. It wasn't dingo but something else. Something else. Maybe bad Satan. And I went back and I came back I was standing there crying, calling, calling my father but no answer. I have to go back and I came back from bush. Still coming back from bush on that road, same road. We used to sing, camping near that, in the funeral. We used to camp there [near the cemetery] and I came back and I sleep myself there covered up with my blanket and went to sleep. And it got dark, dark night and I had a bad dream. I had a bad dream and cry and something will come. Make me jump and cry. And that minister he came, Reverend Dyer. Mr Dyer he made that cross and he helped me, that man. He put a cross there and he gave me wine. Was drinking and he killed all the bad things. Jesus came and they went away. I always go church…

Long time ago, I dunno what number today, I know what year, I had a good dream from heaven. Two years, I had a good dream from heaven. All the angels they been singing for me. I was sleeping that night and I heard this people, angels, they been singing for me. Last one. My country they used to sing, all the angels. Oh, second they been singing Marwamara, my son's country. I used to take them and listen that people they would sing again. I'm still here. I won't forget. I got my Bible, prayer books, hymn books. I still got it.

The school

We like to learn how to speak little bit English so we understand. That what my father said. I came here, my father brought me here. And they teach us at school that's why I am speaking little bit English. My father brought me from bush.

I, we went to school here and we used to learn little bit how to speak English, even understand.

[They would teach me] learning how to little bit read. Reading. But I like to learn more about reading. Some long words I don't know much about, but I only know short words.

They teach me about the sums, sums and lessons, ABC start. ABCDEFGHIJKLMNOPRSTUVWDXYZ for start and all the sums, Twice times table 3 times table, 4 times table a little bit of… But I forgot other time.

The mission songs

Everybody was clap hands. All the ladies, children they came over there. And they went back, I used to sing for them… All my sisters, they used to play for dancing. We used to live in dormitory and they been singing that song:

O Miss Maree when you go to your home
I will never forget you.
Good bye my teacher I do love you
O Miss Maree when you go to your home
I will never forget you.
Goodbye my teacher I do love you

When you go home, like I can sing, you can sing to somebody, you say good bye… I got lotta song but my throat no good. Blackfella song and English song from church.

I can sing *yuwadi* song. *Yuwa* that means Christian song.

Flowers are baby… Take each one is coming – take from God to you. Telling one secret of his paradise. Baby … of the home above. All these flowers of summer – angel like a … Listen to the message which they bring today. They said all the message which they bring today.

My sister son she made that song. From Bible, she make it, but he died, was minister.

Jesus set me free
– I love – Jesus
Jesus coming to you –
Jesus. Remember me my Lord. As I pray to you.
Thank you Jesus you save me please.
Thank you Jesus You set me free
My … Where down we were …
On the cross. Jesus bugandaken.
Thank you Jesus bugandaken.
Praise god Hallenehlu

Mission Christmas

We used to dance every Christmas and my father used to be dance too… One Christmas time used to be old people used to dance. They had a big tree, Christmas tree all tied up. All kinds of things every time, material, all kinds. Every time up in the tree, one big tree. Only saw trees about that high. They used to make that trees turn. Then you had happy Christmas.

And Christmas time they used to dance, make the people happy. And they used to making big tree and cover that tree with branches. They tied up everything like clothes, smoke all kinds. They been sending up that tree on Christmas time. Make the people happy, they used to be smoke every time up in smoke. All kinds of material they tie him up with the branch. Some branches they cutting that tree make it small. And everybody was sitting right down and watch people dancing and some races, people racing, some young boys little boys, some girls, little girls too. They used to dance. Now we had Christmas party. There used to be races and this was the first time we didn't know this country.

Christmas time there used to be dancing make themselves happy, play football and dancing. Women dancing, all the ladies would be dancing... [I] was dancing.

Living conditions in the mission days

We used to camp there... We had a cottage lying there and we had a garden patch here. We had potatoes, banana, cassava, peanuts, all kinds sugar cane. We had a little garden right along, right along there. We had another garden. We had one farmer, farmer man used to teach us to grow the garden, planting garden, right along over there. We had garden. Potatoes... Each woman, each lady, one lady she had five row potatoes. Like me I had five rows potatoes. They were nice potatoes, planted there right along. And this one, after them, plenty mango. This one, other side, we call that corner there, that corner there can you see that big mountain there? On your back. We call that Kunnanj: Fish Creek. Great Mum, Great mother used to be. Great Mummy country but she died. And the Father, old man. They died. We call that place Kunnanj: Fish Creek.

Building one [line of] house straight down, one house for hospital wife and the children, one house other house for husband and wife and the children each one they been built that cottage... They been building one house each. First time. And after this when other people they came this mob all the *balanda*. All the staff they came after and built new houses and big houses, built shop.

Work outside the mission

We had a big road there, been walking right up to crossing, bit of foot walk all the way right up to Madjinbardi. They been skinning; all the boys, they had big contract here. Other man from that time Doyle and son is Maden [Gaden]. Doyle used to be Boss Jack Mays. All that there, ah, everybody said from Oenpelli people, 'Where are we going... we all going, all my people. Come on we go! We go and look like smoke!' And other people got smoke at Madjinbardi! [laughs]

Alright, we been walk now carrying the suede. Still walking right up to crossing, right past, kept on walking, never name there... We went this way. Madjinbardi way. People look for baccy, smoke. But other people got smoke at the station. They been working other contract. Went there. And skinned, cleaning all that hide, put the salt. I used to clean hide too. Put the salt and make it dry like blanket. But we didn't get paid money. We been hard work. It was very hard work we women all the ladies. We couldn't get paid money. We didn't get money it was very hard work. We used to work morning, dinner time, afternoon.

'All you ladies I only give you food when you knock off. When you finished going back to your homes at Oenpelli I give you baking flour, baking sugar, all kinds of food you can take it back with you.' All that used up ah! They been carry the most because we was walking back with a load – no car [laughs]. We used to camp halfway at Needen crossing there but bit farther up.

When we were at Madjinbardi we used to camp there. Camp there one week, two weeks. We used to camp there. Work with that hide. Alright, we can lift that hide there. There two men, three men there who had a car there. They brought a big truck. They been loading, taking all that hides and they all came there from Madjinbardi, right along there. We used to work there and that man said, 'Alright. Alright all the people, you can go back home now we got enough hides'.

'Alright you can smoke now, baccy.' They been smoking, some people they been smoking, give them smoke, black one, long one.

We roll them with the paper. Some cigarette they been using. They been making that pipe with a stick with a hole and smoke him. Sometime make him like pipe. We call that pipe, used to smoke with that tin now.

Nobody get paid. They wouldn't get paid from that food at all. When we came back no money. All the ladies wouldn't get paid… You couldn't get money. And all the men they didn't get paid. All the men they been walking along and they been showing him all the buffalo and they been skinning and bringing all the hides back in the camp. Tomorrow, 'Come on all you ladies – you are cleaning the hides! Wash it, put on salt – make it dry!' We wouldn't get paid.

And I said, 'No, we only give you pay'. Oh! That's right, I forgot. We wouldn't get paid. No money but only get alcohol. They been bringing carton with a boat. On that Cannon Hill way. Cannon Hill way on that river, they brought the alcohol with a boat.

And I saw these people they been drink. Ah they had a drink there. They been drunk. And I say, 'What these people doing?' There was a meal here and I walk back with my mum. Some other people turn back we came back we brought the meal back here. Ah Graeme Bardon he was here, army man, used to work here. I went back, we went back and I found these people they was drunk. And I said, 'What are you doing? How come they are all drunk and what do you have to do?' 'Nah, you can have a drink little bit', 'What's that!?' We didn't know, some church people, my family.

My sister-in-law Elizabeth, her name Elizabeth, Heather, myself and Deborah – old Deborah, Rachel, we weren't do that, that country. Or Trudy. That being the men, clean the hide and we saw these people they been get paid in alcohol and everybody was drunk in afternoon time night time. And I said, 'What are they doing? What these people doing?'

'Oh, they all drunk, all that mob, but I give you little bit one to taste.'

And I said, 'No, I might die'. I said no.

'Come on all you church people! Little taste!'

And I said, 'No, we don't taste, no good. We only drinking wine that's all, port wine'.

'Now you can taste! All you men you can have a drink, not only ladies. You can take all that carton of beer, bottled wine and all kinds of names.'

I been telling that Boss one, 'You can take it back please! We can't have that all the carton, you know, the people might get mad'. You know I been telling the boss one Jim Doyle and Geoff Mace.

'You can take it back please', I said. 'You can give them little bit of liquor, ah, not too much', but I can tell they got gun. 'I'm frightened all these people they might get murdered, they shoot themselves!' And this time I had good mind to think.

'Alright!' that boss man said, 'I take it back with the boat.'

'With the carton, carton. Carton had to go home. Take it back!' 'Alright, Aunt Esther we take it back. Can't have too much. Very dangerous they might kill themselves, and they will take it back in Darwin.'

And I been thinking all these people there got gun. They always go hunting shooting buffalo and I say, 'they might get murdered. They shoot themselves!' That's what I been tell that man, that boss one. And he was standing there and think, 'But you can send him back with the carton. It very dangerous for all these people might kill themselves because they got gun, all of them'. And then he said, 'Alright! Alright Jessie!'

Ceremony and ancestral beings

Bininj ceremony… I can't go near, I stay away. They tell me we had it before, that other one. One, two, three: we had three ceremony in here at Oenpelli. But after that, Jesus he taught me other way. Well, I forgot everything, but all my people they been teaching me that other way. This time I am finished with ceremony anything. No anything.

I been the ground there. You know you been seen the people – where they live? That's the place we had the ceremony. I went there with my sister, she died, I saw her. She was boss of that ceremony, my big sister, other one. And two, one more, three ceremony, we had ceremony here and all the people, all the boys, I saw them. They brought that ceremony maybe from Pine Creek way. This way they didn't know what that ceremony for Pine Creek way. And then the places what they call? Menburu [Mainoru]. Pine Creek way, but Katherine way but other place [Burrumbin?]. Maybe that place now, they put the ceremony. We didn't know, and we saw them, them dancing there. And all the people there used to dance only corroboree here. That bishop, Philip used to sing and other one – old man Philip and Umbalang.

I used to camp [on Injalak Hill] with my husband. And… my son. He's still there. He is staying in his country Kabbari. That country's name Kabbari – my son's country name. That Rainbow [Serpent] there Rainbow dreaming. And that little boy was crying. Was crying long time ago, they didn't tell him now, but my grandmother was telling me too. And my son he know, was crying that little boy. This Rainbow he came from sea. He came from blue sea. He was crawling under the ground and all the people they used to live there at Kabbari. I say country, my son's country. He got red cliff there. Rainbow was vomiting. From all the people, he was eating all the people. He ate all the people. And two little boys they sit there on the rock. They turned to rock. They turned to stone.

That place name. Undupulun next Arrmarnda, near airport, we call that place Arrmarnda. They have a story. The dog was running there. They reckon that dog been turned to dingo ground and didn't know everybody. But telling you about a dream. Baby dog, girl dog and boy one, in the ground. Water did come up. We call that place 'Brokdanakpom' on that corner, airport but that corner that side, we call that place. At that place two dog came and dig the ground. Now the ground was very dry and that two dogs they been dig. They been dig, they reckon, that man reckon, that old man reckon, he was telling us, Old Nipper. They dig the ground and water can come up now. They been drink and before they went to the waterfall that two dogs. That two dogs name: Arrkuluk, Omwarl. Girl one Omwarl. Arrkuluk boy one, like the hill. Their names. They went to the waterfall now and they lived there. They been stay there too long to the waterfall… [Those two dogs] they been turned to rock. Like my son's country. That two little boys. Two brother: first brother and second brother, they been turned to rock. They ended up top hill; they been turned to rock, those two boys. They still there. They been turned to rock, still there. My son country. 'Kabbari' we call that place, 'Kabbari'. There my son's country. They are still there.

Figure 6.3: Esther Manakgu, 2012.
Source: Sally K. May.

BIBLIOGRAPHY

Albrecht, Glenn, Clive R. McMahon, David M. J. S. Bowman and Corey J. A. Bradshaw. 'Convergence of Culture, Ecology, and Ethics: Management of Feral Swamp Buffalo in Northern Australia'. *Journal of Agricultural and Environmental Ethics* 22, no. 4 (2009): 361–78. doi.org/10.1007/s10806-009-9158-5.

Allen, F. Jim. 'Archaeology and the History of Port Essington'. PhD thesis, The Australian National University, Canberra, 1969.

Altman, Jon. *Hunter-Gatherers Today: An Aboriginal Economy in North Australia.* Canberra: Australian Institute of Aboriginal Studies, 1987.

Austin-Broos, Diane. *Arrernte Present, Arrernte Past: Invasion, Violence, and Imagination in Indigenous Central Australia.* Chicago: University of Chicago Press, 2009. doi.org/10.7208/chicago/9780226032658.001.0001.

Australia Royal Commission on the Northern Territory and N. K. Ewing. *Minutes of Evidence.* Melbourne: A.J. Mullett, Govt. Printer, 1920.

Baker, Gwenda. 'Crossing Boundaries: Negotiated Space and the Construction of Narratives of Missionary Incursion'. *Journal of Northern Territory History* 16 (2005): 17–28.

Berndt, Ronald M. and Catherine H. Berndt. *Man, Land & Myth: The Gunwinggu People.* Sydney: Ure Smith, 1970.

Bowman, David M. J. S. and Cathy J. Robinson. 'The Getting of the Nganabbarru: Observations and Reflections on Aboriginal Buffalo Hunting in Northern Australia'. *Australian Geographer* 33, no. 2 (2010): 191–206. doi.org/10.1080/00049180220151007.

Centre for 21st Century Humanities. 'Colonial Massacres Map'. University of Newcastle. Accessed 17 July 2019. c21ch.newcastle.edu.au/colonialmassacres/map.php.

Chaloupka, George. *Journey in Time: The World's Longest Continuing Art Tradition: The 50,000-Year Story of the Australian Aboriginal Rock Art of Arnhem Land.* Chatswood, NSW: Reed, 1993.

Choo, Christine. *Mission Girls: Aboriginal Women on Catholic Missions in the Kimberley, Western Australia, 1900–1950.* Crawley: University of Western Australia Press, 2001.

Church Missionary Society of Australia. *Decade: The Story of the Australian C.M.S. from 1953–1963.* Sydney: Church Missionary Society of Australia, 1963.

Clark, Marshall and Sally K. May, eds. *Macassan History and Heritage: Journeys, Encounters and Influences.* Canberra: ANU E Press, 2013. dx.doi.org/10.22459/MHH.06.2013.

Clarke, Henry Lowther. *Report of the Church Congress Held at Melbourne, 19th to 24th November, 1906.* Melbourne: [The Congress], 1906.

Clarkson, C., Z. Jacobs, B. Marwick, R. Fullagar, L. Wallis, M. Smith, R. G. Roberts, E. Hayes, K. Lowe, X. Carah, S. A. Florin, J. McNeil, D. Cox, L. J. Arnold, Q. Hua, J. Huntley, H. E. A. Brand, T. Manne, A. Fairbairn, J. Shulmeister, L. Lyle, M. Salinas, M. Page, K. Connell, G. Park, K. Norman, T. Murphy and C. Pardoe. 'Human Occupation of northern Australia by 65,000 years ago'. *Nature* 547 (2017): 306–10. doi.org/10.1038/nature22968.

Clinch, M. A. 'Cahill, Patrick (Paddy) (1863–1923)'. *Australian Dictionary of Biography.* National Centre of Biography, The Australian National University. First published 1979. Accessed 17 July 2019. adb.anu.edu.au/biography/cahill-patrick-paddy-5461/text9277.

Cole, Keith. *From Mission to Church: The CMS Mission to the Aborigines of Arnhem Land, 1908–1985.* Bendigo: Keith Cole Publications, 1985.

——. *A History of Oenpelli.* Darwin: Nungalinya Publications, 1975.

——. *Oenpelli Pioneer: A Biography of the Reverend Alfred John Dyer, Pioneer Missionary among the Aborigines in Arnhem Land and Founder of the Oenpelli Mission.* Parkville, Vic.: Church Missionary Historical Publications, 1972.

——. *Sharing in Mission: The Centenary History of the Victorian Branch of the Church Missionary Society, 1892–1992.* Bendigo: Keith Cole Publications, 1992.

——. *A Short History of the C.M.S. Roper River Mission, 1908–1968.* Parkville, Vic.: Church Missionary Historical Publications Trust, 1968.

Cruickshank, Joanna and Patricia Grimshaw. *White Women, Aboriginal Missions and Australian Settler Governments: Maternal Contradictions*. Leiden: Brill, 2019. doi.org/10.1163/9789004397019_002.

David, Bruno, Paul S. C. Taçon, Jean-Jacques Delannoy and Jean-Michel Geneste, eds. *The Archaeology of Rock Art in Western Arnhem Land, Australia*. Terra Australis 47. Canberra: ANU Press, 2017. doi.org/10.22459/ta47.11.2017.

Dewar, Michelle. *The 'Black War' in Arnhem Land: Missionaries and the Yolngu 1908–1940*. Darwin: North Australia Research Unit, 1992.

Elkin, A. P., R. M. Berndt and C. H. Berndt. 'Social Organization of Arnhem Land'. *Oceania* 21, no. 4 (1951): 253–301. doi.org/10.1002/j.1834-4461.1951.tb00176.x.

Emilsen, William. *Fighting Spirit: A History of Christianity at Warruwi, Goulburn Island*. Unley, SA: MediaCom Education Inc., 2016.

Ganter, Regina. *The Contest for Aboriginal Souls: European Missionary Agendas in Australia*. Canberra: ANU Press, 2018. doi.org/10.22459/cas.05.2018.

Griffiths, Tom. *Hunters and Collectors: The Antiquarian Imagination in Australia*. Cambridge: Cambridge University Press, 1996.

Harris, John. *One Blood: 200 Years of Aboriginal Encounter with Christianity: A Story of Hope*. Sutherland, NSW: Albatross Books, 1994.

Harris, Stephen. *The Field Has Its Flowers: Nell Harris*. Darwin: Historical Society of the Northern Territory, 1998.

Hill, Barry. *Broken Song: T.G.H. Strehlow and Aboriginal Possession*. Milsons Point, NSW: Knopf, 2002.

Johnstone, Samuel Martin. *A History of the Church Missionary Society in Australia and Tasmania*. Sydney: The Church Missionary Society, 1925.

Jones, Rhys. 'Recommendations for Archaeological Site Management in Kakadu National Park'. In *Archaeological Research in Kakadu National Park*, edited by Rhys Jones, 299–304. Special Publication 13. Canberra: Australian National Parks and Wildlife Service, 1985.

Jones, Rhys and Tia Negerivich. 'A Review of Previous Archaeological Work'. In *Archaeological Research in Kakadu National Park*, edited by Rhys Jones, 1–16. Special Publication 13. Canberra: Australian National Parks and Wildlife Service, 1985.

Kenny, Robert. *The Lamb Enters the Dreaming: Nathanael Pepper & the Ruptured World*. Carlton North, Vic.: Scribe Publications, 2010.

Leichhardt, Ludwig. *Journal of an Overland Expedition in Australia, from Moreton Bay to Port Essington: A Distance of Upwards of 3000 Miles, During the Years 1844–1845.* Vol. 1. London: T. and W. Boone, 1847. doi.org/10.1017/cbo 9781139107617.

Levitus, Robert. *Everybody Bin All Day Work.* Canberra: Australian Institute of Aboriginal Studies, 1982.

———. 'Social History since Colonisation'. In *Kakadu: Natural and Cultural Heritage Management,* edited by Tony Press, David Lea, Ann Webb and Alistair Graham, 64–93. Darwin: ANCA and North Australia Research Unit, 1995.

Loos, Noel. *White Christ Black Cross: The Emergence of a Black Church.* Canberra: Aboriginal Studies Press, 2007.

Lydon, Jane. *Eye Contact: Photographing Indigenous Australians.* Durham: Duke University Press, 2005.

Macknight, Campbell. *The Voyage to Marege': Macassan Trepangers in Northern Australia.* Carlton, Vic.: Melbourne University Press, 1976.

Mangiru, Hannah. Unpublished oral history with Robert Levitus, 27 July 1981.

Masson, Elsie R. *An Untamed Territory: The Northern Territory of Australia.* London: Macmillan and Company, 1915.

Morris, John Arnold. *The Tiwi: From Isolation to Cultural Change: A History of Encounters between an Island People and Outside Forces.* Darwin: Northern Territory University Press, 2001.

Mountford, Charles. *Records of the American-Australian Scientific Expedition to Arnhem Land.* Vol. 1: *Art, Myth and Symbolism.* Melbourne: Melbourne University Press, 1956.

Mulvaney, Derek John. *Paddy Cahill of Oenpelli.* Canberra: Aboriginal Studies Press, 2004.

Mulvaney, Derek John and John H. Calaby. *'So Much That Is New': Baldwin Spencer, 1860–1929.* Carlton, Vic.: University of Melbourne at the University Press, 1985.

Pybus, Carol Ann. '"We Grew Up This Place": Ernabella Mission 1937–1974'. PhD thesis, University of Tasmania, 2012.

Rademaker, Laura. *Found in Translation: Many Meanings on a North Australian Mission.* Honolulu: University of Hawai'i Press, 2018.

Robinson, Catherine J. 'Buffalo Hunting and the Feral Frontier of Australia's Northern Territory'. *Social and Cultural Geography* 6, no. 6 (2005): 885–901. doi.org/10.1080/14649360500353285.

Sheehan, Colin. 'Strangers and Servants of the Company: The United East India Company and the Dutch Voyages to Australia'. In *Strangers on the Shore: Early Coastal Contacts in Australia*, edited by Peter Veth, Peter Sutton and Margo Neale, 6–34. Canberra: National Museum of Australia Press, 2008.

Silverstein, Ben. 'The "Proper Settler" and the "Native Mind": Flogging Scandals in the Northern Territory, 1919 and 1932'. In *Intimacies of Violence in the Settler Colony: Economies of Dispossession around the Pacific Rim*, edited by Penelope Edmonds and Amanda Nettelbeck, 89–112. Cham, Switzerland: Palgrave Macmillan, 2018. doi.org/10.1007/978-3-319-76231-9_5.

Simpson, Colin. *Adam in Ochre: Inside Aboriginal Australia*. Sydney: Angus and Robertson, 1951.

Spencer, Baldwin. *Native Tribes of the Northern Territory of Australia*. London: Macmillan, 1914.

——. *Wanderings in Wild Australia*. London: Macmillan, 1928.

Spillett, Peter. *Forsaken Settlement: An Illustrated History of the Settlement of Victoria, Port Essington, North Australia 1838–1849*. Melbourne: Lansdowne, 1979.

Taçon, Paul S. C., Sally K. May, Stewart Fallon, Meg Travers, Daryl Wesley and Ronald Lamilami. 'A Minimum Age for Early Depictions of Southeast Asian Praus in the Rock Art of Arnhem Land, Northern Territory'. *Australian Archaeology* 71, no. 1 (2010): 1–10. doi.org/10.1080/03122417.2010.1168 9379.

Taylor, Luke. *Seeing the Inside: Bark Painting in Western Arnhem Land*. Oxford: Clarendon Press, 1996.

Theden-Ringl, F., J. N. Fenner, D. Wesley and R. Lamilami. 'Buried on Foreign Shores: Isotope Analysis of the Origin of Human Remains Recovered from a Macassan Site in Arnhem Land'. *Australian Archaeology* 73, no. 1 (2011): 41–48.

Warburton, Carl. *Buffaloes*. Sydney: Angus and Robertson, 1934.

Wesley, Daryl, Sue O'Connor and Jack N. Fenner. 'Re-evaluating the Timing of the Indonesian Trepang Industry in North-west Arnhem Land: Chronological Investigations at Malara (Anuru Bay A)'. *Archaeology in Oceania* 51, no. 3 (2016): 169–95. doi.org/10.1002/arco.5091.

Archival files

Mitchell Library

ML MSS 6039, Resigned Missionary Files.

ML MSS 6040/1, CMS Federal Council.

ML MSS 6040/3, Church Missionary Society Federal Office.

ML MSS 6040/4, CMS Committee for Aborigines.

ML MSS 6040/12, Oenpelli Reports.

ML MSS 6040/35, Resigned Missionary Files.

National Archives of Australia

NAA A431/1, Oenpelli Mission Station.

NAA A3, NT1917/427, Department of Home and Territories Aboriginal Station, Oenpelli, Attempted poisoning of staff by natives.

Northern Territory Archive Service

NTRS 226, TS 102, Les Perriman Oral History, 1981.

NTRS 226, TS 517, Ruby Roney Oral History, 1985.

NTRS 226, TS 735, Ruby Roney Oral History, 1974.

NTRS 337, Les Perriman, Personal records and photographs relating to Groote Eylandt Mission and Aborigines in Northern Australia, 1921–1972.

NTRS 693, Alfred Dyer, Records relating to mission life in Northern Australia, 1907–1966.

NTRS 694, Records, photographs and research material about mission life in Northern Australia, 1915–1985.

NTRS 1099, Mission reports and station council minutes of the Oenpelli Community, 1925–1977.

NTRS 1105, Publications featuring Arnhem Land missions, 1953–1981.

Other

Historical Oenpelli Slides, Church Missionary Society, complied by K. Hart, A. Wilson and W. Kennedy, 1996.

APPENDIX A: ABORIGINAL NAMES MENTIONED IN THE RECORDS, 1925–31

The paucity of Aboriginal names in the mission records is sadly reflective of the time. Despite over 60,000 words of correspondence published in this volume, only 25 names are given for people living at or around the Oenpelli mission. Many of these are only mentioned once, often regarding baptism classes or death. We present here a list of Aboriginal names for people who were associated with the mission at this time. Table 1 includes all references to named Aboriginal people in the sources published in this volume. Table 2 includes further names in other documents. This is not a comprehensive list of all at Oenpelli at the time, but a compilation of those mentioned in some written sources. The original sources may have made errors or omissions.

Table 1: Aboriginal people at Oenpelli mentioned in documents used in this work

Name (as recorded)	Other names and alternative spellings	Who they were
Arawingi	Arrawindji Arawindju Lazarus	Young man living at mission station. Lost a leg in buffalo camp incident.
Argawalmie		Woman living on station
Buranali		Man living at mission station
Carabumba Carambumba	Garabbunba Elizabeth Gumurdul Ngalmandjurlngunj (clan) Ngalkodjok (skin name)	Young girl/woman living in dormitory
Caryl	Karil Rachel	Young girl

Name (as recorded)	Other names and alternative spellings	Who they were
Denajong		Young boy suffering from leprosy
Elmareri		Young girl living in dormitory
Elmynjalinmag		Young girl in dormitory
Elwyndiwyndi		Young girl in dormitory
Galinower	Galinawa	Young girl in dormitory
Gamarad	Joseph Gamardadj Girrabul Sarmard Samard	Young man living in dormitory, married Elizabeth Garabbunba ('Carabumba'). One of first pupils in Mrs Dyer's school class.
Garijala (Garreejarlar) Gurijula		Woman suffering from leprosy
Garijala	Garidjala Rebecca	Young girl living in dormitory
Garynjulu	Gurindjulu Mary Garnarradj	
Hazel		Aboriginal-Malay girl living in dormitory
Jaragalgal	Djeragalgal Nadanek (clan)	Young girl in dormitory
Nagal	Nagel Philip	Young man living in dormitory
Naganiki		Young stockman
Naluwad	Frank Naluwud Naluweed Narlowieol Narluweed Girrabul	Lost a leg after being accidentally shot in a buffalo camp. Former cattle killer turned worker at the mission station. Known to use his crutch to hit missionaries and their wives.
Narlbrett	Nangalbered	Young boy in dormitory. Child of Bagul and Madjiagu.
Narlumbeal	Billy	Old man living at mission station
Narlym	Narlim Naalim Ngalmandjurlngunj (clan)	Stockman. Son of Nipper Marakarra and Alaamin (Ngalamin). Brother to Elizabeth Garabbunba ('Carabumba'). Married to Djeragalgal. Daughter was Guluba (Peggy Balmana).
Narma Ramagul		Young stockman

Name (as recorded)	Other names and alternative spellings	Who they were
Narpyn	Napaim	Living in the dormitory. Younger brother to Elizabeth Garabbunba ('Carabumba').
Nipper	Marakarra Gumurdul Maraggara Kumutun Ngalmandjurlngunj (clan) Nawamud (skin name)	Senior Traditional Owner for Oenpelli
Paddy		Stockman. Had originally worked for Paddy Cahill and stayed on after he left. First person Dyer baptised after his ordination (Paddy was dying). Buried in cemetery near 'white' settler.
Quilp		Quilp was originally Paddy Cahill's main stockman and continued to work in Oenpelli when the mission took over. It is rumoured he was either a survivor of massacre near Wave Hill adopted by Cahill or he was Cahill's biological son. Quilp was married to local woman Magarorda.
Stumpy		Man living on station. Former cattle killer who came into mission when sick. First Aboriginal person buried in Oenpelli cemetery (but traditional ceremony took place).
Waranbiyga	Biddy	Woman living on station, good cook, stepmother to Elizabeth Garabbunba ('Carabumba'). Wife to Nipper Marakarra. Left mission to live out bush.

Table 2: Aboriginal people at Oenpelli recorded in other documents

Name	Other contemporary and later names and alternative spellings	Association	Reference
Alaamin	Ngalamin	Mother of Mick Walumak (from her first husband). Mother to Elizabeth Garabbunba ('Carabumba'), Narlim, Kuluba, Narpyn (Napaim), and Manmuruk from second husband Nipper Marakarra.	Cole, *History of Oenpelli*, 23
Algandali		Young girl in class	Harris, *Field Has Its Flowers*, 18
Bagul		First wife called Madjiagu. Together they had four children: Galiwal, Nangalbered, Merdeki and Narin.	Harris, *Field Has Its Flowers*, 20
Bill Neidji	Neiji Nakamarrang (skin name)	Brought to Oenpelli mission by relative called Maudie. 'The smartest Aboriginal kid I ever taught' (Nell Harris).	Harris, *Field Has Its Flowers*, 18
Cingoomba		Young wife to Nipper Marakarra	NTRS 693 part 1 (Dyer Story 8), n.p. 'A black prince and princess'
David Namilmil	Mangiru Namirlmirl Nawamud (skin name)	Married to Hannah	Harris, *Field Has Its Flowers*, 18
Dolly Yarnmarlu	Ngalkodjok (skin name)	Wife of Nipper Marakarra. Two children died in infancy.	Cole, *History of Oenpelli*, 23
Gadjag		Brother to Caryl (Rachel). Had leprosy. Died out bush.	Harris, *Field Has Its Flowers*, 16
Galiwal		Eldest son of Bagul and Madjiagu	Harris, *Field Has Its Flowers*, 20
Ganawulu		From Fish Creek	Cole, *History of Oenpelli*, 23

Name	Other contemporary and later names and alternative spellings	Association	Reference
Gararu	Sarah	Worked in kitchen	Harris, *Field Has Its Flowers*, 16
Herbert Yupidj		Originally worked for Paddy Cahill and stayed on with mission	Cole, *History of Oenpelli*, 23
Jingumi		Wife of Nipper Marakarra. Mother of Frank Djenjdjulng (adopted by Nipper).	Cole, *History of Oenpelli*, 23
Kanowla		Man living at station. Discussed rock paintings with Dyer.	NTRS 693 part 1 (Dyer Story 8), n.p. 'Native Drawings'
Mabrima		Girl in dormitory. Died from snake bite.	Harris, *Field Has Its Flowers*, 13
Madjiagu		First wife of Bagul. Mother of Galiwal, Nangalbered, Merdeki and Narin.	Harris, *Field Has Its Flowers*, 20
Magarorda		Wife of Quilp. Helped Mrs Dyer with dispensary on Saturdays.	Harris, *Field Has Its Flowers*, 21
Mainbara		Wife of Nipper Marakarra Mother to Donald Gumurdul, Julie Julunguru (Narndal), Anne Marrabib, Agnes Birriwilik and Helen Alngalgindja.	Cole, *History of Oenpelli*, 23
Majumbu		From Nimbuwar area. First wife named Badjbadjuk. Father of Namadomarndo.	Cole, *History of Oenpelli*, 23
Mamarandja		Girl in dormitory	Harris, *Field Has Its Flowers*, 13
Manakini	Priscilla	Girl in dormitory	Harris, *Field Has Its Flowers*, 13
Manguru		Father of David Namirlmirl	Cole, *History of Oenpelli*, 23

Name	Other contemporary and later names and alternative spellings	Association	Reference
Marawuna	Rebecca	Girl in dormitory	Harris, *Field Has Its Flowers*, 13
Mary		Baby of Elizabeth Garabbunba ('Carabumba') and Gamarad. Died during whooping cough epidemic. Buried in cemetery against her father's wishes.	NTRS 693 part 1 (Dyer Story 8), n.p. 'A black prince and princess'
Mengudja	Samuel Garnaradj	Baptised Easter 1933	Cole, *History of Oenpelli*, 74
Merdeki		Child of Bagul and Madjiagu	Harris, *Field Has Its Flowers*, 20
Minyeiwi		Worked in kitchen	Harris, *Field Has Its Flowers*, 16
Munipa	Esther (baptism name) Jessie Muniba Manakgu	Taken to live at Oenpelli mission by her family when very young. Lived in dormitory.	Chapter 6, this volume. See also Cole, *History of Oenpelli*, 45; Harris, *Field Has Its Flowers*, 13
Namadomarndo		Son of Majumbu from Nimbuwar area and Badjbadjuk	Cole, *History of Oenpelli*, 23
Namala		Worked in the garden. Husband of Dorcas Garmarradj.	Cole, *History of Oenpelli*, 23
Narin		Child of Bagul and Madjiagu	Harris, *Field Has Its Flowers*, 20
Ngandali	Dorcas	Girl in dormitory	Harris, *Field Has Its Flowers*, 13
Old Major Burrirlirl		Originally worked for Paddy Cahill and stayed on with mission. Skilled artist who made bark paintings for Dyer.	Cole, *History of Oenpelli*, 23 NTRS 693 part 1 (Dyer Story 8), n.p. 'Native Drawings'
Rambler	Nadambala Cahill	Given strap for continually running off with other men's wives	NTRS 693 part 1 (Dyer Story 8), 43

Name	Other contemporary and later names and alternative spellings	Association	Reference
Ramilla	Romula Romlo	This is most likely Romula, who also worked with Paddy Cahill. Noted as having been in contact with mission since its inception. First man Dyer trained to use plough. Dyer knew he had escaped from prison for poisoning Paddy Cahill.	Cole, *History of Oenpelli*, 42 NTRS 693 part 1 (Dyer Story 8), 49
Ruth Nellie		Baptised Easter 1933	Cole, *Oenpelli Pioneer*, 74
Walamada		Boy in school. Father to Jacob. Mother called Perriwig.	Harris, *Field Has Its Flowers*, 19, 21
Yarraminni		Storyteller, male	NTRS 693 part 1 (Dyer Story 8), 32
Yimulugulu		Girl in dormitory. Died from snake bite.	Harris, *Field Has Its Flowers*, 13

APPENDIX B: OENPELLI MISSION STAFF, 1925–31

Alfred Dyer	Superintendent	1925–35
Mary Catherine Dyer	Teacher & nurse	1925–35
Mr R. J. Ivin		1926–28
Mr F. A. Thorne	Stockman	1926
Mrs Thorne	Nurse	1926
Florence Sherrin	Teacher	1927–31
Ion Taylor	Builder	1927–29
Philip Taylor	Builder	1927–29
Edgar J. Clymo		1929–33
Betty Clymo	Nurse & kitchen	1929–33
G. R. 'Dick' Harris	Stockman	1929–
Florence Nevill	Teacher	1931–
Miss L. Grieve	Nurse	1931–33

www.ingramcontent.com/pod-product-compliance
Lightning Source LLC
Chambersburg PA
CBHW040154270326
41929CB00041B/3397